IN SEARCH OF KING SOLOMON'S MINES

IN SEARCH OF KING SOLOMON'S MINES

TAHIR SHAH

JOHN MURRAY
Albemarle Street, London

First published in 2002
by John Murray (Publishers) Ltd,
50 Albemarle Street, London W1S 4BD

A catalogue record for this book is available from the British Library

ISBN 0–7195–6324 0

Typeset in 12/13.5pt Bembo by Servis Filmsetting Ltd, Manchester

Printed and bound in Great Britain by
Creative Print and Design (Wales),
Ebbw Vale, Gwent

Contents

Illustrations

All the photographs except that of Frank Hayter were taken by the author.

Acknowledgements

ETHIOPIA IS ENCIRCLED by mountains and shrouded in misinformation. In the West, our impressions of this African country have been moulded by what we have seen on television: enduring images of drought, famine and starvation. But there is far more to Ethiopia than that, and I hope that this book helps lift the veil on a land which has captivated travellers and scholars for centuries.

In acknowledging the enormous amount of guidance and support that I received during my search for King Solomon's mines, I must first thank the Ethiopian people. In few countries have I been welcomed with such extraordinary warmth and hospitality, whether in the capital Addis Ababa or in the remotest villages.

So many people in Ethiopia have helped me that it is impossible to list them all. I would, however, particularly like to thank Getachew Tessfai and his team at the Ministry of Mines, the experts at the Geological Survey of Ethiopia, and the staff of the British Embassy in Addis Ababa. Sincere thanks must also go to Dr Araga Yirdaw, Petrus Visagie, Wayne Nicoleta and their colleagues at Midroc Lega Dembi; and to Yasmin Mohammed and her family. In addition, I am indebted to the many Ethiopians who are mentioned by name in the text. Most of all, I would like to thank Samson Yohannes, who stayed by my side even during times of considerable hardship.

Many others elsewhere have endured my petitions for information, advice and help. Sir Wilfred Thesiger was the first person to suggest I go to Ethiopia, the land of his birth, and he has assisted me at every step. I am also extremely grateful to Dr Richard Pankhurst and his wife Rita for their support. A large number of others have likewise given guidance and advice. They include Fisseha Adugna, Paul Henze, Wak Kani, Alex Maitland, Professor Alan Millard, Dr Konstantinos Politis, Professor Beno Rothenberg, Claus Schack, Rob Kraitt, Josh Briggs, Tarquin Hall, Robert Twigger and Gail Warden.

Above all, however, I am indebted to the hundreds of ordinary Ethiopians who assisted me during my travels. They have probably long since forgotten the day I stumbled into their lives. But I have not forgotten them, nor their acts of kindness. It is to them, and to their compatriots, that this book is dedicated.

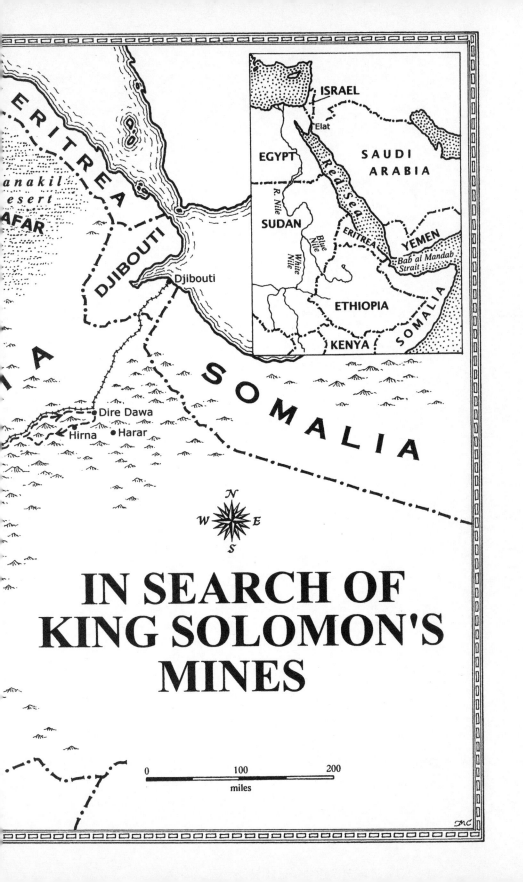

IN SEARCH OF
KING SOLOMON'S
MINES

'He who does not travel does not know the value of men.'

Moorish proverb

'Now the weight of gold that came to Solomon in one year was six hundred threescore and six talents . . . And king Solomon made two hundred targets of beaten gold: six hundred shekels of gold went to one target. And he made three hundred shields of beaten gold; three pounds of gold went to one shield . . . Moreover the king made a great throne of ivory, and overlaid it with the best gold . . . And all of king Solomon's drinking vessels were of gold . . .'

Kings I, x: 14–21

I

Ali Baba's Map

'So geographers, in Afric-maps,
With savage-pictures fill their gaps;
And o'er unhabitable downs
Place elephants for want of towns.'

Jonathan Swift, 'A Rhapsody'

AN INKY HAND-DRAWN map hung on the back wall of Ali Baba's
Tourist Emporium. Little more than a sketch, and smudged by a
clumsy hand, it was mounted in a chipped gold frame and showed
a river and mountains, a desert, a cave and what looked like a trail
between them. At the end of the trail was an oversized 'X'.

'Is that a treasure map?'

Ali Baba looked up from the back page of the *Jerusalem Herald*
and peered at me. He was an old dog of a man, whose pot belly
hinted at a diet rich in fat-tailed sheep. His chin was covered with
bristly grey stubble; he was bespectacled and he spoke through the
corner of his mouth. Like all the other merchants in the bazaar, Ali
Baba had gone from rack to ruin, but he didn't care. He lit a filter-
less Turkish cigarette and let his chest swell with the smoke.

'That is not for sale,' he said.

'But is it a treasure map?' I asked again.

The shopkeeper grunted and returned to his paper. You couldn't
accuse Ali Baba of hard salesmanship. Times had never been worse
for tourism since the fighting had flared up again, and all the other
traders in Jerusalem's Old City were falling over themselves to do
business. But then none of them had a treasure map hanging on
their walls.

'Where's the treasure supposed to be?'

'Africa.'

'Diamonds?'

'No, gold.'

'Oh,' I mouthed with mounting interest, 'pirate treasure?'

Ali Baba glanced up again from his newspaper. Then he straightened his white skull-cap, scratched a broken fingernail through his beard and replied.

'Gold mines, it is a map for the gold mines.'

'*The* gold mines?'

'The mines of Suleiman,' he growled, 'King Solomon's mines.'

The Via Dolorosa is packed with poky shops touting the latest in Virgin Mary T-shirts, playing-cards bearing the head of John the Baptist, Jesus Christ bottle-openers and Last Supper baseball caps. Several merchants that morning had even offered me 'splinters' from the Cross, and one had shown me what he said were Christ's thumb bones. The prices mentioned suggested they were fakes: they only cost two hundred dollars each. Holy Land kitsch surpasses all other forms. It seemed amazing that anyone would ever buy any of the merchandise, especially since tourists were now few and far between. Most had been scared away by the renewed Intifada.

As anyone who's ever set foot in the maze of backstreets of Jerusalem's souk knows, everything has a price. After forty minutes of drinking dark sweet tea with Ali Baba, the map was mine. Wrapping it in his copy of the *Jerusalem Herald*, Ali Baba licked his thumb and counted my wad of notes. Then, after counting them once, he turned them over and counted them again, checking for forgeries.

'Six hundred shekels,' he said. 'Cheap at the price.'

'It may be little to you, but it's a lot to me. It's nearly a hundred pounds.'

'What do you mean?' exclaimed Ali Baba. 'This map could lead you to a treasure greater than the farthest limits of your imagination. It's been in my family for six generations. My father would slit my throat if he were alive. And my mother must be turning in her grave. I can hear my ancestors cursing me from the next world!'

'Why haven't you ever gone off to look for Solomon's mines yourself?'

'Hah!' said the merchant, recoiling. 'How do you expect me to leave my business?'

'Then why are you selling the map after so long, and why to me?'

'You seem an honourable man,' said Ali Baba, opening the door. I thanked him for the compliment.

'You are wise too, I can see that,' he added, as I stepped into the street, 'so hang the map on your wall and leave it at that.'

All over the world unscrupulous shopkeepers have palmed me off with their most suspect merchandise. Most tourists instinctively avoid such objects, but I can't help myself. I have an insatiable appetite for questionable souvenirs. My home is filled with useless junk from a hundred journeys. The highlights include a lucky painted sloth jawbone from the Upper Amazon, a boxed set of glass eyes from Prague, and a broken boomerang purchased in a Moroccan souk, and supposedly once owned by Jim Morrison. I have a West African divining bowl too, made from whale bone, and a fragment of an Ainu warrior's cloak, a human hair talisman from Sarawak, and a ceremonial executioner's sword from the Sudan.

But Ali Baba's map was different. From the moment I saw it, I knew that a great opportunity was spread out before me. No names of places or co-ordinates were marked, but it was the first fragment of a journey. Such leads are rare in life, and must be seized with both hands.

Before Ali Baba could regret the decision to sell his heirloom, I hurried out into the web of streets, past the fruit stalls and perfume-sellers, the caverns heaped with turmeric, ground cinnamon and paprika, dried figs and trays of oily baklava. The Old City was full of life, moving to an ancient rhythm which could have changed little since the time of Christ.

The Intifada might have frightened away the package tourists but, as I saw it, a visit to Jerusalem in a time of peace would strip it of a vital quality – danger. My wife has grown used to hastily planned holidays in the world's trouble-spots. As soon as there's a bomb, an earthquake, a tidal wave or a riot, I call the travel agent and book cut-price seats. I'm no fearless war correspondent, but I have come to realize that the news media has a knack of exaggerating the perils of even the worst national emergency. In any case, a little danger is a small price to pay for ridding a place of tourists. We spent our honeymoon in Alexandria, living it up in the presidential suite of a grand hotel a couple of days after a bomb had wiped out a tourist bus in the Egyptian capital. At first my wife grumbled – she had been looking forward to Venice – but over the years she's got used to holidays that come with a Foreign Office health warning. But even she wasn't prepared to accompany me to the West Bank during the worst fighting since the Six-Day War.

In more peaceful times I would have had to fight my way through the crowds to get up to the Dome of the Rock, which stands on an outcrop known to Jews as Temple Mount, and to Muslims as Haram al-Sharif, the Noble Sanctuary. The small plateau is one of the holiest sites in Islam and is revered by Jews as well.

The Cotton Merchants' market, which was built by the Crusaders and which leads up to the sanctuary, was deserted. A pair of Israeli soldiers were standing guard at the far end of the tunnel, lit by octagonal skylights in the vaulted stone roof. Their fatigues were well-pressed, but their expressions were heavy with the boredom that only conscripts know. In a synchronized movement they lifted automatic rifles to my chest and told me to turn back. Tourists were not welcome, they said. If I took another step towards the shrine, I'd be arrested and charged.

I explained that I was no tourist but a pilgrim. My father, my grandfather and his father before him had prayed at the Dome of the Rock. Now I had come to continue the tradition. Nothing would make me leave without fulfilling my duty. As I delivered my harangue, a beggar with no legs swam desperately over the flagstones, his arms flailing. He kissed my feet, rejoicing at the sight of a tourist. Until my arrival his livelihood must have been in doubt. I handed him a few small coins, for charity is one of the central pillars of Islam.

The conscripts lowered the barrels of their weapons to groin height. They were giving me a moment to persuade them of my faith.

'Tourists degrade what is holy. They are the agents of the Devil,' I exclaimed, as I spat on the ground.

The guards' eyes widened and, perhaps worried that I was a lunatic and would give them trouble, they let me through the cordon. A pair of great doors were swung open on rusting hinges, and I caught my first sight of the fabulous golden dome.

Before I had taken a single step towards the shrine, an old Arab guard hurried over and insisted that I required his services. Only he could keep me safe, he said, and besides he needed the money. His honest eyes were pale green, the colour of rock opals, his unshaven cheeks leathery and walnut brown. His front teeth were missing, causing him to whiffle when he spoke. His name was Hussein.

'My seven sons have been hungry for many weeks,' he said. 'Thank God that you have come! You were sent by God to help restore my family's fortune. I have been blessed by your arrival, and my family have been blessed! May you live for a thousand years!'

After such a welcome I had little choice but to hire the guide. He motioned to the dome and clamped his hand to my forearm, so that I might pause to savour the moment. Resting on an octagonal mosaic-tiled base, and framed in the brilliant blue afternoon sky, the great golden dome blinds all who look upon it. We shaded our eyes in the sunshine and then began to climb the steps up towards the shrine.

The floor of the main chamber is almost entirely taken up by the Rock – a broad rolling slab of stone – which Muslims call Kubbet al-Sakhra. It is from here that the Prophet Mohammed is said to have ascended to Heaven on his Night Journey to receive the Quran. Hussein pointed out the hoof-print of the Prophet's steed Buraq where he leapt into the air to carry his master heavenward. The Rock is sacred to Judaism, too, supposedly the very spot where Abraham prepared to sacrifice his son Isaac, long before the rise of Islam.

Hussein had tears in his eyes as he led me around the shrine. I was unsure whether his emotions were stirred by the thought of my custom or if, like me, he was genuinely affected by his surroundings. Perhaps it was a mixture of both, for you could stare upon the Dome of the Rock for hours and never tire of it.

As he led me down to the Well of Souls, the subterranean chamber where legend says the dead congregate to pray, Hussein wiped his eyes.

'God rewards all believers,' he said. 'Islam is the true path, of course, but we do not frown on those of the other faith. Hostility is bad for us all and it's an affront to what is sacred. Abraham is after all a prophet mentioned by the Holy Quran, just as Suleiman – whose great temple stood here – is honoured by Muslims.'

'Suleiman, *Solomon* . . . his temple was built here?'

Hussein paused to show me the niche where a strand of the Prophet's hair is kept. It is brought out only during Ramadan.

'Solomon, the wise king,' he said slowly, 'he built the most spectacular temple right here where this sanctuary now stands. How it must have looked, its walls and roofs covered in fine gold!'

'Gold . . . from the mines, from Solomon's mines?'

'Yes, of course,' said Hussein.

We left the Dome of the Rock and walked towards the El Aqsa mosque which stands at the southern end of the plateau. Hussein was talking, extolling the merits of Islam, but I wasn't listening. The mention of Solomon and his golden temple had distracted me.

I asked Hussein to stop for a moment. I'd stashed the map from Ali Baba's Tourist Emporium in my rucksack. We sat on the ground beside the fountain where ablutions are performed while I rummaged. Hussein was eager to tell me that Anwar Sadat had come to pray at the mosque, and to recount the day King Hussein of Jordan's grandfather, King Abdullah, was shot dead as he entered El Aqsa. With his own eyes he, Hussein, had seen the bullet enter the old king's head, his turban fall and the dignitaries scatter like rats.

I unwrapped the gilded frame and stared at the map. Hussein glanced at the image, the bright sunlight reflecting off its glass, and fell silent.

'Solomon's mines,' he said, 'the mines in Ophir.'

I was surprised that he could recognize the map so easily, especially as there were no place names marked.

'What is Ophir?'

'The land of gold,' said the guide, 'from where the finest gold on earth was brought.'

'Where is it, this land of Ophir?'

Hussein hunched his shoulders and shook his head.

'Read the Bible for your answers.'

King David was a man of war and so was forbidden by God to construct a great temple in honour of his faith. God guided

David's hand as he drew the plans, but he decreed that it would fall to his son, Solomon, to build the temple, for such a building needed a man of peace to craft it. David paid fifty shekels in silver to a man called Araunah for a piece of land on Mount Moriah, and there, four years after David's death, Solomon began work on the temple.

First he sent word to the Phoenician king Hiram of Tyre, ordering him to fell cedar trees from his forests in Lebanon. The cedars, a symbol of strength and power in biblical times, were the most highly prized trees in the ancient world. Hiram sent timber as instructed and also skilled metalworkers, carpenters and masons. The masons knew the secret science of geometry, some of whose cryptic codes are kept alive today by the Brotherhood of Freemasons, and it was they who cut and polished the immense stone blocks. The accuracy of their work was so great that no hammers were used while the temple was being built, or so the Bible relates.

The temple was built on a conventional Phoenician design, suggesting that King Hiram's draughtsmen helped with the plans. It comprised an outer hallway, the *ulam*; a central courtyard, the *heikal*; and an inner sanctum, the *debir*, or 'Holy of Holies'. It was here, in the inner sanctum, sequestered away from the eyes of laymen, that the Ark of the Covenant was to be kept.

The stone for the temple is thought to have been quarried from beneath the city of Jerusalem. In 1854 one of the royal quarries was discovered by an American physician, Dr Barclay, who was taking an evening stroll with his dog. The dog suddenly disappeared down a narrow shaft. Barclay enlarged the hole and found himself peering into an immense cavern. The entrance to the cave, known today as Zedekiah's Grotto, can still be seen not far from the Old City's Damascus Gate.

When the temple was finished, its decoration began, as the Second Book of Chronicles records:

And the porch that was in the front of the house, the length of it was according to the breadth of the house, twenty cubits, and the height was an hundred and twenty: and he overlaid it within with pure gold. And the greater house he cieled with fir tree, which he overlaid with fine gold, and set thereon palm

7

trees and chains. And he garnished the house with precious stones for beauty: and the gold was gold of Parviam. He overlaid also the house, the beams, the posts, and the walls thereof, with gold: and graved cherubim on the walls. And he made the most holy house, the length whereof was, according to the breadth of the house, twenty cubits, and the breadth thereof twenty cubits: and he overlaid it with fine gold, amounting to six hundred talents. And the weight of the nails was fifty shekels of gold. And he overlaid the upper chambers with gold. And in the most holy house he made two cherubims of image work, and overlaid them with gold.

The temple was completed in the seventh year of Solomon's reign and on the day of its dedication the Ark of the Covenant was carried from Mount Ophel in a grand procession, led by King Solomon himself. Priests dressed in pure white linen followed the king, blowing their trumpets, and behind them came a jubilant cavalcade. Every six paces oxen were sacrificed, drenching the road in blood. By the time the Ark was in place in the Holy of Holies, and the temple was dedicated, 22,000 oxen and 120,000 sheep had been slaughtered.

The temple served the people of Jerusalem for almost four centuries after the death of Solomon in 926 BC, but Solomon's successors lacked his wisdom and the land was misruled. The final blow came when the Babylonian king Nebuchadnezzar invaded Judah, almost annihilating its population and laying waste its cities. Jerusalem itself was besieged for a year and a half, and when the starving defenders finally capitulated, their capital was plundered. Solomon's temple was destroyed and every ounce of gold was stripped away, and carried back to Babylon.

In the Church of the Holy Sepulchre, in the Christian quarter of Jerusalem, a gaggle of nervous Russian tourists were taking in the sights and trying to remain calm. Gunfire was ricocheting off the walls outside, but the priests said there was nothing to worry about. They'd seen much worse. One at a time the Russians stooped to kiss the Stone of Unction, where Christ's body is said to have been anointed after his death. Then they filed into 'Christ's tomb', the holiest site in Christendom.

The mood in the church was subdued, the air filled with the smell of burning beeswax and incense. The walls were filthy, especially at waist height where millions of pilgrims' hands had stroked them as they filed past. I sat on a low wooden bench and waited for the gunfire to stop, but it didn't.

I had already spent two days reading the Old Testament and staring at Ali Baba's map. The West Bank's Intifada was claiming new casualties on a daily basis and making it tricky to see the sights or even to sit in a café. To pass the time I'd bought a tattered third-hand copy of Henry Rider Haggard's *King Solomon's Mines* near the American Colony Hotel, where I was staying along with much of the world's press corps.

The book, which first appeared in 1885, was written by Rider Haggard when he was twenty-nine, as the result of a shilling bet with his brother, who doubted he could write a bestseller. Advertised by its publisher as 'THE MOST AMAZING BOOK EVER WRITTEN', the novel was a runaway success, and more than thirty thousand copies were sold in the first year alone.

In the novel, Solomon's mines lie in what is now South Africa, but they are diamond mines, not gold mines. Rider Haggard was capitalizing on the diamond fever of the time. As a laborious introduction in my copy points out, he set the book in southern Africa because he had spent time in the Colonial Service in Natal and Transvaal, and so knew the region well. As well as an introduction my copy also contained a map. It was even sketchier than the one I'd bought from Ali Baba, marking little more than a river, a pan of bad water, 'Sheba's breasts', a kraal and a treasure cave. After going through the Old Testament for a second time, I came to the conclusion that Rider Haggard's novel, although a rattling good read, was of no use to anyone engaged in a serious search for Solomon's gold mines.

From the outset, I'd grasped that the biblical land of Ophir was the key clue to follow. The Bible can be deciphered in many ways, with an interpretation often hanging on the precise meaning of a single word. For that reason I chose to use the Septuagint version, the earliest known translation of the Old Testament. Made during the third and second centuries BC, it is still the official text of the Orthodox Greek Church. At the time it was written, the Hebrew version of the Bible still wasn't standardized.

The First Book of Kings relates that

king Solomon made a navy of ships in Ezion-geber, which is beside Eloth, on the shore of the Red sea, in the land of Edom. And Hiram sent in the navy his servants, shipmen that had knowledge of the sea, with the servants of Solomon. And they came to Ophir, and fetched from thence gold, four hundred and twenty talents and brought it to king Solomon . . .

Now the weight of gold that came to Solomon in one year was six hundred threescore and six talents . . . And king Solomon made two hundred targets of beaten gold: six hundred shekels of gold went to one target. And he made three hundred shields of beaten gold; three pounds of gold went to one shield . . . Moreover the king made a great throne of ivory, and overlaid it with the best gold . . . And all king Solomon's drinking vessels were of gold . . . For the king had a navy of Tharshish with the navy of Hiram: once in three years came the navy of Tharshish, bringing gold, and silver, ivory, and apes, and peacocks.

Stop a man in the street today and ask him the meaning of Ophir and he is likely to shake his head. But for centuries the word was steeped in myth.

The Bible reveals what came from Ophir, but it does not say where it was located. Its authors took it for granted that everyone knew where it was and recorded only that those who journeyed to Ophir were away for three years. Interpreting this literally, some scholars took it to mean that the actual travelling time was three years. So they, and others, pointed to the most distant lands they knew. Ptolemy, in his maps, placed Ophir in the Malay peninsula and Christopher Columbus believed he had found Ophir in modern Haiti. Some suggested India, Madagascar, Ceylon, Arabia or even Peru, while others postulated that Ophir may merely mean 'remote'.

It was the discovery of an immense set of ruins in southern Africa – known as Great Zimbabwe – that led the Victorians to believe that they had finally discovered the Bible's Ophir. The ruins, after which Rhodesia was renamed at Independence, were found in the 1870s. To the Victorian mind, the stone workings, which lie nearly two hundred miles inland, resembled Solomon's temple. Though this was amateur archaeology at its most suspect, at the turn of the last century dozens of books appeared claiming that the riddle of Ophir had at last been solved. Rider Haggard's novel was but a fictional account of an astonishing discovery.

These days the Great Zimbabwe theory has been discredited and the location of Ophir remains a mystery.

If Ophir is the first real clue to finding the mines, then the second lies in the most famous consort of King Solomon – the Queen of Sheba. Just as we are never told the location of Ophir, so the Bible fails to give the exact location of the Queen of Sheba's kingdom. In fact, it doesn't even tell us the queen's name, but the First Book of Kings does hint that she hailed from a land which was rich in pure gold:

> And when the queen of Sheba heard of the fame of Solomon concerning the name of the Lord, she came to prove him with hard questions. And she came to Jerusalem with a very great train, with camels that bore spices, and very much gold, and precious stones: and when she was come to Solomon, she communed with him of all that was in her heart . . . And she gave the king an hundred and twenty talents of gold, and of spices very great store, and precious stones . . . And king Solomon gave unto the queen of Sheba all her desire, whatsoever she asked, beside that which Solomon gave her of his royal bounty.

As I sat in the shadows of the Church of the Holy Sepulchre that afternoon I thought of Ophir, the Queen of Sheba and King Solomon's gold. It seemed absurd that so many generations of amateurs and experts should have searched for King Solomon's mines in such far-flung lands. The answer, surely, must lie closer to hand.

My Michelin map of the Middle East included a large part of East Africa, stretching south as far as Lake Victoria and east to the Persian Gulf. I spread it out before me. If Solomon's ships left the port of Ezion-geber, thought to be near modern Elat in the Gulf of Aqaba, then his fleet would have headed south down the Red

Sea in search of gold. Solomon's people had reached the Promised Land after fleeing from Egypt. They were a land-based people, not accomplished mariners, and it seemed unlikely that the king's ships would have gone further than necessary to find gold.

I knew that Ophir might have lain in southern Arabia, which may have been the Queen of Sheba's homeland, but the Sabaen kingdom probably stretched across the Bab al Mandab Straits to the African continent. The more I sat and deliberated, the stronger Africa, and in particular Ethiopia, beckoned me. I had been to a great number of African countries but had long yearned to explore Ethiopia. Like thousands of adventurers before me, I'd been bewitched by the country's history, its folklore and the strange tales of life there. Years before, I had learned that the imperial family of Ethiopia traces its descent from Menelik, the son supposedly born to the Queen of Sheba and Solomon. A sacred Ethiopian text, the *Kebra Negast (The Glory of Kings)*, tells the story in full.

After becoming pregnant by Solomon, the Queen of Sheba returned to her native land. She left the wise king to his seven hundred wives and three hundred concubines, and departed with seven hundred and ninety-seven camels, all of them laden with gifts. The Queen, who is known as Makeda in the Ethiopian texts, brought up Menelik on her own. When the boy reached adulthood, he journeyed north to Jerusalem to meet his father. The *Kebra Negast* says that as they left Jerusalem, Menelik's companions stole the hallowed Ark of the Covenant and took it back to Ethiopia. The Ark is supposedly still kept in the northern city of Axum.

I could see from the map that Ethiopia would have been easily reached from Solomon's kingdom – it was no more than a short boat trip down the Red Sea. In ancient times Ethiopia was a source of apes, ivory, frankincense and myrrh; precisely those items which the Bible says came from Ophir. And in ancient Egypt, Ethiopia was known as a land where gold could be easily mined. Even today the country has extraordinary reserves of gold and other valuable minerals and, unlike in southern Africa where you have to dig down thousands of feet to reach the ore, in Ethiopia's highlands the gold seams lie close to the surface.

I stood up, folded my map away and walked out into the after-noon sun. To the right of the main entrance to the Church of the

Holy Sepulchre there is a doorway that leads to a chapel maintained by Ethiopian Christians. Once there was an Ethiopian monastery in Jerusalem, but in the seventeenth century when the monks could no longer afford the Ottoman taxes, it was forced to move here, to a series of dank rooms that lead off the roof of St Helena's Chapel. Now a handful of monks continue to maintain a presence in Jerusalem as their forebears had done for centuries.

In one of the rooms I found a small shrine, its walls black with soot, its benches shiny and worn where thousands of robes had brushed against the wood. The walls were hung with colourful paintings showing the Queen of Sheba being greeted by King Solomon. I walked through the chapel and up a flight of stairs, out on to the roof. A bearded Ethiopian priest, dressed in a flowing black robe, a prayer book in his hands, was asleep beneath a weeping willow. As I watched him sleeping I thought about my map, and about Ophir, and about a journey. Ethiopia was awaiting me.

On my way back to my hotel, I passed Ali Baba's Tourist Emporium once again. I glanced in through the open door. The shopkeeper was dozing in his chair but he awoke with a start when he heard my footsteps cross the threshold. Even to the ears of such a reluctant salesman, the sound of feet meant tourists, and tourists meant trade.

When he'd wrapped the loops of his glasses around his ears and squinted in my direction, Ali Baba asked how I was enjoying the gunfire. He said that there was nothing like a little shooting to keep everyone on their toes. I told him that I'd been unable to think of anything but King Solomon's mines since buying the map, and that I had decided to look for the mines myself. I was heading for Ethiopia, I said.

Ali Baba warned me against making the journey. It would be full of dangers. He should never have sold me the map. His mother would be turning in her grave, his father would be cursing the day he was born. As he spoke I noticed something familiar hanging on the far wall of the shop. Little more than a sketch, and smudged by a clumsy hand, it was an inky hand-drawn map. I went over and compared it with my own map. Although obviously executed by the same unskilled artist, and set in identical chipped gold frames, they were different.

Furious, I demanded to know why another map was hanging in the very same spot as the one I'd purchased. Ali Baba ran a calloused hand across his cheek. Times were desperate, he said woefully, and desperate times called for desperate measures.

'That's all well and good,' I said with mounting anger, 'but this is fraud. I've got a good mind to call the police.'

Sensing trouble, the old shopkeeper started to board up his emporium. He packed away the splinters from the Cross, the Virgin Mary fridge magnets, the fluorescent pink rosaries and the kitsch Nativity scenes.

'The map I sold you was the *real* one,' he said slyly, 'I'm giving you a head start in your search. You see, this other map is a fake. It'll keep the competition from your heels. Look on it as after-sales service!'

2

Seven Stones

'The first condition of understanding a foreign country is to smell it.'

Rudyard Kipling

WHEN THE BLIND Mauritanian woman's deranged guide-dog sank its front teeth into my thigh, I doubled over in agony. The pain was terrible, but it was soon replaced by an overwhelming fear. Since my arrival in Addis Ababa, two days before, dozens of people had warned me to watch out for rabies. Ethiopian dogs, they all told me proudly, are very rabid indeed. Pressing a hand to my bloodied leg, I looked down at the dog. It was panting wildly, its eyes seemed to flash manically, and its tongue lolled out of a frothing mouth. The dog's owner called the creature to heel. I told her that her pet was a danger to society.

'Oh,' she exclaimed frivolously, 'isn't *petit* Bertrand a naughty little one?'

An hour later I found myself sitting in a doctor's surgery on the other side of Addis Ababa. A pair of impressive medical certificates on the far wall advertised the physician's skill. I pointed to the crescent of puncture marks in my thigh and grimaced. The doctor asked if the dog's eyes had glinted. I replied that they had.

'Was there milky froth around its mouth?'

I said that there was.

The surgeon licked his lips.

'Rabies,' he declared menacingly.

'The woman was blind,' I said, 'she couldn't see the animal's condition. Are you going to give me twenty-one jabs in the stomach?'

'There's no anti-rabies serum in Ethiopia,' said the doctor. 'You'd better go back to your hotel and rest.'

He began to write out his bill.

'What if I start frothing at the mouth?'
'Don't bite anyone,' he said.

Back at the Hotel Ghion I sat on the lawn with a map of East Africa spread out before me. Blind people from across the continent had converged on the hotel for their annual conference, and some of their savage guide-dogs had escaped their sightless masters. Now they were tearing around the hotel grounds, hunting as a pack and snapping at the unsuspecting. Spying me from across the garden, and clearly eager to join in the fun, *petit* Bertrand slipped his collar and bounded over, eyes flashing, mouth foaming. I leapt up and seized a deck-chair, holding it out in front of me like a lion-tamer, and as we danced across the lawn I yelled for help. When at last Bertrand was dragged away, I returned to the matter in hand. I had arrived in the Ethiopian capital charged with a solemn mission to locate the source of King Solomon's gold.

There's nothing quite like a good quest for getting your blood pumping. In faraway Jerusalem, the idea of seeking out King Solomon's mines had seemed irresistible and Ali Baba's map, though perhaps not the genuine article, seemed the key to a magical journey. Now, faced with a real map, I began to feel daunted by the task I'd set myself.

In London, I had snapped up all the books I could find on King Solomon, the Queen of Sheba, biblical history, Ophir, Ethiopia and gold. Most were still unread and lay wrapped in newspapers and packed in a wooden tea-chest in my hotel room. The background reading would have to be done *en route*.

I looked at the map again.

Ethiopia is a reddish-brown anvil of mountains, nestling in the Horn of Africa. Everything about it hints at remoteness, and for three thousand years its name has been synonymous with mystery. Herodotus was the first to tell of its strange beasts, its ebony trees and its exotic inhabitants, 'the tallest, handsomest and longest lived of men'. Cosmos wrote of the emporia of frankincense and myrrh. Then there were the great explorers who risked life and limb to penetrate the country – men like Juan de Bermudez, Christovao de Gama, James Bruce and Henry Salt.

A well-known geologist in London had suggested I look for gold in the Afar region, near the Red Sea coast. The ferocious Danakil people who live there have, until recently, judged a warrior's standing by the number of testicles hanging around his neck. Someone else told me to seek out the hyenas of Harar which, a legend says, guard Solomon's golden treasure. Another friend pointed to the north. Deep in the mountains there was, he said, a monastery which kept safe the secrets of the wise king. Another acquaintance told of a church in Lalibela, said to have the 'Gold of Sheba' in its treasury.

Almost fifty years before, my father had also searched for King Solomon's mines. He'd unfurled a great map of the Middle East and, taking a handful of stones, had placed them on key points. He had put one stone on the Sudan, another on Petra, others on the holy city of Mecca, on Damascus, Cyprus and Beirut, and on our ancestral home of Paghman, in Afghanistan. His journey had eventually led him to deep caverns north of Port Sudan on the Red Sea coast. Thirty years before my father set out for the mines, his father, Sirdar Ikbal Ali Shah, had spent months criss-crossing southern Arabia on the same quest. The search for King Solomon's mines was a family obsession.

Sitting on the hotel lawn, I took out of my pocket seven pebbles of my own. I placed the first on Afar, where the testicle-hunters once roamed. The next I put on Harar, home of the hyenas. I dropped the third pebble on the northern border with Eritrea, and the fourth on Lalibela. Then I placed another on Gondar, once Ethiopia's seat of imperial power, and home to the Ethiopian Jews. That was five. Where else?

The sound of guide-dogs mauling a newly arrived traveller distracted me for a moment. I glanced at the map again. Herodotus had said of western Ethiopia 'there is gold obtained in great plenty'. So I placed a pebble due west. I had one left. That morning's newspaper had spoken of a legal gold-mining operation in the south of Ethiopia. So I put the last pebble there.

Uncertain of where to begin my search, I decided to go for a walk. For two days I'd been cooped up in the hotel, tormented by insomnia and savage West African guide-dogs. It was time to get to grips with Addis Ababa.

Leaving the grounds of the Hotel Ghion, I headed north-west. The red clay-like soil, the morning dampness after heavy night rain, the bitter green oranges and roasted maize laid out on makeshift stalls, and the grinding gears of battered blue Peugeots brought back memories of other journeys in Africa. The sky was grey, low clouds threatening more rain, and the air was thick with diesel fumes and the noxious stench of old plastic bottles being burned on open fires. Taxis honked as they swerved to miss each other. Roadside hawkers whistled through their front teeth at passers-by. A flock of sheep bound for market ambled along the road, their bells ringing as they walked.

Addis Ababa, the 'New Flower', is not as new and fresh as its name suggests. In the years since 1975, when Haile Selassie, the last Emperor, was smothered with a pillow in the bedroom of his palace, the capital has dwindled. The street-lamps are broken and birds now make their nests in them. The concrete office blocks are crumbling, and the pavements are full of people who seem to have nowhere else to go. Cars are held together with bits of string, their bodywork patched with makeshift repairs, and the roads are pocked with craters. Every detail of daily life reflects the confusion of the country's recent history.

Once he'd dispatched the Emperor and buried him standing upright under his lavatory bowl, President Mengistu set to work on pacifying the tribes whose leader he'd become. For seventeen years his torture-rooms worked overtime, taming a proud people. He managed to achieve notoriety even in a continent where despots are commonplace. Few Ethiopians will talk of those terrible Mengistu years. Perhaps they are trying to forget, or perhaps they are still in shock. When at last Mengistu's Marxist government collapsed in May 1991, the streets ran with blood once more. Promises were made and then broken, and the cycle of hardship has persisted. People live from one day to the next, keeping their heads down, making do as best they can. Many fear the present and most have little hope for the future. As for the country's 3,000-year-old history, that is a taboo subject. The government's greatest worry seems to be that Ethiopians will remember the exiled imperial family and demand their return. Ask anyone about the glorious legacy of the past and they will place a finger to their lips.

I walked on as if in a daydream. Hundreds of men and women were swarming down the road, their heads veiled in white cotton shawls with embroidered borders, their feet squashed into ill-fitting shoes. Some of them were singing, their voices high-pitched yet solemn. Others were chanting verses softly to themselves. Many more were clutching Bibles to their chests. One woman was carrying a gaudy painting of the Virgin Mary and another was crawling on her knees, with a silver cross cupped in her hands. At the centre of the crowd a plain pine coffin was being carried at shoulder height. A posy of violet-coloured flowers had been placed on top, along with a scruffy straw hat.

Across from the mourners a man without legs dipped his head in respect. He seemed numbed by pain, his eyes welling with tears. Like veterans from a secret war, he and his countrymen had seen too much, had endured the unendurable. Worst of all was the thought that the world had forgotten them.

As I stood watching in silence, a dilapidated turquoise taxi pulled to a halt beside me. I assumed the driver was looking for a fare, but I was wrong. Instead, he climbed out of his cab, strode over to the solemn procession and said a prayer. He looked as if he was in his late twenties. His back was ramrod straight, his hands clenched together over the buckle of his belt, and his head bent towards the ground. When the cortège had moved on, the taxi-driver returned to his vehicle. Curious, I asked him if he knew the deceased.

'No, sir,' he replied courteously in English, 'but when an elder dies our entire nation must mourn . . .'

Before he could finish his sentence the first drops of late morning rain splattered down. I leapt into the taxi. A second later the shower became a torrent. In the distance the funeral procession moved forward, the white cotton shawls now soaked and clinging to frail bodies.

The driver was waiting for the name of a destination. He said his trusty Lada would take me to the ends of the earth if I wished. Ducking his head humbly, he smiled broadly and introduced himself. His name was Samson, son of Yohannes.

I had heard that Haile Selassie's body, now retrieved from beneath the presidential lavatory, was being kept at the tomb of Emperor Menelik II until a fitting burial could be arranged. Since Ethiopia's imperial family claim descent from King Solomon and the Queen of Sheba, the tomb seemed an obvious place to visit, so I asked Samson to drive me there.

'There's no money to pay for the Emperor's funeral,' he said as we drove along. 'The government won't give any money, and Haile Selassie's own family are too miserly. They don't want Ethiopians to know how rich they are. As for the Rastafarians, they could easily afford to pay, but they won't.'

'Why not?'

'The Rastas named themselves after Ras Tafari, the title of the Emperor Haile Selassie. They say he is God, and since God cannot die, they won't pay for his funeral. It's not right, there's no dignity for the man.'

In a country where the study of history is frowned upon, I was impressed by my driver's knowledge.

'I only drive a taxi because I have to,' he said. 'I support my brothers and sister, my mother, my father and so many others. They all rely on me.'

The tradition of one man supporting a whole host of relatives is known in the Middle East as 'living off Abdul's job'. As soon as one man gets work, the rest of his family give up their own jobs and sponge off him. Samson tapped me on the knee with his thumb.

'I long to have a real job with respect and honour,' he said. 'Then my girlfriend's father will think I'm a worthy man. But secretly I have an even greater wish.'

'What is it?'

'To know every detail of our history.'

'Can you buy history books?'

'The government's bought them all up,' he said. 'They burn them or tear out the subversive pages. It's much easier to forget about the old days and keep quiet. That's the best way to stay alive.'

'Do you have any history books, though?'

My questions were making Samson uneasy. In Ethiopia, as I was fast finding out, you couldn't be too careful. But he was well aware that the government had no funds to hire foreign spies.

'Yes, I have a history book,' he confided. 'It tells an astonishing story. It has taught me about the Emperor and his ancestors – about Menelik and Mekonnen, King Tewodros, and the great battles they all fought. I have learned, too, about the British explorers James Bruce and Nathaniel Pearce, about the kings of Harar, Queen Makeda and Solomon.'

'What if the book was discovered?'

'It's well-hidden,' he replied. 'I bring it out only at night when my prying neighbours have gone to bed. I lock the door and bolt the window of my room. Sometimes I pretend to snore loudly even though I'm awake. Then, still snoring, I light the candle, hold its flame close to the pages, and read.'

As he spoke Samson span the wheel through his hands and we turned off the road. Then he revved the engine as hard as he could and drove up a steep path that led into a copse of eucalyptus trees. A sentry in grubby fatigues was standing guard and he raised his Kalashnikov as a cloud of oily exhaust engulfed him.

'Follow me,' said Samson, leading the way towards an octagonal Orthodox church.

Rain was still falling, rustling through the eucalyptus like a shamanic rattle. A handful of pilgrims were clustered at each of the church's doors. Most had shuffled up the steps on their knees and were now pressing their lips to the door-frames. We mounted the steps, removed our shoes and sought refuge inside.

In Jerusalem I had visited the Ethiopian church tucked away behind a wall on Etyopya Street. This one was laid out in the same way. The main hall was covered in threadbare carpets and lit by dozens of crackling neon strip lights. Dotted around it were tremendous drums and *makwamya*, ritualistic prayer sticks. The air was pungent with the smell of frankincense. The walls were decorated with murals and hung with bright paintings of biblical scenes, and in the middle of the chamber there stood a grand cube-shaped structure, shrouded by curtains. Here, hidden from the eyes of common men, was the 'Holy of Holies' in which lay the *tabot*, a replica of the Ark of the Covenant.

Hearing our voices, a deacon appeared. He was muffled in a blue shawl, and in one hand he carried a collection tin. Voices hinted at visitors, and visitors suggested donations. I asked politely if I could look inside the Holy of Holies, as I was eager to see the Ark. The deacon recoiled in horror and shrieked. Not even he, he said, was permitted to set eyes on the mystical Ark. So I asked about the murals. They showed Makeda and her entourage making the journey across desert sands to Jerusalem, where the queen presented Solomon with golden treasures. A trainee priest, who could not have been more than thirteen, was dusting the paintings with a rag tied to a long bamboo pole. The deacon looked at his collection tin and then at me. I asked where the tomb of Emperor Menelik could be found. The deacon snapped his fingers, and the young trainee priest struggled to lift a flagstone in the floor, revealing the entrance to a crypt.

Time spent in Cairo's great cemetery – known locally as 'the City of the Dead' – had introduced me to the delights of subterranean mausolea. In one fabulous Cairene tomb, an ancestral guardian had once brought me a pasha's head. I'd never seen such a fine set of teeth but, anxious to avoid the wrath of the dead nobleman's family, I'd ordered the warden to put the head back as quickly as he could. Now, the former Emperor's mausoleum brought back those days and nights spent in Cairo's cemetery.

The crypt housed three colossal marble tombs, belonging to Menelik II, his consort the Empress Taitu and their daughter Zawditu. My interest in Menelik, the modernizing Emperor, had begun years before when I'd read a book on the history of execution. In it I came across a tale about Menelik. The Emperor was told by his advisers that in far-away America a new and ingenious technique for dispatching criminals had been devised. The victim was strapped into a wooden chair and subjected to a strange and dangerous substance called 'electricity'. The Emperor was told that the process was excruciating and that death followed only when the prisoner's eyes had popped like ripe grapes, and his head had sizzled. Menelik liked what he heard and, so the story goes, he placed an order for a pair of chairs. It took months to transport the chairs to the Ethiopian kingdom. When at last they arrived they were assembled and taken to the palace where the Emperor surveyed them. He was impressed by their craftsmanship and asked for a demonstration. Only then did the courtiers realize that the devices were useless – electricity had not yet reached Ethiopia. Undeterred by this setback, Menelik ordered that the electric chairs be used as imperial thrones.

Next to Menelik's grey marble sarcophagus stood a long glass-fronted cupboard set into the wall. Inside was a delicate, finely tooled coffin. The deacon bowed his head, and Samson the taxi-driver looked glum.

'Here is our former Emperor, Haile Selassie,' said the priest. 'We are waiting to bury him according to the ancient rites. But there are problems . . .'

I raised an eyebrow.

'The Rastafarians!' he exclaimed, rolling his eyes. 'They come in their hundreds to see him, but they say that he's still alive. He is in their hearts. That's what they say. So they don't give any money for the burial.'

The deacon rubbed a hand across his face and stared longingly at the empty collection tin. I dropped a folded note into it and stepped aside, as a throng of Rastafarians entered the crypt, their dreadlocks hidden under crocheted hats, their Jamaican accents echoing through the shadows.

Samson led the way back to his taxi. He told me that Haile Selassie had striven to bring Ethiopia into the modern world, just as Menelik had done before him. Both men had also recognized the great natural wealth of the country and had hoped to exploit its treasure.

'What treasure?'

Samson narrowed his eyes.

'Gold,' he said.

From the mausoleum we drove on through rain-soaked streets to the National Museum. Tourists are few and far between in Ethiopia these days. Rastafarians may visit the coffin of their deity, but they rarely bother with the dilapidated state museum. Some of the former Emperor's ceremonial robes were on show, along with tribal crafts and a jumble of bones labelled 'Lucy, the oldest Humanoid in the world'. Samson said they'd been found in the Danakil region in 1974 and had been named after the Beatles' song 'Lucy in the Sky with Diamonds'.

'Lucy has made us famous. There's even a ballet about her in America. It's all about her life.' He glanced down through the cracked glass case at the assortment of bones. 'Lucy's made us famous, but she hasn't made us rich.'

Unable to resist, I asked him about Ethiopia's gold.

'The Bible speaks of Ophir,' he said, 'a great golden treasure, hidden, but waiting to be dug up. A little hard work, a little sweat, and we'd all be rich like they are in America. Gold is the future of Ethiopia.'

Samson told me that he was from Kebra Mengist, a small town far to the south of Addis Ababa. His father, a schoolteacher, had instilled in him a love of the Bible and a thirst for knowledge. But at an early age he had strayed.

'My parents told me that history was a good thing,' he said. 'After all, the Bible is a kind of history and that is the best thing of all. They told me to study, but my friends tempted me with riches.'

'Were they thieves, stealing from the wealthy?'

'No, no, they were prospectors,' he replied, 'digging gold from the giant open mines.'

I felt my pulse begin to race. A possible source of Solomon's gold suddenly seemed within reach. Anxious not to appear too enthusiastic, lest he take advantage of me, I asked Samson why he had abandoned mining and become a badly paid taxi-driver instead.

'For three years I dug gold from the ground,' he replied. 'Stripped bare to my waist, I worked like a rat in tunnels below the surface. It was infernal down there: hot, stinking, dangerous beyond words. The men who laboured there used to say that they had died and gone to Hell. The Devil was our employer. There was no escape. Yes, I earned good money but, like all the others, I spent it on liquor and bad women. If there was any cash left we gambled it away. The more money we earned through mining, the more we drank, and the more desperate we became.'

We moved on through the museum, past cases filled with imperial crowns, carved gourds, baskets in every colour of the rainbow, and manuscripts written in Ge'ez, the ancient language of Ethiopia. As we walked, Samson continued his story.

'There were dangers everywhere. Sometimes a tunnel would collapse and the miners would be buried alive. I lost many friends that way. Others were killed for their pouches of gold dust, their throats slit with a razor-blade during the night.

'My parents begged me to return home. They said Beelzebub was inside me. But I laughed at them and made fun of their poverty. Then one morning as I was shaving, I saw my face in the scrap of mirror. My eyes were bloodshot from drink and filled with anger. They were not *my* eyes – they belonged to the Lucifer.'

Back at the taxi, Samson showed me his prize possession – an extremely large leather-bound Bible which he kept under the passenger seat. It had been printed near St Paul's in London in 1673.

The good book, Samson said, reminded him of the true path. But it also taught him that gold could be beneficial if given respect, if used for the good of all men. He had read the Books of Kings and Chronicles and knew all about King Solomon and the land of Ophir. Unable to believe my good fortune at meeting a man who was familiar with biblical history and who had worked as a gold miner, I took out my map and told Samson about my quest to find Solomon's mines.

'Travelling in Ethiopia is hard,' he said. 'It's not like America where the roads are as smooth as silk. Here the buses break down and the police want bribes. A foreigner searching for gold would surely be locked in a cell and beaten with a thorny stick.'

I boasted that I had experience, that I'd only recently travelled to see the Shuar tribe who live deep in the jungles of the Peruvian Amazon. I told him how they shrink the heads of their enemies to the size of a grapefruit, and how they make manioc beer with the saliva of their ugliest crones. I omitted to say that the once feared Shuar warriors are now all fanatical Evangelists, desperate only for tambourines.

'It sounds as if you are a man with no fear,' Samson replied, blowing into his hands. 'But how will you find your way to the gold mines? You are a stranger in a foreign land.'

'I need an assistant,' I replied meekly, 'someone with a knowledge of history and gold. And if I'm to find King Solomon's mines, I'll need someone with a gigantic Bible to keep the Devil away.'

3

The Father of Madness

'There is little doubt that Abyssinia is the real emporium of Ophir.'

Frank Hayter, *The Gold of Ethiopia*

IN 1894, TWO engineers sought an audience with Emperor Menelik II, who had recently moved Ethiopia's capital from Ankober to Addis Ababa. One was Swiss, the other French. They had realized that Menelik's new capital would only expand if it were connected to the Red Sea coast; and so they proposed building a fabulous railway, linking Addis Ababa with the French port of Djibouti. The project would be a masterpiece of engineering skill. Never one to shun a modern idea, Menelik was intrigued by the scheme. But before he would agree to it, he set the two Europeans a task to test their expertise. They were confined to a room under armed guard, given some twine, an awl, a knife and a sheet of tanned leather, and ordered to make a pair of shoes before the sun rose at dawn. The engineers unpicked their own shoes and used them as patterns. They worked all night and, as the first rays of light swept across the capital, they presented the Emperor with a fine pair of leather shoes. Menelik pledged his support and three years later the railway was built.

In the century since its completion, the railway has gradually decayed. In Ethiopia, if something breaks it stays broken. Now the paint on the railway carriages is peeling and the floorboards have cracked. The light-fittings have been stolen, the clock dials have lost their hands and the bolts have lost their nuts. Even the station-masters' whistles no longer whistle. Packs of wild dogs feed on the rats which eat the cockroaches, which feast on the larvae which infest the wooden boards of the rolling stock.

Samson and I turned up at the station in time to watch the third-class passengers being whipped into line with batons. As far as the police were concerned, third class were fair game. When the railway police had finished beating their passengers into submission, they turned their attention to the beggars. Addis Ababa is awash with desperate supplicants, lured from the countryside by the dream of streets paved with gold.

I knew the journey to Harar was going to be bad when the train broke down three minutes after leaving Addis Ababa station. Samson, who had not been on a train before, pleaded with me to jump out into the sidings while we still had a chance to escape. Our cramped carriage was packed with a troop of riotous Somalis, and Samson was not happy. Understanding their language was, he said, a curse greater than any other imaginable. But the Somalis were nothing compared to the rain. The carriage leaked like a rusting sieve. In the summer such ventilation must be a boon, but during the heavy rains it soon drives you wild. Samson kept getting up to rearrange himself, frantic at the thought that the rain might drip on to his cherished Bible.

I had promised him a considerable wage if he would lead me to the gold mines. I suspected I'd kick myself later for hiring someone about whom I knew so little, but Samson had agreed willingly and he seemed amiable enough, if a little preoccupied with the Devil and biblical passages. Leaving his brother to look after the taxi, he packed a plastic carrier bag with a few old clothes and waved his girlfriend goodbye.

Before heading south to Samson's ancestral home, we would make a detour. I wanted to visit the walled town of Harar in the east, for it is there that hyenas are said to guard King Solomon's gold.

Three hours after breaking down, the train came alive, pulling out through the endless shantytowns that surround the capital. Corrugated iron shacks stretched to the horizon, slotted together like tinplate toys. A band of shoeless children were playing hide-and-seek in thickets of bamboo while their older sisters thrashed clothes on a rock in a stagnant pool. Five men were drinking beer from dark brown bottles beneath a eucalyptus tree. A blind man hobbled down to the tracks to relieve himself. As the train struggled to gather speed, the stench of raw sewage and methane became overpowering.

I found myself watching the Somalis in fascination. Quite different from the Ethiopians, who frown on boisterous behaviour, they spent the journey passing a demijohn of hard liquor around. When they were not drinking they sang, and when they were not singing, they chewed *qat*, the mildly narcotic leaf that is so popular in the Horn of Africa and southern Arabia. Periodically Samson would look up from his Bible and mutter darkly. He said they would rob us in the night and might even throw us out of the train altogether. Somalis, he said, are in league with the Devil.

Just before dusk, the rain eased and allowed the dying sun to illuminate a mass of grey clouds on the horizon. Ten minutes later we were sitting in total darkness. The carriage's lights had long ago burnt out. As the hours slipped by, our eyes adjusted to the darkness, and the Somalis' unruliness reached new heights. One man stood up and urinated the length of the aisle. Then two others had a competition to see how far they could spit. The man sitting across from us, a soft-spoken engineer with a cross pinned to his lapel, informed me that they were not Christians. The depraved conduct of the Somalis was not their fault, he said, but that of their religion.

Samson had brought out a candle stub and was reading the Psalms by its flickering light. He promised to stay awake, to ensure that the Somalis kept their hands off our baggage and our throats. I drifted in and out of sleep, dreaming of the hyenas of Harar and their cache of treasure.

By nine o'clock the next morning the Somalis had passed out, and the sun was burning high above a desert. I gazed through the window, still half asleep, and thanked God for the change in climate. Low thorn trees and cacti threw shadows across the panorama of sand. Rabbits scuttled about in search of food. We passed a huge herd of camels hobbled near the tracks, their clay-coloured hides reflecting the light. There were camel calves, too, tied together like convicts in a chain. When the carriage halted at a small station, herdsmen swarmed up to the windows, selling fresh camel milk and salted cheese. I bought some of the milk, which was passed up in an old tin can. It was still warm.

Twenty-six hours after leaving the capital, we pulled into the terminus at Dire Dawa. Given the state of the track and the train, it was a miracle that we had arrived at all.

As usual, I had far too much luggage with me. I had left most of my books in Addis Ababa, selecting only a few at random to read along the way. Even so, I was surrounded by military canvas sacks full of supplies. I like to be prepared for any eventuality. What I was not prepared for was a full luggage inspection. All alighting passengers were frisked before they could leave the station and every piece of luggage was searched by a team of officious female guards. They were looking for contraband. When I had heaved my belongings on to the inspection table, all the guards ran over to rifle through them. I might not have had any contraband, but I did have all manner of imported curiosities, including an electric razor and an inflatable camping chair. The chair was viewed with great suspicion and I was ordered to inflate it. Then, to my great annoyance, it was confiscated.

I was eager to press on to Harar, but Samson had fallen into conversation with a fruit-seller on the station platform. The man spoke of an immense cave on the outskirts of Dire Dawa, in which gold had once been mined. Deciding to investigate further we took rooms at the Hotel Ras and then made a beeline for breakfast. The hotel had seen better days. The telephones had lost their dials and the ceiling fans were missing their blades. The lavatories leaked, and the floor tiles were hideously chipped. We took seats at one end of the dining-room and ordered a large quantity of buttered toast. Samson seemed very happy and said that he always tried to stay in hotels when he had the chance. I asked which was his favourite hotel. Rubbing his eyes with his thumbs, he confessed that he had not stayed in one before.

I am not sure why, but caves and gold tend to go hand in hand. Throughout Africa, Arabia and the Indian subcontinent, I've come across snippets of folklore which link the two firmly together. Underground caverns are of course the perfect place to hide treasure, just as they're a good starting-point for digging shafts to reach gold-bearing veins. Of all the stories I have heard on the subject of caves and gold, the strangest was related by my father in his first travel book, *Destination Mecca*.

Following Arab folklore, which says that Solomon took gold from the region north of Port Sudan, he prepared for an extensive search. Everyone he met on the Red Sea coast alerted him to the dangers he would face. Some warned of bandits. Others told him to beware of the Hadendowa tribe whom the British called 'Fuzzy-Wuzzies' during their occupation of Sudan. They were reputed to hack off the limbs of intruders for sport. Still others spoke of death through thirst or hunger, or at the hand of supernatural forces. Undeterred, my father journeyed up the Red Sea coast. He hoped to meet a lone Irishman who had supposedly spent the previous twenty years prospecting the area for gold. He never found the Irishman but, after a long search, he came across hundreds of immense slag heaps that reminded him of the piles of coal tailings in Yorkshire. He reckoned they were probably thousands of years old and that the ancient Egyptians and perhaps Solomon's legions had mined gold in the area.

Not far from the slag heaps, he found a series of tunnels, many running more than three hundred feet into the ground. 'Once inside the workings,' he wrote, 'there is something eerie about the silent maze of intersecting galleries, the abandoned piles of earthenware crucibles, the strange silence of the place.'

But more peculiar still was the absence of carbon on the walls. Lamps or burning torches would have been required to illuminate the long tunnels and shafts, and they would have left a residue of carbon. When my father asked local people about the mines, they all gave the same reply. Obviously there was no sign of carbon, they said, because these mines were worked night and day by Solomon's army of jinn.

After breakfast Samson and I left the hotel, walked past the Coca Cola factory and made our way to the bazaar. On either side of it were hundreds of refugee tents but in the bazaar itself business was thriving. The stalls were piled high with dried ginger and spices, garlic and onions, rose-water, dried dates and limes, and on every table sticks of sandalwood incense were burning to ward off the flies.

Now and again Samson would stop to ask a stallholder about the legend of the cave filled with gold. Everyone he spoke to nodded vigorously. There was a legend, they said, and there was a cave filled with treasure. They were certain of that much. But when I enquired where the cave could be found, they swished at the flies and shook their heads.

We pressed deeper into the bazaar. The entire market was roofed with a patchwork of sacking, but it didn't keep out the heat or the flies. Children were whipping their homemade hoops through the streets past yet more stalls. I took a close look at the merchandise. As well as spices and fruit and vegetables, there were sacks of flour and oil donated by US Aid. Thousands of empty tin cans were on sale as well, and rusting car parts, tattered clothing and a sea of broken telephones, bicycles, kettles and shoes.

A boy in a bright red shirt said he knew the cave. It wasn't far and he would take us if his friend could tag along as well. What about the treasure? The boys shook their heads. No one ever went down there, they said, on account of the bats.

Twenty minutes later, after rambling through a maze of back-streets and an enclosure filled with goats, we found ourselves looking down on a substantial crater that led to a wide-mouthed cave. From the smell it was evident that the crater and the front part of the cave were used as a public lavatory. Reluctantly, we climbed down.

One of the boys' older brothers offered to take us deep into the cave if we bought an old rubber boot and a cup of petrol. He needed these for a fire, which would provide light and keep away the bats. I handed over funds, and someone was sent to fetch the required materials.

I was ready to endure hardship in my quest for Solomon's mines but I'd not expected the first obstacle to be so unpleasant. The boy in the red shirt said it was the refugees who used the cave entrance as a lavatory. He didn't know where exactly they'd come from, but he said they squatted night and day.

Eventually the wellington boot arrived, along with a cup of petrol and a metal tray. The oldest boy took charge. First he ripped the rubber boot into strips. Then he put the strips on the tray, poured the petrol over them, and struck a match. A few seconds later, the strips of boot were alight and belching black smoke. By now a crowd of children had joined us down in the hole. None of them seemed to mind sliding around in the faeces and choking in the smoke. They were determined not to miss the opportunity of watching a foreigner make a fool of himself.

The blazing boot was carried ceremoniously into the cavern.

Samson and I kept close behind. Thousands of orange-yellow eyes shone from the walls like stars on a clear night, but as soon as the first fumes billowed into the chamber all hell broke loose. Suddenly we were attacked by screaming harpies, diving, swooping and flapping, their leathery wings bombarding us from every direction. Then the rubber boot, which had heated the tray to an industrial temperature, went out, plunging us into darkness. Provoked beyond all reason, the bats redoubled their attack. I stood stock-still, hands drawn over my face to protect my eyes, trying desperately not to panic.

Another boot was brought into the cave and ignited. I called out to Samson. Could he see any mine-shafts leading off or any sign of gold? Choking, he pointed to the far wall of the cavern. I peered through the mass of wings and dense smoke. In the lowest part of the wall there appeared to be a doorway which had long since been filled in with neatly cut blocks of stone. The boy in the red shirt said that a hermit used to live in the cave and that he drew paintings on the walls in bats' blood. Behind the doorway there was a room, and in the room was the hermit's skeleton. Local people had bricked up the doorway when the hermit died.

The children didn't know whether the hermit had been secretly searching for gold. What about the refugees? Had they ever been found digging for gold? The boys didn't know that either. The refugees were very poor, they replied, in fact so poor that they lived in tattered tents and had almost no food – which made me wonder how such an ill-fed people could produce such monstrous amounts of sewage.

After a cold shower back at the Hotel Ras, we took our places in the dining-room once again. The waiter watched me show Samson how a formal table is laid, with multiple pieces of cutlery. He leaned over and adjusted the fly-paper which hung above our table. His shirt had become discoloured over time and his bow tie was frayed and bleached from years of wear.

'We used to lay the table like that,' he said wistfully. 'That was in the old days, in 1965, when the Hotel Ras was a jewel. Of course I was a young man then, a foolish young man. But I remember those times. The parties, the music, the fine foreign food.'

We ordered spaghetti and boiled potatoes, and the old waiter hurried off to serve a table of rowdy Russians on the other side of the room. I wondered what business had brought them to Dire Dawa. Gold, perhaps. They certainly had a great deal of money to spend, if the number of prostitutes at their table was anything to go by.

Samson tried to count the dead and dying flies cemented to the fly-paper. I looked over at him as he counted energetically, and I congratulated myself. I was pleased with the way he had stood up to the rigours of the cave. He'd hardly complained, even when he realized that, like me, his hair was matted with bat excrement. I suggested we take high-powered torches and return to prize the blocks of stone out of the doorway. A mine-shaft might lie behind the blocked-up entrance. Samson ate his spaghetti without looking up.

'The cave's secret is obvious,' he said. 'The Devil is waiting behind the doorway. He imprisoned the hermit and would do the same to us. As for the bats, they're the Devil's servants.'

Unable to muster support for a second assault on the cave, I told Samson that we'd return to the bats if the hyenas of Harar didn't live up to expectations. We left our bags at the hotel and then hailed a minibus heading for Harar.

The road up to the walled city had been recently constructed by the Chinese. A sea of crooked-horned cattle ran down the olive-black asphalt as we approached, parting only long enough to allow us through. Like the road on which it drove, the minibus was brand-new and we were the only passengers, which made me suspicious. In a country like Ethiopia no vehicle travels if it's not laden to bursting. The driver, whose face was tormented by a severe nervous tic, said he had won the vehicle in a game of cards. When I quizzed him why he had no other passengers, he changed the subject, declaring that Harar was the Pearl of Ethiopia. Once I'd set eyes on it, he said, I would weep like a child whose mother had died.

I asked him if he'd ever heard the legend of the hyenas and the gold. He let out a shrill cackle of laughter.

'Ah, yes,' he said, 'the hyenas – there are thousands of them. They come to the city walls each night, and they take children. Dozens of babies vanish every year. It's a problem for our peace-loving town.'

He paused to feed the steering-wheel through his hands.

'There's little we can do. You see, if you kill a hyena, ten more are born.'

'Has it always been so?'

'Yes, of course, since ancient times. Everyone knows that the hyenas were once men like you and me. They were all in love with the Emir's most beautiful daughter. Each night they'd try to climb up to her bedroom in the palace. The Emir got so enraged that he turned all the suitors into wretched dogs.'

Most sub-Saharan towns have an air of torpor, brought on by the heat and a general eagerness to relax. But Harar has a distinctly Eastern bustle about it. Everyone was busy. Some were counting money. Others were running errands or making butter by shaking plastic bottles full of milk. Even the lines of lepers were hustling for handouts.

In the market, wide cane baskets brimmed with *qat*, okra, melons and lentils, mangoes and black-bellied fish. There were cupfuls of peanuts on sale too, and macaroni, blocks of grey salt and prickly pears. The range of fruit and vegetables was impressive, but nothing could compare with the range of contraband.

Shops in Ethiopia generally have only a few meagre goods on sale, little more than basic foods, Chinese cooking-pots, plastic buckets, rubber boots and scouring pads. But Harar's proximity to Djibouti has made it a refuge for illicit merchandise. The shops were full of the latest widescreen TVs, videos, blue jeans, cartons of Marlboro and bottles of Scotch. Wherever I looked, bales of illegal stock were being off-loaded from trucks.

I tried to imagine what Harar was like when Richard Burton, the Victorian adventurer and linguist, reached the walled city in 1854. The British East India Company had commissioned him to explore the Somali coast and he came in disguise, uncertain whether he would be treated as a guest or as a prisoner. In fact he was the first European to visit the town and not be executed, and he later described his journey in *First Footsteps in East Africa*.

The backstreets of the old city were crowded. Old men sat playing draughts with upturned bottle caps, reclining on charpoys or sipping glasses of mint tea. Lines of women in traditional Harari pantaloons loitered outside the many mosques, hoping for alms. There were children too, tottering along with great bundles on their heads, savage dogs snapping at their heels. And everywhere there were donkeys and goats, tattered chickens and underfed dairy cows. Doorways led from the narrow streets into courtyards shaded by sprawling acacia trees. Barbers ran cut-throat razors over cheeks, then rubbed kerosene into the skin. Mothers washed clothes in tubs. The faithful prayed in silence, and in every doorway sat bearded men, their mouths stuffed with *qat*, their eyes glazed like those of the Lotus-Eaters. By early afternoon, most of Harar's men were in a trance.

A shopkeeper had told us where to find the hyenas. Outside the city wall a crude whitewashed building stood in the shade of a tree. In its courtyard a shrine had been built, and on the shrine a beggar was sleeping. The ground outside the house was littered with hundreds of jaw-bones and sets of front teeth.

In the courtyard a young woman was squatting, picking nits out of her daughter's hair. She chatted to Samson for a few minutes without looking him in the face. He told me that we had come to the right place: the woman's husband was a hyena-man. The woman brought us glasses of sweet tea and said her husband Yusuf would return shortly.

Ten minutes later, a fiendish-looking man arrived at the house. Yusuf had thin lips, a greasy complexion and no eyebrows. He was leading a scrawny cow by a rope. I introduced myself and asked him what exactly a hyena-man's duties involved. He motioned for me to sit and watch. Wasting no time, he sharpened a pair of long knives against each other and led the cow to a spot beneath the tree. He tied a rope around the neck of the animal and bound another around her front feet. A gentle push and the cow was forced to kneel like a convict before an executioner. She let out a mild bellow of protest but seemed resigned to her fate. Yusuf held one of the blades high above the jugular and recited the traditional prayer: '*Bismillah ar-rahman ar-rahim*, In the name of Allah, the Beneficent, the Merciful'. With that he carved the knife into the animal's neck and a fountain of blood gushed out. The cow collapsed as blood continued to pump on to the ground beneath her. Then, just as I thought the grim event was over, her back legs struck out wildly in a last struggle for life.

Yusuf started to dismember the carcass. He drained the remaining blood into buckets, hacked away the head, carved off the limbs, gouged out the lungs and the offal, and emptied the stomachs of their half-digested grass. Then he chopped the carcass up into small, bite-size chunks.

I asked him why he had slaughtered the beast.

'Every night I feed the hyenas,' he said, 'just as my father did and his father did before him. My eldest son Abbas will do the same. It is a tradition in our family, a responsibility we pass through the generations.'

'Is the cow sick?'

'No!' he shouted. 'We only feed them the very best cows, and we kill them in a *halal* way, bleeding them to death.'

'What happens if you don't feed the hyenas?'

Yusuf's already sullen expression froze.

'If we do not feed them,' he said, 'they'll descend on Harar and carry away all the children.'

'Have they ever bitten you?'

'So many times,' the hyena-man replied, as his bloody fingers stuffed his mouth with *qat*. 'But better I am bitten than our children eaten.'

'How many hyena-men are there in Harar?'

Yusuf burped loudly.

'At one time there were so many – a dozen or more. The town was very safe because the hyenas were happy. But now the young don't want to carry on the duty. They don't realize the terrible price they will pay. If no one feeds the hyenas, the animals will become enraged and will run wild!'

'Who pays for the meat?'

'That's a big worry,' he replied uneasily. 'Some people with young children donate money, but it's not usually enough. You see how we live, like beggars. I spend all my extra money to make sure the hyenas get the very best meat.'

I asked about the gold.

'These creatures are not mortal,' Yusuf replied. 'That's certain. They are ghosts or jinn. It's true, they protect Solomon's golden treasure and keep it from Satan.'

'Have you ever tried to find the treasure?'

'Only a lunatic would risk his life to follow the hyenas to their lair,' Yusuf replied. 'Any man who has dared to climb down into their burrows has been torn limb from limb.'

Muttering to himself, Yusuf wandered away. Each night, before he feeds a bullock or a cow to the hyenas, he goes off to wash, to collect his thoughts, to pray and to chew a great deal of *qat*. He asks God to make sure he's not bitten badly, to keep the hyenas happy, and to protect the city's children until dawn.

By nine o'clock the moon was high above Harar, casting ivory light over the whitewashed walls of the house. Yusuf had chewed *qat* since early afternoon, and his eyes were dilated to capacity. The mild amphetamine gave him the strength he needed to face the hyenas.

Before the feeding began, he hurled the buckets of cow's blood as far as he could over the baked earth outside his house. The hyenas' sharp sense of smell would quickly alert them to the killing. Then, sitting on an upturned pail, he started to call the animals by name.

At that moment the first hyena appeared. Cowering and snarling, its head hung low, it darted over to where the blood had been thrown and began to lick the ground feverishly; its mottled fur reflecting in the beam of light from my torch, its eyes glistening like shards of crystal. Yusuf spoke to it in a language I did not understand. Then he tossed over a hunk of offal. When I looked again I saw others, many now, their shadowy forms moving through the darkness like phantoms. Whistling, calling names and chanting mysterious words, the hyena–man lured the animals towards him.

As Yusuf skewered a chunk of roughly cut beef on a stick and held it in his teeth, I stepped back from the buckets of meat. Lurching, snapping, the hair on their spines bristling, the hyenas crept forward. More were joining the pack. Before I knew it there were too many to count accurately, at least sixty, perhaps more. One by one they seized the meat from the stick. Then gradually they forgot their fear and seethed around their master, filling the air with the sound of crazed laughter. From time to time greed would get the better of them, and they would turn on each other. For an hour or more Yusuf continued to feed them, until the entire carcass had been devoured.

Before driving back down to Dire Dawa, Samson and I stopped for some food at a small café. All the tables were occupied by men who were smoking, laughing and chewing piles of fresh *qat*. We asked three or four of them about Yusuf and the hyenas. To my surprise they all said the same thing. They agreed that without fresh meat, the wild dogs would descend on Harar and butcher the town's infants. They were convinced that the hyenas guard a treasure more fabulous than any other known to man. Sometimes, they said, a hyena is shot and in its ear is found a gold earring. Lastly, they explained that at night, after he has fed them, Yusuf transforms himself into a hyena and runs off with the pack. Until dawn the next day he reigns as the hyena king.

On hearing this we rushed out of the café and down through the narrow streets to the gate in the old city's wall. Jumping across a ditch we made our way to Yusuf's house. The smell of offal and blood still lingered beneath the tree where the hyenas had fed. Samson declared that he'd prove that the tales of superstition were a load of nonsense, and so we scoured Yusuf's home, the courtyard and the surrounding area. But the hyena-man wasn't there.

Travel in Africa is generally something to be endured rather than enjoyed. The bus-ride back to Addis Ababa was the kind of experience that makes you question the purpose of even the most well-intentioned journey and long for the luxury of home. Shunning the train, I had insisted that we race back to the capital on the local bus. After numerous false starts, the vehicle rolled out of Dire Dawa at walking pace. It was the middle of the night. Very soon it became clear that the bus had severe mechanical problems. The gearbox was badly in need of repair and the bus had no brake pads.

We discussed the hyenas. Samson was convinced that there was no gold mine or hoard of treasure waiting to be found at Harar. To my irritation he declared that the expedition so far had been a waste of time.

'Gold drives men mad with greed,' he said. 'You can see it in their eyes. If there was a treasure,' he went on, 'Yusuf would be the first man to kill the hyenas and take it all.'

The man sitting in the row behind us was dressed in a patched boiler-suit with a canary-yellow scarf wound around his throat. He was clearly deranged. For fourteen hours he pretended he was a radio announcer, chattering manically into his thumb. Someone whispered that he'd been a soldier during Mengistu's regime and that he had been tortured. As the hours passed my sympathy wore thin. The other passengers grew sick of his noise as well. They held an impromptu vote, and then threw him off the moving bus.

We broke down more times than I can remember. At each breakdown the occupants trooped off with all their belongings and sat at the side of the road. At the regular checkpoints the vehicle was searched and searched again. Each time, the passengers would struggle to conceal their contraband – cartons of imported cigarettes, pink Lycra shell-suits, fake Ray Bans and tubs of French margarine.

By local standards the journey was not unusual, but in a dusty village called Hirna something happened which confounded me.

The bus was undergoing repairs at a blacksmith's stall. Samson had gone off to find some food. I wandered about the village aimlessly and a group of children followed in my wake, taunting me with the usual chorus of '*Faranji, faranji!*' I hardly looked up, but then I noticed that away from the gaggle of children a boy of about ten was standing all alone. He was barefoot, covered in dirt and dressed in rags like the others. But the strange thing about him was his complexion – he was white. In African countries you often see albinos, but I was sure this boy wasn't one of them and his appearance brought to mind a newspaper story that I'd once read.

In the 1970s a man and a woman turned up at the US Embassy in Addis Ababa, claiming to be American citizens. They explained in Amharic – they spoke no English – that they were brother and sister and that they had been abandoned by their parents twenty years earlier. The woman was called Tegest Gadessa, and her brother was named Mariam. In the intervening years both had been badly treated and Tegest had been raped on several occasions.

The details of the tale are sketchy, but it seems that their parents were driving alone through the Ethiopian highlands when their vehicle broke down. Some people said they were missionaries, others that their father had a contract to search for oil. The mother and her two children stayed with the vehicle, while the father took to the road in search of help. He was never seen again, probably killed for his wallet and his shoes a few miles on. When the car was attacked by *shiftas*, bandits, the mother died. The boy and girl were taken to a remote village, sold into slavery and given Ethiopian names.

The loss of awareness of one's identity, a condition called fugue, is very rare and I might not have given the white boy at Hirna further thought had I not remembered the Gadessas' story. I called the boy over and gave him some bread. He didn't speak English or Amharic, only Oromo. The other children said he was sleeping in the open and that he'd arrived in the village six months before. Samson confirmed that his speech was slurred and his knowledge of Oromo only mediocre.

Where were his parents? With the other boys taunting him, he replied with growing apprehension. He didn't know where his family were, he said. He had been left to fend for himself. I asked him to lift up his tattered shirt. His chest and back, although very grimy, were undeniably white.

The more questions we asked, the more frightened the boy became. I slipped him a wad of *birr* notes and gave him some more food. Then, bursting into tears, he ran away.

Three toots of the horn warned us the bus was about to leave. There was no time to search for the boy, but I decided to report the incident to the British Embassy when we reached Addis Ababa.

For two more days that accursed brakeless bus inched its way towards the capital. At night we stopped at roadside dens where music blared, warm beer flowed freely and prostitutes caroused with clients. Diesel was heavy on the air, and oily mud thick on our shoes. Outside the dens truck drivers slept beneath their vehicles, wrapped in no more than a *shamma*, a white cotton shawl.

On the second night we stopped at a particularly vile bar and decided to sit outside instead. A meal of *injera*, Ethiopian bread, and *doro wot*, spicy chicken stew, was brought out and set before us. As we ate, Samson talked of his home town of Kebra Mengist, of his family and his beloved girlfriend. Did he plan to marry her? He looked sombre at the question.

'If God wills it, we will marry,' he said gloomily, 'but weddings are expensive. When I mined gold I was rich, but the Devil was inside me. Now that I have returned to God I am penniless.'

After the meal he opened the great Bible at random and started to read. As far as Samson was concerned, a man who didn't read the Bible had no hope of succeeding at all. He never said so, but I knew he regarded me as an especially wretched case. While he ploughed through the Book of Revelation, I started the life story of an Englishman called Frank Hayter. The book was entitled *The Gold of Ethiopia*, and it had been published in 1936. With such a title it had seemed an obvious book to buy.

Every few minutes Samson would pause, glance up at the starlit sky, and thank God for walking beside him. Then he'd return to the text, his lips trembling as he mouthed each word. Across the table I had a revelation of my own.

The frontispiece showed a moustachioed Hayter in a pith helmet, a safari shirt and khaki shorts, with a long cigarette-holder between his lips. He was standing against a backdrop of a giant leopard skin. I started to read, and by the end of the first chapter I was hooked.

Frank Hayter was born in 1902, into a farming family on the Welsh borders. From his earliest youth he dreamt of becoming a great white hunter and of travelling to the Dark Continent. The first step towards his goal came when he got a job at the London Zoo as a taxidermist. He took pride in his work and was thrilled when he was selected for a special African expedition. He was to travel to the Abyssinian highlands to collect a hundred baboons for the zoo.

In 1924 Hayter took the boat-train to Marseilles, and then a steamer on to Djibouti. There he caught the train to Dire Dawa, where he made his base. In those days the now quiet railway town was full of shady characters. Greek and Armenian merchants ran every type of scam, and Danakil warriors would meander in from the desert, shields held tight across their chests, testicles dangling round their necks. Hayter even came across the resplendent entourage of the socialite and traveller Rosita Forbes, camped out on the outskirts of Harar.

After buying guns and supplies, and hiring guides and camels, Hayter and his small caravan set out across the desert towards Afar. By day the party was ravaged by heat. At nightfall the jackals arrived. Eventually they reached marshland. 'For three hideous days, and three even more hideous nights,' Hayter wrote, 'we were in those reeking, fever-stricken swamps, moving not mile by mile, but foot by foot.'

While trapped in the marshes, the caravan was ambushed by

Danakils, who were eager to add fresh trophies to their necks. Undaunted, Hayter forced his men to charge through the warriors' lines. Several were slain and most of the supplies were lost. Remarkably, Hayter managed to complete his mission, rounding up a hundred Abyssinian baboons. But as they were carried away, a monk put a curse on Hayter for stealing sacred animals. Thinking nothing of it, Hayter loaded the baboons on to a ship bound for London. The animals' crates were lashed to the deck but one night a storm blew up. The waves that broke over the ship split many of the crates, so freeing the baboons which ran wild. The curse had begun to take effect.

In the years that followed, Hayter returned time and again to Ethiopia. He was bewitched by the country. Travelling to the most distant outposts, he struggled to earn a living. He worked as a rat-catcher, as a rare butterfly hunter, as a muleteer and as a debt-collector, but it was as a gold prospector that he made his name.

The 1920s were buoyant times in Ethiopia. Although Menelik II had sought to open up his kingdom to the outside world and to modernize it, the economy was still largely feudal. A handful of Europeans took advantage of the country's lack of sophistication and introduced luxuries for the few who could afford them, while others leased mining concessions from the government and prospected for gold.

Frank Hayter spent years panning rivers and digging alone in the untamed reaches of western Ethiopia. The locals nicknamed him Abba Kuta, 'The Father of Madness'. They'd never come across a man so set on searching for gold. Hayter was certain that the precious metal had been mined in Ethiopia for millennia and that ancient Egyptians must have worked the region even before the time of Solomon. For Hayter, Ethiopia was the 'Land of Sheba', whose queen travelled to Jerusalem to shower the wise king with gold.

Somewhere lost in the Simien Mountains Hayter believed there lay a network of shafts from which fabulous quantities of gold had once been mined. He had heard of monasteries built over cave entrances where the monks refused to let foreigners enter the gold-filled caverns: they were waiting for the 'Great White Queen' to return.

Hayter never relinquished his search for what he called 'the

Queen of Sheba's mines', but gradually the curse began to exact its terrible revenge. Each day, he grew a little weaker. A once athletic young man was slowly becoming a physical wreck. Then, after years of solitary prospecting, he stumbled across a series of cave entrances which led to mine-shafts. The doorways, faced with carved stone, stood high on the ledge of a remote mountain called Tullu Wallel.

Cautiously, Hayter entered one of the portals, fearful of disturbing a wild animal in its lair. Deep in one of the shafts, he said, there lay a fabulous treasure. But before he could cart away the gold and other riches, the curse of the baboons struck for the last time. A river which flowed through the cavern suddenly swelled to a torrent and Hayter was forced to escape. By the time he had returned with fresh supplies, the entrance to the caves had been mysteriously sealed. However hard he tried, he could not break in.

Samson had never heard of Tullu Wallel; nor had anyone else I asked. But he did agree that Ethiopian curses are something to be taken very seriously. He'd seen with his own eyes a cursed man die a slow and painful death. The spell had been cast by a high-ranking priest on a shopkeeper whose only crime was to enter a church wearing shoes.

By the time we reached Addis Ababa I was determined to find out more about Frank Hayter and Tullu Wallel, and I knew there was only one man who might be able to help. Dr Richard Pankhurst has spent most of his life in Ethiopia. His grandmother, Emmeline Pankhurst, was the founder of the suffragette movement, and his mother was equally spirited, moving to Ethiopia in the 1930s in order to help support the resistance against the invading Italians. Dr Pankhurst has written extensively on Ethiopian society and history, and is regarded as the foremost expert on all matters Ethiopian.

Tracking down the distinguished scholar was far easier than I had expected. He lives with his wife and their dogs in a cottage on the outskirts of Addis Ababa. An hour after speaking on the telephone, he pulled the front door wide open and ushered me in for tea.

We sat in a conservatory at the back of the house, drinking mint tea and nibbling at slices of toast spread with home-made jam.

Despite this veneer of Englishness I very soon realized that my host had an unusual sensitivity towards the African continent and, in particular, Ethiopia.

Dr Pankhurst has spent most of his life travelling in the country's remote areas and he speaks faultless Amharic. I was worried that he might regard my search for Solomon's gold as frivolous. I did not know much about Ethiopian culture and so far I'd only been as far as Harar. So when I was invited to talk about my project, I gave the details uneasily.

Pankhurst stared into space for a few moments.

'Ethiopia has a great history of gold,' he said at last. 'Herodotus, Cosmos, Agathachides, Barradas – they all spoke of it.'

I asked if he'd heard of Tullu Wallel or Frank Hayter.

'Tullu Wallel is not far from Beni Shangul, as I recall,' he said. 'Historically the area was renowned for the quality of its gold. Menelik seized the province in 1886 to exploit its rich mineral resources. The most valuable licence was granted to a prospector called Ilg. He found what he believed was an ancient Egyptian gold mine at Nejo. As for Frank Hayter,' he continued, 'yes, I know the name. He wrote some letters to my mother. Like her, he was against the Italian Fascist invasion of Ethiopia.'

Pankhurst paused to sip his tea.

'Even so, as a credible point of reference, I'd have to say that Hayter is rather unreliable.'

Later that day I thumbed through my books, searching for the references that Pankhurst had mentioned. Agathachides, a Greek geographer writing in about 140 BC, told how prisoners-of-war were used to mine gold. 'Vast numbers of them are bound in fetters,' he wrote, 'and compelled to work night and day without pause, with no hope of escape. For they are under savage soldiers who speak a foreign tongue.'

Cosmos, a Greek-speaking merchant – writing seven centuries after Agathachides – said that 'a land of frankincense and gold lies at the farthest end of Ethiopia'. Arriving at the Axumite port of Adulis in about AD 524, he heard that gold was mined by the Agau people in the west and bartered through a system known by anthropologists as 'dumb commerce'. Every other year, the king of the Axumites sent forth his agents to trade with the Agau. The agents arrived with a great entourage, bringing oxen, iron, salt and other merchandise to exchange for gold. They would set up camp, and surround it with thorny fences. Oxen would be slaughtered and the meat hung on the thorns along with other goods. During the night the Agau would take what they wanted and leave nuggets of gold in their place.

A thousand years after Cosmos, the Portuguese explorer and patriarch Juan de Bermudez travelled west along the Nile. Bermudez, nicknamed 'the Lord of Wealth', had become famous for discovering the Caribbean island of Bermuda which is named after him. (He actually found the island by chance, when he was shipwrecked on a voyage from Virginia.) In his chronicles of Ethiopia, he wrote that the land was barren but that the soil was red, for it was two parts gold and one part earth. The precious metal was more common than iron, and was fashioned into wondrous objects by the locals.

From the earliest times explorers have been fascinated by Ethiopia and particularly by its western regions and the barbarous tribes who once inhabited them. Famed for their strange rituals and their expertise in mining gold, the tribes of Wollega and Beni Shangul are the stuff of legend. It is no surprise that for people like Frank Hayter – who was inspired by Rider Haggard's novel – western Ethiopia was an obvious place to search for King Solomon's mines.

Though Pankhurst had dismissed Hayter as unreliable, I was gripped with an overwhelming desire to follow in his footsteps. I knew that my chances of success were slim, but the idea of seeking out the mountain seemed important. I searched for Hayter in my other books but only one mentioned him. *In the Land of Sheba*, written by Captain E. J. Bartleet, Hayter's contemporary and friend, tells the story of Tullu Wallel. Opposite the text, there is a black-and-white photograph of a cave and a shaft entrance. Beneath it, the caption reads: *The entrance to the Queen of Sheba's caves*.

4

The Mines

'The real voyage of discovery consists not in seeing new landscapes, but in having new eyes.'

Marcel Proust, *A la recherche du temps perdu*

WE MUST HAVE been mad to swap the comfort of our beds for the snarl of the bus station. Long before dawn we turned up to search for the bus heading south to Samson's home town of Kebra Mengist, walking through ankle-deep mud and wishing we were anywhere but here. A dozen battered buses were being mobbed by crowds of would-be passengers, all of them frantically trying to get aboard. Their belongings were wrapped in blankets and held above their heads, as if they were wading through a flood. The engine of each bus roared wildly in competition but, as I'd already discovered, noise had nothing to do with reliability.

Our vehicle rolled up at high speed, its single headlamp lighting the way. A sea of pickpockets and ticket touts, priests, soldiers and porters lurched towards it. Behind them all, soft-spoken Samson and I tiptoed through the mud as bravely as we dared.

A few *birr* were sufficient to give us the pick of the wooden benches. As all Ethiopians know, the best place to sit is at the front, and the worst is beside the rear door. We stuffed our bags under our seats. Samson had spent his first wages on a Chinese-made tartan bag. He winced when I made fun of the purchase but he wasn't dispirited. The case had somehow transformed him. He was no longer a taxi-driver. Instead he had become a traveller. As he drew my attention to the bag's stitching, a tidal wave of people swept up into the bus. At first I couldn't make out individual passengers, for it was still dark. But gradually the dawn brought detail to their faces. Many looked fearful at the thought of the journey

47

ahead, as they struggled to find space for their children and their baggage. No one but me seemed to care about the bus's dilapidated state, or that its driver looked like an axe-murderer.

At home I'm the first to complain at the prospect of a road trip. The hum of radial tyres on tarmac and the tedium of the motorway are enough to drive me to road rage. But elsewhere in the world a long drive is quite different. The wooden seats, the exhaust fumes, the loud discordant music and the press of passengers, fattened chickens and dingy sacks are only minor irritants. What matters is survival.

On an African road trip you're a gambler. Every passenger has a lump in his throat, like the man who slips one bullet into the chamber of a revolver, spins it and holds the weapon to his temple. You pay your money and you take your chances. As in Russian Roulette, the thrill lies in surviving.

Peer out of the grimy windows if you dare, and you will see the wreckage of those who have lost the gamble. A great truck laden with crates hurtles past. Minutes later you pass the same vehicle, lying on its side at the foot of a ravine. Its crates have been reduced to matchwood and their contents lie strewn across the ground. The driver's body sprawls out of the cab's open door. The vultures begin to descend, and soon locals from the nearest village swarm down like locusts to pick the wreckage clean. Within a matter of hours everything that can be carried away has gone. The merchandise is the first to go. Then the splinters of wood from the crates are taken and the diesel is siphoned from the tank. The wheels are plundered, then the truck is stripped of its engine, its bodywork, wiring, wing-mirrors and seats. Soon all that is left is the chassis. Ethiopian hillsides are littered with them. A serious crash is something to be relished, an unexpected bounty for the whole village to share.

There was a time when Ethiopia's roads were safe, but Menelik II, the great modernizer, heard news of a new-fangled invention. The electric chair might have been a disappointment, but he'd been told of another toy – the motor-car – and he wanted one desperately. Word spread far and wide that the first man to drive a car to the Emperor would be rewarded beyond his wildest dreams.

Three thousand miles away an Englishman called Bede Bentley heard of the challenge. He was already a respected adventurer and had fought against the Boers and against the infamous Mad Mulla in Somaliland. He'd even proposed building a motorized armoured vehicle, which he called a 'tank'. But he'd made the mistake of sending the designs to Lord Kitchener, who thanked him politely and promptly stole them.

In 1907 Bentley bought the newest model of Siddeley motor-car and had it painted in green and white stripes. The expedition's party included Bentley's uniformed chauffeur Reginald Wells, a Somali gentleman who went by the name of George, and a brindle bulldog called Bully. A few supplies were loaded up, and the adventure began. Soon after leaving England, Bentley heard that a German team had set off at the same time and were racing them to reach Menelik first.

After covering the roughest terrain ever navigated by a motor-car, Bentley, the chauffeur, the Somali and the brindle bulldog arrived at Menelik's palace in Addis Ababa. The journey had taken them many months, but they'd beaten the Germans and upheld British honour. Best of all, the Emperor was delighted with his new toy.

The landscape flattened once we descended from Addis Ababa and we drove through rolling ranges of farmland, edged with eucalyptus trees and peppered with low *tukul*, traditional huts. In the yellowing afternoon sunlight oxen pulled ploughs, goaded on with pointed sticks by farmers who had worked since dawn. The fields were tiny, divided up again and again as each generation received its inheritance. In some, tall strands of maize rustled in the breeze. In others grew *teff*, the grain from which *injera* is made; it was feathery like pampas grass, swaying as the wind rippled through its long stems. Young girls, some of them no more than four or five years old, trudged barefoot along the roads and across the fields, stacks of firewood on their heads. For them, childhood is an apprenticeship for a life of extreme hardship. In Ethiopia it is the women and children who do most of the work.

The bus passed a small town's quarry. Its ragged labourers were all old women ferrying blocks of dusty stone on their heads. Nearby their overseer, a man, sat primly on a cushioned chair. When I commented on the plight of the women Samson made excuses. The government was rotten, he said. It encouraged men to do nothing.

'It is the way of our country. Old ways cannot change.'

From time to time the bus would stop on the outskirts of a village. Soldiers would frisk everyone and then pillage their luggage. Sometimes they would seize a passenger at random and beat him. Samson said that the ploy was used to frighten all the rest. If so, it worked. The other passengers shuffled their feet and stared down at the ground, too frightened to stand up for the innocent.

Sometimes the stops were more pleasant. Droves of hawkers would come crowding up to the windows, holding up their wares for sale. The passengers would buy all they could afford: baked maize and peanuts sold in twists of paper, hair combs and oranges, unripe plums and roasted barley, rubber shoes, cooking pots and packets of seeds.

The highlight of the bus journey was the fight. As anyone who's ever taken an Ethiopian bus knows, there is an unwritten rule that the windows *must* remain firmly closed. I was never quite sure of the reasoning behind this, but the only time I opened a window Samson told me to shut it quickly before I was beaten up. Late in the afternoon, a quiet, unassuming man decided to open the window beside him just a fraction to let in a little fresh air. The man next to him immediately leapt up and began to shout. At first the two men just yelled at each other, but then they started to brawl. Within seconds, fists were flying, nails were slashing and sticks were raining down. The commotion, which had begun at the far end of the bus, spread like wildfire as all the other passengers took sides. The driver looked in the mirror and clapped his hands. If they didn't stop at once, he shouted, he'd drive the bus off an approaching cliff.

Despite the brawl, the cramped seats and the lurching motion of the bus, I found myself brimming with energy. Frank Hayter's story and his discovery of a mine-shaft could have come from Rider Haggard's own pen. Hayter's book spoke of ferocious tribes and ravening wild beasts, of hunters without fear, of treasure maps and gold beyond measure.

From what I could make out, Hayter never prospected in the south of Ethiopia, perhaps because the rich southern seam, known as the Adola greenstone belt, was not discovered until after the Second World War. In Hayter's time, prospectors worked the rivers and mountains of the west, and the great gold seam on the Eritrean border.

The problem with searching for ancient gold mines is that, like any mineral, gold can be mined out. Hundreds of thousands of slaves would have been able to work through entire hillsides, extracting almost all the ore. In the same way, a man in search of oil wells in three thousand years' time will probably find not a trace of oil left.

As we drove Samson rambled on about Kebra Mengist. He said his home town was the finest place in Ethiopia, blessed with the best food, the cleanest water, the most beautiful girls and the most chivalrous townsfolk. As for the gold mines, he claimed they were very extensive indeed. I was nervous that a foreigner arriving on the scene, even escorted by a local, would be regarded with suspicion. Samson said that Kebra Mengist was *his* town, and the miners were *his* people. They knew him and he knew them. He would protect me.

Late afternoon became early evening, and the bus rolled on. The earth turned from red clay to sand and back to red clay again. Gradually the scenery changed. The land became more fertile, dotted with banana plants and tall trees bearing flame-red flowers. The huts were different, too, their walls fashioned from wickerwork, with a pot woven into the apex of each thatched roof. Until then, most of the huts we had seen were made from wattle and daub.

Outside each hut a woman sat plaiting fibres to make baskets. As the road climbed again, we looked down across a swathe of emerald grassland rolling towards the horizon. When I tried to describe the lushness of the landscape in my journal, I knew that no one would believe me when I got home. We think of Ethiopia as a place of starvation, where the land is barren and the soil scorched by drought. Nothing could be further from the truth.

Ten miles from Kebra Mengist the bus pulled over at a police checkpoint. We trooped out and stood in line with our luggage. In the flickering light of a pressure lamp all the bags were inspected, and the passengers frisked. Then one of the soldiers climbed up into the bus and searched it. He whistled loudly to his officer. Contraband had been found. A moment later the driver and his companion were being marched away. The search was at an end, said the officer. They'd caught the culprits. The rest of us could go. I had heard that smugglers sometimes slip their goods under the seats of innocent travellers, and one glance at the driver's face suggested that he wasn't an innocent. Still, I asked, could he not be allowed to take us the last few miles into town? Quite impossible, came the reply. The driver was transporting contraband and had to be punished. So, like refugees walking with their worldly possessions, we took to the road. I regretted bringing so much equipment with me but none of the other passengers complained. Perhaps they were just thankful that it wasn't they who were locked up in a cell.

Fortunately the moon was full and it led us like a beacon through the darkness. The road was flooded with soupy grey mud and we trudged through it like soldiers broken by defeat, our packs heavy on our backs.

Three hours after leaving the checkpoint, we reached Kebra Mengist and staggered into the Holiday Hotel. It doubled as a butchery – a bull's heart had been nailed to a post in front of the building, in a crude advertisement. Drenched in mud and aching, I was too tired to complain. I flopped down on the mattress in my room, still in my boots and filthy clothes, and fell into a deep sleep.

When I awoke hours later, the sun was high above Kebra Mengist. My back and legs still ached and I knew that I needed some pampering. Samson wasn't in his room, so I walked through the muddy streets in search of some luxury.

Having listened to Samson's enthusiastic description of his home, and knowing that on the map the town was labelled prominently, I had had high hopes of Kebra Mengist. A couple of minutes' walk was enough to shatter the illusion. There was no electricity and no running water. No petrol was on sale and there was no tarmac on the roads. Most of the houses had crumbling walls and corrugated iron roofs, rusted through and pocked with holes. The only place to eat was a bar where a dozen or so prostitutes were already touting for business. I sat on the veranda, ordered something to eat and tried to keep the flies away from my face.

Like so many towns in Ethiopia, Kebra Mengist was living from day to day. No one gave any thought to the weeks or years ahead. They were making do as best they could, struggling through the present. The only certainty was that life would get worse. The streets were teeming with people, many of them drifting desperately from one place to the next offering a single object for sale.

One woman clutched a bruised apple; others had only a stalk of maize, a worn-out tyre, a bar of soap, a basket, or a handful of eggs. And here and there boys pushed homemade barrows over the rocky red dirt, on the lookout for odd jobs.

A few feet from where I was sitting a cow was licking a discarded engine block. There were goats, too, foraging for non-existent scraps. And all around there were beggars, wrapped in a web of rags, some blind, others lame or maimed with leprosy.

I sat swishing the flies and sipping sweet tea, and wondered what had happened to Samson. Perhaps he'd sloped off to see his family or had hurried away to church.

Then, in the far distance, I spotted a well-dressed man walking towards the town centre. Every few moments he would pause to greet an old friend, pressing his shoulders to theirs, kissing cheeks, nodding in satisfaction. He seemed to know everyone. His head was held high and there was a spring in his step. But most surprising was his get-up. He was wearing a mint-green three-piece suit and a scarlet tie. I screwed up my eyes to get a better focus. With each step, the figure became more familiar. It was Samson.

He saw me and, rather sheepishly, ambled up to the veranda where I was sitting, still caked in dried mud. There had seemed little point in changing my clothes or washing if we were going to go down a mine.

'This is my home town,' he said grandly, 'I have a reputation here. And I've been in the capital, so people are asking how well I have done for myself.'

I could sense every young man in Kebra Mengist packing their bags for Addis Ababa at that very moment.

'Aren't you leading them astray? After all, Addis is awash with people from small towns who can't get jobs.'

Samson straightened his tie and dusted an imaginary piece of fluff from his shoulder.

'Look at this place,' he said gently. 'If you lived here, wouldn't you want a little hope as well?'

Tesfaye was Kebra Mengist's barber, an Ethiopian version of Sweeney Todd. He'd have pulled your teeth out, slit your throat and chopped you up for pies before you knew it. His hands were muscular, their veins thick with blood, their nails chipped, with dirt beneath the tips. He invited me to sit in his chair, and he sharpened his scissors on a strip of black leather. They hadn't been used for months. In times of hardship people cut their own hair. Samson told me to watch my throat. Tesfaye had, he said, worked in Mengistu's torture-rooms. It didn't surprise me in the least.

While Tesfaye chopped my hair, Samson strolled about town in his suit, showing it off to his friends. He was enjoying his newfound status as a celebrity, and he seemed to have forgotten that we were just passing through on our way to the gold mines. When I reminded him of the project, he cupped his hands over my ears and replied that he was doing research. Before we could set out for the illegal mines at Shakiso, we were expected to put some money into the local economy. If we didn't spend enough cash in town, he said the locals would lay a trap for our vehicle, push it off a cliff, and strip our bodies of their clothes. I was about to curse Samson for talking such rubbish, but one look at Tesfaye stopped me. Then, to my astonishment, the barber put down his blunt scissors, picked up his pet tabby cat and blew kisses in her ear.

We returned to the local bar. I was expected to buy drinks for a string of regulars. Samson said the place was notorious as the haunt of *shiftas*. Satisfy them, he said, and we'd go unhindered.

On the porch there sat a tall man whose face was painted white, and spotted with black and red dots. His shirt was open to the waist, revealing a chest smothered in grey ash. He was drinking a glass of tea, and he looked very much out of place. I was overcome with a great urge to stand and stare. I couldn't help myself. Samson said the man was from the Karo tribe – a people of strong traditions, who hail from the south-west of Ethiopia. I would have asked a dozen questions, but Samson tugged me into the bar by the collar.

The drinking den was like so many others on the African continent. Before my eyes could adjust to the dark, fly-ridden room, the smell of warm beer, vomit and urine hit me squarely in the face. Around the edges of the room, a handful of prostitutes sat looking bored. Business was slow. In the middle of the room twenty or so middle-aged men were slouched at tables. One of them was polishing a knife blade on his sleeve, and most had scarred faces. They were a rough bunch by any standards, and they were clearly suspicious of strangers.

'Foreigners don't come to Kebra Mengist,' said Samson in a worried tone. 'So when they see a white face they get nervous, and when they get nervous they get violent.'

'So what should I do?'

Samson rubbed his thumb and forefinger together.

'Spend some more money,' he said, 'buy more beer and treat them to prostitutes. Everyone here knows that spies are stingy men. And besides, if they're enjoying themselves with the women they'll leave us alone.'

So I asked Samuel, who owned the bar, to tell every whore in town to hurry over. His customers were to be treated to as much beer as they could drink, followed by a bawdy time in the back rooms. A wave of anticipation rolled through the joint. The prostitutes winked at me all at once, grateful for my philanthropy, and the male customers raised their beer bottles high above their heads in a drunken salute.

Samuel took my cash and nodded solemnly. I'd be safe from vagabonds on the road, he said. He had learned English from a book, and he pieced together his sentences with exquisite care. When he had counted my money four times, he asked how much he'd need to bribe the American Embassy to give him a visa. Would a hundred *birr* be enough?

Before I could reply, the door was swung back and two dozen working women strutted in, flaunting their thighs and their breasts, and pouting lasciviously. The drinkers saluted again. I've never seen so many grinning, glowing faces in a single room. Samson suggested we leave while the men were occupied, so we made a hasty exit.

To my surprise, a vehicle was waiting to transport us to the mines. It was owned by Peter, one of Samson's schoolfriends. He was a thin, soft-spoken man and in the first minute of our meeting he told me three times that he was a Christian. He thanked the Lord for bringing us to Kebra Mengist, and then he thanked Him again for blessing his friend Samson with such good fortune.

At some point in the recent past Peter's Toyota van had been in a head-on collision. Its front was hideously disfigured. In any other country the vehicle would have been condemned, and flattened into a block of steel for recycling without so much as a second thought. The doors had been welded shut, which meant you had to climb in and out through the windows. The steering-wheel had been replaced by an iron spike, a severe hazard in itself. As for the windscreen, it was so cracked that it seemed miraculous it hadn't shattered.

Peter agreed that there'd been trouble on the roads and said he'd lost a wagon-load of passengers. The carnage had been terrible but, thankfully, his vehicle had been resurrected from the dead.

The ends of two wires were touched together to create a spark. A moment later and dense blue diesel fumes were billowing around us. Then we were off, crawling out of Kebra Mengist and heading south-east towards the mines.

The first small community we reached was Shakiso, a frontier town in the gold-mining belt. We halted for a cup of freshly roasted coffee, while Peter carried out emergency repairs to his vehicle.

The main street was lined with shops selling Western contraband – Walkmans and televisions, Swiss Army knives, Russian vodka, lacy underwear, Marlboro cigarettes and CDs. Profits from the gold mines put luxury purchases within the reach of ordinary men.

There were a few vehicles too. Most of them were painted yellow and belonged to Midroc, the only company licensed to mine the Adola gold seam, at a place nearby called Lega Dembi. Midroc was founded and owned by Mohammed Al-Amoudi. In fact Al-Amoudi seems to own almost every major enterprise in Ethiopia. His photograph greets you wherever you go in the country, smiling widely, with a scrap of beard on his cheeks. As well as the gold mine, he owns the leather tanneries, the foreign car dealerships, the main construction company, mineral companies and soft drink franchises, office blocks and even the new Sheraton Hotel in Addis Ababa. I had known that getting access to the legal gold mine at Lega Dembi would be very difficult. Everyone I asked, including Samson, had said there wasn't any hope. Even so, before leaving Addis I had sent a gushing letter to the chief executive of Midroc, asking for permission to visit. But African bureaucracy is never fast moving, and in the end I had decided to forget about Lega Dembi and concentrate instead on gaining entry to the illegal mines.

Shakiso doesn't feature in guidebooks, nor was it on my map. In more usual circumstances it would have been a place to avoid. The central bar in town was full of surly customers. I assumed they were miners, but they made the *shiftas* at Kebra Mengist's drinking den look like saints. We sat down at an empty table near the far wall and waited for the coffee. A man of about forty reeled in, already drunk. He made for our table and ordered a bottle of beer. The whites of his eyes were straw yellow and his brow was a mesh of interwoven lines. When he spoke, his lips trembled and splayed outward, revealing flushed gums. I paid for his drink, hoping it would ease the tension. Then I asked his name. He spat on the floor. Names, he said, were for friends, and I was no friend of his. Samson kicked me under the table and suggested we leave before there was trouble.

Two hours later, when the sun was high in the sky, we saw the first signs of mining. A row of elderly women were panning a river, swirling the dirt with a smooth sweep of the arms. Around their necks were leather pouches in which they kept the precious gold dust. We had reached the Adola greenstone belt, Ethiopia's richest gold seam.

The authorities had licensed the one official mine at Lega Dembi, but they were powerless to stop the dozens of small illegal mines dotted throughout the region. The illegal mines all focus on alluvial gold, that is gold which has been washed down by rivers and which is panned from the silt. Solomon's miners would have used the same technique, for blast-mining didn't develop until the nineteenth century. Modern gold mining concentrates on break-ing down the rock around a gold seam, pulverizing it into dust and extracting the metal from that dust. It is, however, an extremely expensive process. In most places alluvial deposits do not contain enough gold to make modern, large-scale industrial mining worth-while.

Samson warned me that the illegal mines were dangerous – a place where there was no honour, no brotherhood of men, and where Christianity was a dirty word.

As he spoke, I made out a line of thatched huts in the distance. It was hard to see much through the windscreen's cracks, but it looked as if we had reached a village. The driver said the encamp-ment had been deserted. The gold had run out, so the miners had moved on a few miles down the road. The empty village, its ghostly huts sloughing their walls and roofs like an unwanted skin, was my first glimpse of a mined-out seam. With so much at stake, the miners were willing to leave perfectly good huts and build new ones elsewhere.

Eventually we spied another village on the horizon called Bedakaysa. It was framed by eucalyptus trees which grew straight up from the ochre-red earth, and above it buzzards soared, riding the thermals of the late afternoon air. The village was made up of dozens of simple thatched huts bordered by *enset*, or 'false' banana trees. And this time there were people, hundreds of them.

A river flowed between us and the village, but it was almost dry: its waters had been redirected to feed panning pools. There must have been about sixty houses, each roofed with long, grey grass, packed cheek by jowl. Narrow plumes of smoke rose from cooking fires, and there was the occasional shriek of a child or the bark of a dog protecting its territory. The closer we got, the more people we saw. They were like ants on the jungle floor, all busying themselves with work.

Samson said the community was no more than a year or two old.

'They come and they go,' he explained, 'rising up from nothing, becoming more and more sordid, and less Christian, as the miners waste their money on drink, gambling and girls. Then, when the gold dries up, the village breaks down and moves on.'

'The Devil is all around us,' added Peter. 'Be careful that he doesn't tempt you.'

We unloaded our belongings from the van. Samson had not wanted to stay in the encampment, but I'd insisted. How could I appreciate the community, I asked, without experiencing it at first hand?

After we'd stopped Peter had kept the engine running. When I looked round again to say goodbye, he had gone, leaving us with no choice but to enter the village.

In moments of great uncertainty on my travels, I have always felt that something is protecting me, that I will come to no harm. Samson would say that God is watching me. I am not so sure, but, as we stumbled down the hill towards the mining village, I sensed a protective arm embracing me.

A voice was calling out to us from the river bank.

'Sammy! Sammy!'

One of the miners had recognized Samson and ran up to us. The two men embraced, nudging their shoulders together in the usual prolonged Ethiopian greeting. The miner was about my age but he was built on a superhuman scale, standing as tall as a black bear on its hind legs. His arms were like pistons, capable of exerting a great force for a long period of time. A halo of hair ran round the outer edges of his balding head in a natural tonsure. His skin was very dark, almost the colour of Indian ink. Samson introduced him as Noah, a miner whom he'd known since childhood. Noah came from Gambela in western Ethiopia, on the border with Sudan, a land where all men are as tall as trees and as dark as charcoal, or so he said. Then, without another word, he heaved my army kitbags on to his back and led the way into the encampment.

An Ethiopian mining village has to be seen to be believed. The camp was like the Wild West – stakes were high, hard liquor flowed, and the value of human life was almost non-existent. Samson likened it to a diabolical inferno. I followed Noah between the rows of thatched huts, struggling to keep up with his giant strides. Many of the huts were drinking dens selling home-brewed *araki*, marked by an upturned can on a pole outside. In others, prostitutes were servicing the needs of young men whose bodies were raw and aching after a shift in the tunnels. More still were packed with gamblers, waging gold dust on the turn of a card.

The main street was a quagmire of mud where forlorn dogs roamed. The place stank of sewage. Despite the dirt and the depravity, there was an air of excitement, a sense that fortune was within any man's grasp. As well as bars, there were other entrepreneurs too. One man was selling old clothes from a wagon. A neighbouring stall offered bruised vegetables, and next to that there was a cobbler who would repair flip-flops for one *birr*.

Our arrival in the village attracted attention. A gang of drunken young men clapped and whistled when they spotted us and began to follow us, but Noah threatened to tear them apart with his hands. He dumped my bags and Samson's Chinese tartan case in his hut and said we were welcome to stay there. The room was entered through a low doorway outside which there was a homemade rack for shoes. The floor was carpeted in spotlessly clean nylon sacking. Above the bed hung a hand-crafted cross, and beside it stood a row of worn paperback prayer books sand-wiched between a pair of bricks. Pride of place was given to a bulky black stereo powered by a car battery. There was no electricity in the village. Noah reminded us to watch out for thieves. Nothing was safe, he said. Then he led us up the hill to the mine.

The crater almost was the size of a football pitch and about a hundred and fifty feet deep at its lowest point. It had been carved out of the rocky African dirt, a fragment at a time. A thousand shades of golden brown reflected in the bright sunlight. The miners were covered in mud. I hardly noticed them at first, but as my eyes adjusted, what I saw took my breath away.

Thousands of men, women and children were digging with their hands. A few had basic implements, shovels or iron pikes. All were barefoot, dressed in ragged wet clothes, their skin glistening with sweat, and all were labouring desperately to dig out the earth and haul it to the surface. It was a sight out of the Old Testament, and at that moment the notion of Solomon's mines fell sharply into focus. For the first time I understood what I was searching for.

In the village I'd been the cause of great interest, but at the mine itself the workers were too busy to look up. Each had a role to play. If one person paused in his work the system would begin to break up, then production would slacken and money would be lost.

At the bottom of the pit were the diggers. Many of them were women and children. They'd chiselled their way further and further down, through layers of clay, rock and earth. You could see the gold seam clearly. It was a honey-yellow strata, which started about thirty feet down. The upper layers of soil had been piled in a bulwark around the edge of the crater, and the precious vein was being chipped away and carried to the panning pools. Moving such an enormous quantity of earth called for brutish manpower. Hundreds of men, perched on fragile ledges, tossed the pans of soil from one to the next in a giant relay. Their biceps were savagely over-developed, enabling them to transfer a forty-pound pan from the bottom of the crater to the surface in thirty seconds flat.

Once at ground level, the gold ore began another relay, to the panning pools. A great deal of water is necessary for panning, which is the usual way to extract specks of gold from an alluvial lode. The river had been dammed, creating a large pond edged with rushes and water hyacinth. A series of sluices had been built to filter out rocks and to allow a constant stream of fresh water into the pool. In fact, the system hasn't changed much since it was invented by the ancient Egyptians five thousand years ago.

Most of the panning was done by women and children, using round, wooden pans about three feet wide. A gentle sluicing movement removes unwanted dirt and, if you're lucky, leaves a fine crescent of gold dust at the bottom of the pan.

The ancient Egyptians turned panning into an art form, and it was from them that Solomon's kingdom learnt the technique. In the late nineteenth century, gold tailings in the Egyptian desert were discovered and processed by archaeologists. They found that almost no gold had been left by the miners working five millennia before. But the cost was high. The Nubian Desert is littered with human bones, no doubt those of slaves who succumbed to the heat and the toil. The main difference between Solomon's mines and the illegal ones in Ethiopia is slavery, or rather the lack of it. The Ethiopian miners were working for themselves. There was no need for whips and threats of death. Greed was their master, goading them to work from before sunrise to dusk.

Noah led the way from the main crater to another area, where many hundreds more were working in a labyrinth of tunnels. The openings were like well-shafts, dozens of them stretching out over a distance of about three hundred feet. Etching out smaller, individual seams, the lone workers labour in an underworld where cave-ins are a constant threat. Samson said that every year the narrow tunnels entomb many young men. But for the men without fear the rewards are high. If they find a nugget, they swallow it or stuff it up their rectum, for retrieval later. In the mining camps, trust doesn't exist.

When I asked how much precious metal had been found, I was always greeted with anxious looks. No one would admit to finding any gold at all, even when everyone knew they had. Although the gold was supposed to be shared out equally in a loose co-operative, everyone lied, cheated and stole from their neighbours. The only people who'd boast were the younger men. They did so to impress the whores, whom they hoped would give them a free servicing. But, as the girls knew very well, anyone boasting about what they'd found, hadn't found anything at all.

5

Children of the Devil

'Where the south declines towards the setting sun lies the country called Ethiopia, the last inhabited land in that direction. There gold is obtained in great plenty.'

Herodotus, *The Histories*

DUSK FALLS SWIFTLY in southern Ethiopia, casting a cape of blackness over the gold mines. The air gradually cools and then comes alive with tremendous bats. Noah said they were the spirits of the miners killed in cave-ins. Enraged at being cheated by death, they were desperate to bite their companions who still worked in the mines.

Soon after dusk the strong young men slunk up from the mineshafts and returned to the village. Even for them it was far too dangerous to stay out after dark. Who knew what a shaft miner had swallowed? Given the right circumstances there were plenty of would-be murderers eager to find out.

'They slit your throat with a razor-blade or a sharpened belt buckle,' Samson explained. 'Then they cut open your intestines and sometimes even your bowels.'

'Very messy,' added Noah.

'How does the murderer get away with it if he's covered in blood?'

'That's not the problem,' said Noah. 'If he's found gold he'll buy some *araki* and everyone will forgive him. The problem is if he *doesn't* find anything and he can't afford a few rounds of drinks.'

There was no church at the encampment, a fact which made Samson increasingly restless. He said he could smell depravity in the air. Noah, also a staunch Christian, had proposed erecting a house of worship, but the other miners had scoffed at the idea.

They said a church was a waste of money, and proposed instead that a team of them should be sent up to the northern state of Tigray to bring back new prostitutes. The ones at the mines were, by all accounts, riddled with venereal disease. Tigrayan women have angelic features and copper skin, and are considered by many people to be the most beautiful women in Africa. A large number of the prostitutes I'd seen at the mining village, not to mention in the bars in Kebra Mengist and Shakiso, were Tigrayan. Samson told me that prostitutes usually work in another region, for fear of bringing shame on their families.

Without a church to pray in, Samson and Noah sat on a bench in the bar and talked about Jesus. They swapped stories of his life and drew morals from his teachings. A pressure lamp lit up the room like daylight, causing the huddle of miners to blink nervously. They preferred the shadows. An empty glass was sitting before every one of them. Bizarrely, the walls of the bar were papered with *The Straits Times*, the Singapore daily. Beside my head was an interesting feature about black magic rites performed by Dyak headhunters in Malaysia. I pointed it out, but no one was interested. They had only two things on their mind – *araki*, and how to get some more of it.

Noah said that little gold had been found that day, so I bought a round of drinks. The *araki* was served warm, straight from the still. Quite often a batch is so strong it turns to a crude form of poison, knocking out everyone who drinks it. Quality control is non-existent.

Samson and Noah shunned the *araki* and pulled out their Bibles. I respected them for staying faithful to their religion in what were testing circumstances. They were like missionaries in a foreign land. But they knew as well as I that saving souls and spreading God's Word was a sure-fire way of getting themselves killed. What surprised me most was that Samson had managed to wrench himself from the debauched spiral of life at the mine.

'Gold mining is like a drug,' he said. 'The more gold you get, the more you need to excite you. Your closest friends are dying around you, but you don't give them a second thought. All you can think about is *araki*, Tigrayan whores and the meaningless knick-knacks you're going to buy.'

Samson's father had stressed the value of education to his sons.

Studying, he'd told Samson as a youngster, was the key which could open the doors to life. I was struck by the clear goals Samson had set himself, now that he had escaped from the world of prospecting. In his spare time, he was learning computer programming, a skill which he had heard would be useful if and when he got to America.

'For years I wasted every moment working at a mine like this,' he said, pressing his Bible to his stomach. 'I turned my back on my parents and my true friends, accusing them of jealousy. But worst of all I turned my back on God. If I'd not got away, I'd have been dead long ago. Yes, I may be much poorer – but driving a taxi is more honourable than this!'

He motioned to the pack of thirsty miners who were ready for more free drinks. Then he begged Noah to leave the mines. But his friend said he was wedded to the profession, addicted to the thrill of danger and the financial rewards.

When I had doled out as much charity as I could afford, a string of tall Tigrayan women trooped into the bar, each wearing yellow vinyl shoes and a transparent top. Their hair was braided tightly and their mouths shone with fuchsia-pink lipstick. None of the miners had any money, but the girls took credit. Samson said some of the men, the older ones at least, had wives. But they liked the prostitutes, whom they considered to be sophisticated. One of the women, plumper than the rest, sat down beside me. Her name was Hannah. When I asked what she thought of the miners, she rolled her eyes and blew me a kiss.

'You go America, tomorrow?' she replied.

I didn't understand.

'No, no, I'll be staying here at the mine for a few days.'

'Not America . . . tomorrow?'

'No,' I said.

She sneered at me and turned her attention to a hulking creature with a fresh gash down one cheek. Again, I heard her asking about America. I doubted if the man even had a passport, let alone a visa to the United States. But as he massaged her thighs, he whispered: 'America, America.'

The evening dragged on, with Samson and Noah discussing the Psalms, and the miners racking up huge bills on credit with the working women and the bar's one-eyed owner. As the hours passed, it seemed that everyone was talking about America, and any man who merely uttered the magic word was assured the Tigrayan girls' attention.

As I settled down to sleep in Noah's hut that night, I wondered how an entire population could have become so desperate to get to a place of which they knew so little. Samson rarely stopped going on about the life he'd lead in that far-off land. Even as he read the Bible or discussed the lives of the Apostles, I could sense him thinking of America.

To him and others, America was a place full of opportunities where Ethiopians were given prospects and a future. Samson had applied to the US Embassy for a visa but had been refused. He knew the chances of gaining entry were slim, and he was turning his mind to more subversive tactics. Someone had told him that you could go to Mexico and cross the border by swimming the Rio Grande. Another had suggested he find a rich American woman and persuade her to marry him.

The following morning, three more women asked me if I was going to America. Then a gang of children selling maize and roasted barley came over to tell me that it was nearly time for America. They would be going over there to have a look.

'When? When are you going?'

'Oh,' one replied dreamily, 'any minute now.'

By the time the first rays of sunlight spilled over into the mine, two thousand workers were busy digging the ground or lugging ore up to the panning pools. As the sun rose it baked the ground, making the business of digging far harder. The miners toiled away like convicts.

A few years before, I'd seen Sebastiao Salgado's extraordinary black-and-white photographs of the enormous Serra Pelada gold mine in Brazil. I remembered images of mud-drenched men, tens of thousands of them, climbing rickety ladders up the sides of the pit. They carried sacks on their backs, filled with soil to pan. The mine near Shakiso didn't have ladders. Rather, the workers would take their positions and stay in them. In some ways their system was more efficient. Hurling pans of earth up in a giant relay was much speedier and far less tiring.

The miners were working together because they had to, but I never got the feeling that they did so willingly. Given half a chance, they would happily have killed the man or woman next to them for the smallest nugget of gold. Noah pointed out three or four characters to keep away from.

'That's Josiah,' he said, pointing to an elderly miner with a limp. 'He killed his own wife after suspecting she'd stolen a pouch of gold from him. He's already asking why you have come here.'

Noah tapped one finger on his nose meaningfully.

'And that's Yohannes over there. He's got Aids, but he still rapes the Tigrayan girls.'

Later that morning I left the mine and walked back through the village. Samson had been complaining that his shoes were being ruined by the ankle-deep mud and I'd offered to buy him a pair of rubber boots. We headed for the market area and had a good look through the heaps of old clothes on offer. The only boots were parrot green and four sizes too big. He took them anyway.

There was a commotion at the far end of the market. In the distance I made out a throng of Tigrayan girls mobbing a stall. They were admiring its stock of impressive merchandise. There were lipsticks and handbags, blankets and bed-sheets, leather footballs and French aftershave, silk shirts, Swatch watches and cartons of 555 cigarettes. Some of the girls sidled up to me and implored me to buy them luxuries.

Samson said it was all contraband, brought from Djibouti once a week by a travelling salesman.

'He goes from mine to mine selling this rubbish. Who needs aftershave in a place like this? Instead of saving their money these foolish people come here, to America!'

'*America*?' I exclaimed.

Samson pointed to a crude, hand-drawn board hanging above the stall. On it, in Amharic, was the word America.

As we wandered back towards the crater I found myself questioning man's obsession with gold. How could a simple, relatively useless yellow metal have been so important for so long? Was it the colour, the weight, or the warmth of it in one's hand? Or was it the fact that gold stays brilliant and clear of rust in even the wettest climate?

Whatever the reason, gold has been hoarded and worked since

the days of the ancient Egyptians, though man discovered the metal long before Pharaonic times. Fragments of natural gold have been found in Spanish caves, apparently put there forty thousand years ago by Paleolithic man. And the lure of gold has been responsible for some truly terrible episodes in history, not least the Spanish conquest of the Americas that brought the Aztec and the Incan empires to a brutal end.

With the sun beating down on our heads, we clambered down the slalom of trails leading towards the floor of the crater. The first thing I noticed as I descended was a sharp rise in temperature. Fifty feet down and I was gasping for breath, asphyxiated by the press of hot air. Another fifty feet and my pores began to run with sweat. The miners tossed up their weighty pans higher and higher in their well-rehearsed relay. They too were sweating, but I never saw one of them pause for water. When they needed to pee, they did it where they stood.

We squatted in the deep glutinous mud at the bottom of the crater, catching our breath and wishing we'd brought a supply of drinking water. Around us were dozens of women and children, all shovelling earth on to the round wooden pans. Up above, the children had been thrilled at the spectacle of a foreigner and eager to cluster around and get a good look. But on the floor of the pit there was no such interest. The children worked like slaves. Indeed, they were slaves, for I doubt they got any share of the money they earned. Working alongside them, their mothers were brawny and well built, with strong backs and muscular hands. Several of them were obviously pregnant.

One of the boys, aged about ten, slipped me an affecting smile. Samson told me that the children start young.

'They work down here in the pit,' he said, 'but they're more useful to bore the tunnels which run along the actual gold seams. You can send a child down a hole just a few inches wide.'

'Don't they ever get stuck?'

Samson nodded.

'Yes. Then they suffocate. Or else they're killed in cave-ins.'

Our timing couldn't have been worse. As Samson finished his sentence, we heard shouts from beyond the pit. The area echoed with sound at the best of times, but these yells rose above the usual noise. Many of the miners dropped their pans and scrambled to the surface. Others were running round the periphery of the crater.

'Cave-in,' said Samson coldly. 'Someone's trapped, probably a child.'

We left the women and children and hurried up the steep banks and over to the maze of tunnels. A crowd of miners were digging furiously with pikes and spades, and one man was shouting out, calling a single name: 'Adi! Adi! Adi!' But there was no response.

A woman came running, tearing barefoot down the track from the village. She was weeping hysterically. I found out later that no one had called her, she had simply known that her son, her eldest boy, was trapped. We listened, all quiet, desperate for a sound. But there was silence, a terrible, haunting silence.

The woman ran from one hole to the next, crying down each tunnel. All the other children had scurried to the surface. They said that Adi had been digging in a separate tunnel, away from the others, when the earth above had collapsed. The mother screamed, her features locked in an ecstasy of pain. Nothing is so agonizing as to see the face of a mother who has lost her child. I couldn't bear to watch. The miners crowded round, comforting her. I wanted someone to reassure the woman that there was hope, that children have been pulled from rubble days after an earthquake. But like everyone else, she knew that her son was already dead.

Adi's body was eventually found a few minutes before sunset. The time that it took to dig the boy out was testimony to the depth at which he had been working. The camp's wild, carefree atmosphere had evaporated. That evening none of the miners joked or boasted, and there was no talk of Tigrayan whores. Instead they banded together like brothers, and for the first time I felt respect for them. One of their own had died. He may have been a child of nine or ten, but he was a miner who'd perished in the line of duty. In silence the corpse was carried at shoulder height down the muddy track into the village. The mother walked beside her son, resting her hand gently on his head. Her eyes were swollen with grief.

The sordid carnival of the previous night was nothing but a memory. No one drank in the bar. The few clients who couldn't stay away simply sat there staring into space, consoling each other. In the back room, the fire under the still was starved of fuel. The drip, drip, drip of transparent liquid had ceased. The whores sat about plaiting their hair, ready for a night without trade.

Adi's crushed body was wrapped in a clean white shawl and laid out in his parents' home. Samson and I stopped there to pay our respects. The hut was already filled with people.

Samson recited Psalm 23 as softly as I've ever heard it spoken:

The Lord is my shepherd; I shall not want.
He maketh me lie down in green pastures: he leadeth me
    beside the still waters.
He restoreth my soul . . .

Samson's eyes were closed as he spoke. Perhaps he was remembering past friends and enemies whose lives had ended under the ground. When we left the hut, he looked up to Heaven and rebuked God. Then he held his Bible to his face and wept.

Next morning, long before the mining had begun, the villagers rose and filed from the camp. Most were wrapped against the early chill in their *shammas*. Their heads were bent towards the ground, their faces long and drawn. Noah led the procession which snaked for a mile or so south of the mine. We walked near him. Behind us Adi's body was carried at waist height, with his mother and father, and their closest friends following behind.

A grave had been carved out of the brick-red soil in an area away from the gold seam. The body was placed in the hole and, with little ceremony, it was covered over. Then the first light of dawn turned the sky steel blue.

By seven o'clock the mine was burgeoning with activity again. The pans of golden earth were wending their way up from the bottom of the pit, and the dark, cramped network of tunnels was busy with infant workers. A young miner had been lost, but hardly anyone stopped to reflect. Contemplation is a luxury, requiring time and alternatives.

In the late afternoon a vehicle could be seen negotiating the jagged track leading to the mining community. We could hear its engine revving for a mile or more before it arrived. The miners didn't have to look: they knew the car. It was the property of a local government bureaucrat. Somehow he'd heard that there had been a death and he had come to get the details down on paper.

Noah told me to go into his thatched hut as quickly as I could. The only thing the bureaucrat would like more than a dead miner was a foreigner to torment. So I hid in Noah's shack while Samson hastened back and forth, filling me in on what was happening. The administrator, he said, was questioning Adi's parents, telling them to go to Shakiso to help with an official report. That was the last thing they intended to do.

'If the government knows about this and other illegal mines,' I asked, 'then why don't they close them down?'

Samson winked.

'They're in it for the money,' he said. 'They buy most of the gold, and they sell it at a big profit. Unless they send the army down here they're never going to be able to stop all the mining, and this way at least they get the lion's share of the profits.'

Despite this, I found that the miners had a pretty accurate idea of international gold prices. For this reason they only sold part of their haul to the officials.

'If they let on just how much gold's coming from this seam,' said Samson, 'then the government would have no choice but to nationalize the place. Then they might have a rebellion on their hands.'

There was already insurrection in the air. Samson reported that hundreds of miners had left the pit and were massing around the official. I could make out loud voices, then shouting, and finally the rumble of an engine as it sparked to life.

'How did he find out that someone had died?' I asked Noah later when he returned from the mine-shaft.

'There are spies, lots of them,' he replied. 'In fact it is strange that they haven't handed you in.'

Now that he mentioned it, I realized that the miners had been friendly towards me. They had welcomed me as courteously as they knew how, and some had offered to show me the surrounding area at night or to feed me.

'You'd better watch out,' said Noah, 'they're probably planning to rob you or kill you.'

'America,' added Samson.

'The market stall?'

Noah frowned.

'No, the *country* America,' he said. 'They see you as their way out of here and over there.'

Like all Ethiopians, the miners had a grand plan which culminated with their arrival in the United States. No other country was good enough – none had the cachet of America. I hadn't been in Ethiopia long, but dozens of people had already asked me how to get a visa for America. I'd even heard of agents who, for a steep fee, could prescribe the best route across the Atlantic.

Noah pointed to a man outside one of the huts lolling back on a homemade chair.

'That man there,' he said, 'he's an expert on America.'

Dawit's head was round, like a small watermelon, and it appeared to balance on his wide shoulders without any trace of a neck. His palms were as soft as a beauty queen's cheeks. They'd obviously never been down the mines. Dawit laughed riotously at the slightest opportunity, and I asked him why he was always so cheerful.

'We Amhara are very happy people,' he replied.

'What's the best way to get to America then?'

Dawit stopped laughing and lowered his head. The only thing he never joked about was business.

'These days it's harder to get an asylum visa,' he said, 'but there are lots of other ways in. You can go through another country, like Germany, France or Britain. You can say you're a priest and get a Christian foundation to sponsor you, or pretend to be a Jew and go via Israel. Or, if you can get to Mexico, you can jump across the river . . .' He paused for a moment, trying to remember its name. 'The Rio Grande, they call it the Rio Grande, and the water's very low at the moment. But the best way to get to America,' he said, flexing his shoulders, 'is to get yourself a foreigner's passport.'

I was struck by how much Dawit knew and the more we spoke, the more impressed I became. There were very few questions he could not answer. At last I asked him which was his favourite American city.

Dawit looked blank and then burst out laughing, and Noah and

Samson collapsed in hysterics. When eventually they stopped, the three of them stared at me as if I were mad.

'He's never been to America,' said Noah.

After meeting Dawit, I tiptoed around the village, gripped by paranoia. If I disappeared and my passport was taken by a swarthy young Ethiopian, it could be months or years before the crime was discovered. I told Samson of my worry and forbade him to leave my side even when I was asleep – in fact especially when I was asleep. That night my dreams were filled with gangs of miners creeping into the hut, snatching my passport and slitting my throat. Then they fought with each other to see who would win my passport for the journey to America.

The next morning I awoke to find Dawit at the foot of my sleeping-bag. He'd had an idea in the night, he said. I was to give a short informal talk about America to the miners. As someone who'd passed through US Immigration several times I had inside knowledge that I could pass on. It sounded like an easy way to please the community, so I agreed to talk in the open space that evening.

Life at the gold mine was pleasant so long as you didn't have to do any mining. There was a perpetual sense of risk, balanced by the lure of instant wealth. The place was like a grand casino. Money raised by communal mining was shared out, but anyone who found a large nugget was permitted by the others to keep it. Whether anyone realized it or not, the system encouraged industriousness. The big problem though was that all of them were unable to stop mining, regardless of how much gold they found.

Everyone I spoke to said they would leave if they found a big enough nugget, but I knew that that was a lie. The miners had become addicted to the gambler's lifestyle. Nothing, except possibly religion, could prize them away. And in any case, anyone cashing in on a big find had debts to pay, and what was left would be blown in an instant.

'If you look at this place,' said Samson as we sat together in the late morning sun, 'you'd think there wouldn't be much in the way of expense. But you'd be wrong. Miners make good money, much more than any other Ethiopians. But they have to pay back the money they owe to other miners, they have to buy clothes and food, and they have to send money home to their families. Then there are illegitimate children to care for, there's *araki* to buy, and Tigrayan girls to employ.' Samson stared at the baked earth as he remembered the corrosive existence. 'The most expensive thing of all,' he added, 'is treating others to luxuries – women and drink.'

'But why pay for others if you can't afford to?'

Samson smiled from the corner of his mouth.

'Just in case one of them finds a big nugget,' he said. 'If you don't help them when they're poor, they won't remember you when they're rich.'

Life must have been much the same for prospectors working in the Klondike, in California, or in Australia in the mid-nineteenth century. The first great gold rush took place near the Sacramento River in northern California in 1848. A carpenter working at a sawmill there found a sizeable gold nugget. Try as he might to keep his find quiet, word soon got out. Within days there were tens of thousands of would-be miners camped out nearby, and within four years more than 250,000 miners had descended on California. Living in the most terrible conditions and blinded by greed, they were risking everything for the sake of gold.

I met an Italian recently whose great-great-grandfather had set out from his native Milan in search of a fortune in California. He saw the prospectors living like dogs, eating rotten supplies and using lousy equipment. The Italian had intended to search for gold like the rest of them. But as soon as he saw the conditions in which they lived, he changed tack. Instead of thinking about gold, he turned his hand to bringing in supplies. Within weeks he'd made a fortune selling saddles and clothes, pans, chemicals, tents and food.

Look at the map and you can see traces of those pioneering days in the names – Bonanza Creek, Gold Hill, Gold Creek, Eureka. But the name which crops up again and again is Ophir. Christian miners were certain that they'd discovered the Old Testament land. In Bedakaysa no one apart from Samson and Noah had ever heard of Ophir. They had no interest in Bible readings. They had been residents of Hell for far too long. Samson called them 'The Children of the Devil'.

We often discussed the idea of Ophir. Samson felt sure that Solomon's gold had come from ancient Ethiopian mines. He pointed out that the Israelites had probably acquired the metal from many mines in one region rather than from a single glorious pit. He said that a giant mine only existed in the minds of novelists and Hollywood, and he reminded me that an entire region, or country, can get mined out, especially where the gold veins are close to the surface, as they are in Ethiopia. Modern industrial mining processes can sift through thousands of tonnes of ore each day. But mining was no less thorough before the days of heavy machinery. Hundreds of thousands of prospectors at the Klondike River did the work of the machines, as they do today in mines like Bedakaysa.

In London I had managed to buy a handful of books written at the turn of the last century which told of Great Zimbabwe, the ruins which the Victorians thought were once Ophir. One of the volumes had been published in 1899 and was written by an eccentric German professor called Carl Peters. The book was entitled *King Solomon's Golden Ophir: A Research into the Most Ancient Gold Production in History*. Peters tackled the subject with Teutonic thoroughness and came up with an interesting theory. The Old Testament writers were usually very precise in giving details. Why then did they give no indication as to the whereabouts of Ophir? They seemed to assume, says Peters, that everyone knew where it might be found. If Ophir was remote there would have been a need to supply the curious with details. Africa was a land known to the ancients, though they knew little of its interior or overall geography. Might not Africa and Ophir be one and the same? In support of his theory, he looked at the etymology of the word 'Africa'. The original root of the name, according to him, was *Afer*, probably meaning 'Red' or 'Red Land', as in the common colour of the continent's soil. *Afri* were its people, and *African* the adjective which described them.

In the century since Peters' book was published, it has been proved that the Great Zimbabwe ruins are not connected with the ancient Israelite kingdom, the land of Solomon. Even so, Peters' theory seems plausible. Ophir might well have been Africa, and Solomon's gold might well have come from a region of the continent that lay close to his kingdom, the mountainous hinterland of Ethiopia.

In the late afternoon I paddled at the edge of the panning pool. The miners were hard at work, ferrying their pans of earth from the bottom of the crater. Children darted about selling sticks of roasted maize, sugar cubes and knitted hats. From time to time women and children came up from the mine where they had been digging and swapped places with the panners. Panning was back-breaking work but it meant that you could at least wade in the thigh-deep water and keep cool.

The male miners were proud of their profession and keen for their sons to follow them. Noah told me that mining gold was con-sidered the most macho thing a man could do. Miners scoffed at farmers and laughed uncontrollably if one mentioned people who did office work. They rated the value of a job by the thickness of the callouses it gave their hands.

Noah was an exception. He had two young sons but he shud-dered at the thought of them entering the mine.

'They're having an education,' he said. 'The only way I can pay for it, though, is by mining. I pray that I'll find a big nugget. Why do you think I spend such long hours in the tunnels risking my life?'

'Where are your family?'

'Back in Kebra Mengist,' he replied. 'I won't let them even come to the mine. I'm not ashamed of the work, but I don't want my wife or my two boys to see the savage people I live with.'

Dawit came over and said it was time for my talk. He'd spread the word through his network of contacts and he expected a bumper audience. We made our way to a flat patch of land to the west of the main mine. Young men would sometimes play football there. Others used it for their ablutions, and the place was running with rats and stank of human excrement. Despite the stench, dozens of miners had already arrived. More were turning up every minute. Most of them knew that a foreigner had been staying in the village, but until that moment they had regarded me as of little use. That was about to change. Dawit had billed me as the man who could put an end to all their problems – he had declared some-what fictitiously that I was the missing link between them and America.

Samson grew nervous when he saw the extent of the crowd. He said there was a danger of the local official closing the event down and arresting us. Having been in big gatherings in India and Africa before, I was more worried by another danger. At a right-wing rally in Nigeria, given by a fanatical Christian preacher from Germany, I'd seen dozens of people trampled to death. The pastor claimed to have the power to heal the sick. He told hundreds of cripples to make a pyre from their crutches and wheelchairs. When they'd done this, the preacher claimed to have healed everyone, and with that he drove off in his stretch Mercedes. Of course no one was cured. Instead, tempers boiled over and the crowd stampeded. The saddest thing was to see all the disabled left lying on the ground without their crutches and wheelchairs, unable to get home.

Dawit assured me that there would be no stampede. Everyone present, he said, had paid one *birr* entrance fee, or at least had promised to pay later. The children sat at the front, wriggling in the dirt, a little unsure of why they had been coaxed to attend. Their parents and the general population of miners stood behind them. There must have been about five hundred people. The Tigrayan girls had donned their best dresses and vinyl high heels, and were sitting with the children. The entire congregation was united by their interest in the title of my talk, 'Getting to America'.

When they were quiet, and we were sure that there were no stragglers still to come, Dawit introduced me, speaking in Amharic, while Samson translated.

'Mr Tahir has come from faraway America,' said Dawit, 'to tell you about his wonderful country and how to get there.'

After a prolonged greeting, I began my talk. Whenever I said the word 'America', the gathering drew a deep breath.

'America is an amazing country,' I said, waiting for Dawit to finish translating my words. 'It's sometimes known as "The Land of the Free" because everyone has rights.'

One of the young men began to heckle me, demanding to know what people in America thought of Ethiopians there.

'People like Ethiopians in America,' I said, reassuringly. 'I've met many Ethiopians there who have a good wage, but they were not frightened of starting in a simple job.'

'Like gold mining in a pit?' called another.

'Not exactly . . . more like working in a restaurant. But it's important to study hard and to learn English. If you have a qualification you can earn a lot of money.'

The audience looked worried. None of them had any qualifications.

'Tell them the best way to get into America,' prompted Dawit.

I thought for a moment.

'It's a big country,' I said, 'with many ports of entry. Some people cross over from Mexico, but that's getting harder; and others come in by sea. But the best way is to get a friend or a relative to sponsor you, or to have a job waiting for you. You see, if you're "uniquely qualified", they can easily bring you from overseas to do the job.'

Dawit struggled to translate the concept into Amharic.

One of the Tigrayan girls had a question. She rose to her feet, thrust her chest out towards me and asked: 'Do American men need *us*?'

I was taken aback by this question, but rather than discourage her, I replied with enthusiasm.

'Yes, I'm sure they do!'

I carried on, padding the talk out with information about life in America, saying it wasn't all like the movies, and that the streets weren't paved with gold. Some of my metaphors must have suffered in translation.

Then, winding up, I said jokingly that they could push me down one of the mine-shafts and steal my passport. That would give one of them at least an easy entry into America. The miners looked at me and then at each other. Then they stared at the ground and giggled nervously.

6

Breakfast with Idi Amin

'In Africa think big.'

Cecil Rhodes

THE MORNING AFTER my talk, one of the miners came to Noah's hut and presented me with a gift. His name was Solomon. I would have asked how he came by the livid scar that ran from his eye to the base of his neck but, reading my thoughts, Samson suggested in a whisper that it was none of my business. Solomon said he'd enjoyed my talk very much and that he knew the details would come in useful when he arrived in America. He had heard about a city where a ferocious wind blew, rarely ceasing for a moment. He couldn't remember its name.

'Chicago?' I suggested. 'It's called the Windy City.'

He smiled broadly.

'You really know a lot about America.'

'There's no need to give me anything,' I said.

But Solomon insisted.

The gift was wrapped in fresh banana leaves, and there were flies swarming all over it. Dreading what I would find inside, I unfurled the leaves. There lay a pair of very bloody and very dead hares, their long bodies rigid with rigor mortis. The very sight of the creatures so early in the morning made me feel nauseous. I gagged at the stench, and asked Noah to dispose of them immediately. He thought I was mad. To him, their smell was like the scent of freshly cut flowers. He rambled on about how roasted hare was one of life's true luxuries. One taste and, he assured me, I would become addicted to the meat.

He hurried off and gave the hares to one of the Tigrayan girls called Taitu, named after Menelik II's consort. She said she'd stew them for us. Hares are a delicacy in Tigray. The Amhara, she said, had no idea how to cook them. Taitu was so beautiful that no one dared look her in the eye, not even Noah when he asked her to cook the hares. Her skin was the colour of burnished brass, rolled over a frame of bones of extraordinary delicacy, and her voice was as soft as a siren's. Noah said she'd been married but had run away from Tigray after being found in another man's bed. Unable to face her husband or her family, she had fled to the south and eventually ended up as a whore.

Taitu cooked the animals and brought them to me for lunch, served in a thick gravy. I invited her to join us and, as we ate, I asked her about her homeland of Tigray.

'In the north,' she said, 'people are so proud that a father will kill his daughter if she brings shame on the family. Then if anyone asks him about his dead daughter he will pretend to forget her name.'

Taitu nibbled at a bone with her front teeth. Her eyes were bright, but I sensed great sadness.

'We all have dreams,' she went on. 'Most of the men here dream of going to America. They don't know what they will do once they're there, or even why they want to go. But,' she said, looking me squarely in the eye, 'they all know that whatever America is like, it must be better than Bedakaysa.'

'What are *your* dreams?'

She fiddled with her braids for a moment before answering.

'I dream of going home,' she said.

That night the first real rains of the monsoon fell. There is no smell in the world as intoxicating as African rain on the red sub-Saharan soil. All the miners' children ran outside and danced in the downpour, laughing and shouting with glee. Samson and I pulled off our shirts, rolled up our trousers and splashed our way to the panning pool. Awed by the power of nature, Samson looked up at the sky, the rain cascading over his face and down his body.

'This is my God talking to me!' he cried.

For once I knew he was right.

By morning all the water had long since been absorbed into the earth. The footprints leading to the mine were a little deeper, the mud a little thicker, the panning pool a few inches higher.

Noah had been down the shaft for two hours by the time we got there. Rather than being exhilarated by the break in the weather, he looked worried.

'Another death,' he said.

'A cave-in?'

'No, another kind of accident.'

The body was lying a few yards from the shafts, covered by a thin white shawl with delicate embroidery around the border. It was the body of an adult miner, a man universally despised. According to Noah he was a well-known thief and was suspected of being one of the official's spies. Unlike the death of the child, there was no display of emotion at this death. Most of the miners didn't even bother to look at the corpse, which had been found early that morning.

Noah took me over and lifted the corner of the shawl. There was a hideous wound on one side of the man's face – a gash from the left ear down to the base of the neck. The jugular was clearly severed.

'A bad accident,' said Noah.

'What do you mean "accident"? The man's obviously been murdered. That's a clean cut made with a knife.'

Noah tapped me on the shoulder.

'No, it's an *accident*,' he said firmly, 'he slipped in the rain and cut his neck. The others are going to bury him right away.'

Two days later we heard the sound of the official's vehicle skidding through the mud. Another spy had no doubt informed him of the murder. A second downpour had turned the track into a thick reddish-brown soup, but the rain was good for the miners. It softened the earth and made the panning easier. An adequate supply of water is always a problem for gold prospectors. In many parts of the country small-scale mine-shafts shut down in the dry season. Samson had said that the main dangers in the heavy rains were from cave-ins or flash-floods in the narrow tunnels where children and the bravest men worked.

As we watched the vehicle lurching up the trail, Noah told me to go to his hut and wait there, as I'd done before. Finding a foreigner in the village at such a time would only complicate matters.

I did as he requested, but then peeped through a hole in the hut's back wall. I had a good view of the official and his assistant as they got out of the car.

They were an odd couple. The assistant's nose had been broken, and he had small ears that lay flat against his shaven head. He was dressed in a grubby beige jacket with oversized lapels; the garment's right shoulder was torn, exposing the lining. His boss wore a chequered overcoat, purple trousers and a felt hat, but despite his eccentric outfit he looked formidable. His thick-framed glasses and cold efficient features hinted at a man who liked to get to the bottom of things. Both men's shoes and ankles were caked in mud. They'd obviously had to push the vehicle *en route*. The official seemed very angry.

In any other part of the country a local administrator, however lowly, would command respect, but not here. The miners were brash and self-confident. They were used to danger, and though their daily work broke the law, they made ten times more than the officials from Shakiso.

No one bothered to meet the car, so the visitors tramped over to the mine itself. I waited in Noah's thatched hut. A few minutes later I heard shouting and a high-pitched whistling. Samson hurried in and said there was trouble. He looked very worried and told me to pack up my stuff at once.

'Is it about the murder?'

'No, no,' he replied, 'they don't even know about that, or they don't care.'

'Then what's the problem?'

'It's you.'

I bundled up my sleeping-bag and stuffed it with odd bits of clothing into my kitbags while Samson laid his precious Bible flat in his tartan case. The case, I noticed, was already splitting at the seams.

'What shall we do? They'll see us if we leave.'

Before Samson could reply, the hut's door swung open and the official and his assistant stood in the doorway. I could sense their delight at finding a foreigner. Noah was behind them, trying to get their attention. I knew from that moment that any efforts to talk our way out of the situation would be futile. The official asked for our papers. I pulled out a photocopy of my passport and handed it to him – I had learned years ago never to give original documents to anyone if I could help it. Samson fumbled in his case for his identity card and passed it to the official. Much conversation in Amharic followed.

As the debate grew more heated, I became worried. In the Indian subcontinent a few crumpled notes slipped surreptitiously into a sweaty palm would have effected our release. But in Africa bureaucrats are usually too proud to accept a bribe, something I admire when I'm not the one being arrested.

The murderer had got away with it, but Samson and I were bundled into the back of the official's car and driven off. There had hardly been time to thank Noah and say farewell to the miners and the Tigrayan girls. Samson was generally talkative, but as we slip-slided through the soupy mud, he said nothing. The officials were also quiet, but I sensed an air of triumph.

We were driven to Shakiso and taken to the police station. Once inside we were told to stand in a corner. A notebook was taken down from a shelf, a pencil licked, and the interrogation began.

Neither the official nor his lackey spoke English, so Samson had to translate. I didn't really know what to say but I decided to tell the truth, though I knew it wouldn't be easy – the reasons behind my journeys are never straightforward. As we stood there, my hands sweating, Samson's brow knotted with anxiety, I attempted to explain.

'I have come from London to search for King Solomon's gold mines,' I said. 'It is known that the Israelites, and before them the ancient Egyptians, mined gold in Ethiopia. That is why I am here. Unlike others before me, I see it as my duty to visit all kinds of mines – legal and informal.'

Samson struggled to translate my words into Amharic. The official didn't look at me – his eyes were on the wide-spaced lines of his notebook – but he scribbled madly. When his pencil had stopped moving I started to talk again.

'The last thing I want,' I said, 'is to acquire any gold. You see, I'm interested in Ethiopian history.'

Samson paused and stared at me in alarm. Had I forgotten that the word 'history' was taboo?

The official put down his pencil and cracked his knuckles one by one. Then he looked at me, glanced at the photocopy of my passport and asked Samson a question.

'He wants to know who you're spying for,' he said.

I sighed. Then Samson sighed.

The man spoke again.

'He wants your film.'

Fortunately I'd learned a trick from the veteran cameraman and war photographer Mohamed Amin. Mo, as he was known, was the man who filmed the original television footage of Ethiopia's famine in the mid-1980s. It was his powerful images that galvanized action which culminated in the Live Aid pop concert. When confronted by officials intent on confiscating his films, Mo would quickly wind in the tapers of unexposed rolls and pass them off as exposed films.

Before we'd left Noah's hut I had hidden my exposed films in a pair of filthy hiking boots at the bottom of one kitbag. Now I whipped out a couple of blank films, slid in the tapers, and ranted on about how valuable they were.

The official looked delighted and demanded I hand them over. Theatrically I tossed them on to the desk. The official passed them to his assistant, who stamped on them. Then he barked a string of orders and we were taken away. Samson was still trying to negotiate us out of our predicament and had become desperately upset. I dared not tell him that I was rather enjoying the experience.

We were taken to a cell and locked inside, though 'cell' is a misnomer. The floor consisted of baked mud, and the walls were merely wooden planks with gaps between them. The roof was built of rusting corrugated iron which let in a draught and leaked when it rained. In the wide gap between the floor and the walls lay shards of broken glass, presumably intended to discourage inmates from sliding out on their stomachs. Five other men were already inside, three of them asleep, the other two playing cards.

Samson was miserable. He didn't say anything, but I knew he was regretting ever having met me. I had become his tormentor and was dragging him further and further away from his objective of getting to America. I told him that I'd double his pay for every day we were incarcerated, but he didn't respond. Instead he sat on his haunches and chewed his knuckles.

After an hour there was the sound of a key turning in the lock and the jailor arrived carrying a lunch of *zill-zill tibs*, shredded beef strips. He said that if we were still hungry afterwards we could have some more, and if there was anything else we needed we were to let him know. The jailor had been miscast by life. He was one of the most gentle and compassionate men I think I've ever met. Samson and I treated him with due courtesy, but the others took advantage of his kindness. They had him washing their clothes, fetching them water and darning their shirts.

I remarked on the jailor's kindness to Samson.

'Of course he's kind,' he said, 'he's an Amhara.'

The first few hours in the cell were quite stimulating. I'd never been in a prison cell before and was quite enjoying the experience. I urged Samson to introduce me to the other felons. Befriending them might lower our chances of getting our throats slit in the night. The two card-players turned out to be Amhara as well, which raised their standing in Samson's estimation. One of them had small shifty eyes. He reported proudly that he'd beaten his wife with a stick for having run off with a neighbour. The second card-player said he was there because he'd stolen a chicken. He had no money to live anywhere better and so preferred to stay in the jail.

The other three convicts only woke up when it was getting dark and then they shouted at the jailor, ordering him to bring them some food. He did as he was told. One of the men, whom I dis-covered later was a miner accused of killing a prostitute, drew a line in the dirt with his thumb and then glared at me. If Samson or I crossed the line, he said, he'd break our necks.

The jailor declared that anyone wanting to go and pee could do so in the bushes outside the police station. The five men trooped out unsupervised. I was surprised that they didn't break free and run off. When they came back a few minutes later they seemed to sense my surprise because they looked rather sheepish. Meanwhile the jailor told Samson that the official had gone home and that he wouldn't be back until noon the next day.

That night I lay on my back and thought about earlier narrow escapes. A journey, I reflected, is of no merit unless it has tested you. You can stay at home and read of others' experiences, but it's not the same as getting out of trouble yourself. Whenever I'm in a tight spot, I think of Mohamed Amin. He was an expert in getting out of tight spots in Africa and, in particular, in Ethiopia.

As well as filming news, Mo ran a small publishing company. In my early twenties, when no one else would give me work, Mo hired me to write books. By then he had already lost one arm, blown off in Addis Ababa, during the fall of Mengistu's regime. During our travels together in many African and Asian countries, Mo passed on some of his knowledge. He taught me to take my own fuel into war zones, preferably high-octane aviation fuel – most petrol engines can run on it as long as their timing is altered. He also showed me how to hide a roll of 35-millimetre film in the heel of my shoe, and he taught me that when dealing with African bureaucracy you should remain respectful and calm.

Mo Amin died during the hijacking of an Ethiopian Airlines plane off the Comoros Islands in November 1996. I remember the day clearly because it was the same day that my father died. A week before his death I'd met Mo in Nairobi. He'd asked me to write the text for a book on Saudi Arabia. He knew I wanted to spend time there. But, as always, he drove a hard bargain.

'I'll give you a thousand pounds,' he said.

Even for Mo this was a pitiful sum, but he was a shrewd negotiator, and was never one to start high.

'That's not enough,' I said.

'Well, double it.'

From past experience I knew to ask for payment in kind as well as in cash.

'What about some transport?'

'I'll give you two club class tickets on Ethiopian, anywhere they go,' he said. Mo had an inexhaustible supply of tickets on Ethiopian Airlines.

'What else?'

He leant back in his chair and thought for a moment. His bionic artificial arm was laid out on the desk before him like a trophy, a reminder of his bravery.

'I'll give you a Somali passport,' he said.

'You've already given me one, for the last job.'

Mo bit his lip.

'Make it a diplomatic Somali passport.'

'Now we're getting somewhere. What else?'

'A holiday to the Seychelles.'

'And . . .?'

Mo drew his hand down his greying goatee beard.

'All right,' he said coldly, 'I'll give you breakfast with Idi Amin.'

A week later Mo was killed, and with his untimely death went my chance of sharing a meal with the infamous Ugandan dictator.

The jailor woke me at dawn with a cup of freshly roasted coffee. He said that if he'd made it too sweet, I was to tell him and he'd try again. The other felons were asleep, all except for the one the others called Wossen. Samson said he had been drinking all night. The liquor had been smuggled in by the jailor as a reward for good behaviour. Wossen's right eye was milky white and suppurating. Every so often a fly would land on it but Wossen had given up trying to brush it away. He was too old, too tired, too drunk.

The night had been uncomfortable but not unbearable. My bags were locked away in the office but the jailor had provided some hay for our heads. He had even offered to wash our clothes, though it would take three days to dry them now that the rains had come. I thanked him but said we hoped to be released long before then. The jailor responded, saying there was little hope of us being given an early release.

At about eleven o'clock the official ordered us to come to the office. He was dressed in the same purple trousers as the day before, but his shoes had been expertly cleaned and they now shone. To lighten the mood, I thanked him for having looked after us so well. The experience had been absorbing, I said, but now we were ready to leave.

The official slapped his hand down on the desk and ordered me to be quiet. He would ask the questions and we were to answer them. But before the interrogation could continue, he wanted to look through our bags. Samson was to show his first. The tartan Chinese case was placed on the table and unpacked. The parrot-green wellington boots were brought out, then the three-piece suit. The official frowned.

'Now unlock your bags,' he said, pointing at me.

Most Ethiopians travel with only the bare necessities. If they bring along any luxuries at all, they're usually intended as gifts for relatives or friends. But, as every African checkpoint guard knows, foreigners carry with them all sorts of appealing objects, and I am no exception. Fearful of leaving a key piece of equipment or an important book behind, I travel with just about everything I own. Unlocking the kitbags' padlocks, I began to remove an assortment of items. First came a plug of soggy, mud-ridden clothes, then a few books on Ethiopian history and on the business of gold. The official rifled through the mounting pile, searching for subversive material, and as he did so his face darkened. Clearly he thought I was a spy, and I began to get worried. At the bottom of one kitbag, I knew, there was something that would confirm his suspicions.

In London I had bought an expensive high-tech metal detector. So far I hadn't even shown it to Samson. The detector – called a Gold Bug II – looked like the sort of thing James Bond would take along on a mission. I had planned to try it out at the mine, but I hadn't had time.

I mumbled that there was nothing left in the first bag and started to take out the contents of the other. The bureaucrat knew that I was lying. He plunged his hand in and triumphantly pulled out various bits of the detector. Then he laid the pieces on the table and told me to assemble the device. As I did so, I tried to explain why I needed it, but the official wasn't listening. He had found a foreign spy and he was clearly already thinking about the likelihood of promotion. Samson glared at me, furious that I'd kept all know-ledge of the device from him.

The official picked up the telephone and barked into the receiver for a minute or two. I couldn't understand the conversation, but I could guess its drift. A pair of spies had been found, he was telling his boss. One of them's a sly foreigner caught red-handed with illegal equipment. The other's a local, an Amhara found in posses-sion of a suspicious three-piece suit.

After the call, the official smoothed a hand down his shirt-front, pressed his fingertips together, and said something in Amharic. Samson was led away. Sweating profusely, his hands trembling, he was unable to look me in the eye. Then I was marched back to the cell. Samson wasn't there. I sat against the far wall, away from the others. The thrill of incarceration was beginning to wear thin. The jailor motioned with his hands and mouth, asking if I'd like some lunch. I shook my head. Now, I said in English, wasn't the time for eating.

Again I found myself wondering how to get away. We probably

could have escaped, but they had Samson's identity card and would have hunted him down. The thought of Samson being hunted by anyone seemed unfair. Mo Amin had always told me to remain calm in a tight spot. Calmness, he used to say, buys you time. He was a great believer in allowing events to take their course. Solutions, he'd say, present themselves if you give them time. But sitting in a small-town cell was a waste of time. I had things to do. I had Solomon's mines to find.

Then I remembered the advice of another friend. When you're in a scrape, she said, the best thing to do is the unexpected. A seasoned opponent of Apartheid in South Africa, she'd once found herself in the midst of a riot in Johannesburg. A vigilante mob had surrounded her car and was rocking it from side to side. She was running out of time. Another minute and she'd be dead. So, instead of screaming or showing fear, she blew the vigilantes kisses. They looked horrified and ran away.

Samson was brought back to the cell a few hours later by a man I'd not seen before. He introduced himself as the commander of the region, and asked some basic questions in English. What was I doing in Ethiopia? Why did I need such a high-tech piece of equipment? What had I seen at the mines? Was I a spy?

As before I answered truthfully. Samson and I, I said, were searching for King Solomon's gold mines. We were not interested in buying gold but rather in its cultural and historical importance. The man rubbed his eyes and then he smiled.

'Are you from America?' he asked.

'No, from England.'

'I want to go to America,' he said. 'Can you give me some advice?'

At first I was wary, suspecting some kind of ploy to get information out of me, but then I realized the man's enquiry was genuine. So I scribbled out some suggestions on a sheet of paper. He thanked me and asked if there was anything he could do to help. I pointed at the cell door.

'You could open that,' I said.

Without a second thought he snapped his fingers. The door swung open from behind. The official, who was pacing up and down in the hallway, scowled as we strode past him. Samson was given back his identity card and our possessions were loaded into the commander's car. He had insisted that his driver take us to Kebra Mengist.

There seemed little hope of gaining entry to the legal gold mine at the nearby Lega Dembi plant, but Samson urged me to follow up my letter with a phone call. To my great surprise, my call was put straight through and I found myself talking to the managing director of Midroc operations. By the end of the conversation I had been invited to tour the legal gold mine, and even to stay at Midroc's headquarters, a few miles from Kebra Mengist.

At the gatehouse, our identity papers were inspected. One of the armed guards spat our names into a walkie-talkie and listened to the crackling reply. Then the barrier slowly lifted and, as it did so, the guards stood to attention and saluted. In the pickup truck that had brought us from Kebra Mengist we rolled ahead into a vast compound. Only hours before Samson and I had been locked up in a cell with convicts. Now our luck had miraculously changed.

Lega Dembi was laid out on a grand scale. From the gatehouse to the actual mine was a distance of about two miles. The plant's perimeter fence was festooned with razor-wire and punctuated at intervals by sentry posts, each manned by soldiers armed with Kalashnikovs. We heard later that there was also a special paramilitary squad that roamed the grounds, searching for intruders.

The road snaked down into a valley, before climbing steeply. We passed a series of enormous pools, where tailings were being processed and then, as the route ascended, we caught our first glimpse of the plant. There were storage depots and power-generation units, mills and foundries, warehouses and rows of geological laboratories. And everywhere there were tracks leading in all directions on which towering Caterpillar crushers and tippers drove at speed.

A well-built man dressed in khaki and wearing thick wire-rimmed glasses strode out of his office to greet us. His name was Wayne and he was Australian. He said he couldn't remember the last time a visitor had come to Lega Dembi. I told him about my search for Solomon's mines and then I asked him about the gold.

'You've come to the right place for gold,' he said, 'but we don't mine it like Solomon's slaves would have done. We use ammonium nitrate.' He paused. 'I don't think Solomon had any of that.'

As Wayne drove us to the mine, he admitted that in the gold business you can't like gold too much. If you do, he said, you get greedy, and if you get greedy, you make mistakes.

Five minutes later we stood on a ridge above the lip of a vast crater. Below us lay an enormous mine, so big that it made me shiver. A dozen trucks were being loaded with rocks. When they were full they'd hurry away through deep mud to the crushing plant. I was surprised to see that some of the biggest trucks were being driven by women. Midroc was an equal opportunities employer.

On one side of the crater a group of men in yellow hard hats were busily unloading boxes guarded by a man with an AK-47.

'That's the ammonium nitrate,' said Wayne. 'It can blow a mountain into dust, but actually it's just fertilizer.'

'What about the bullion?'

'I'll show you.'

Wayne took us to the gold room where the molten metal was about to be poured. Once through the rigorous security system, we were locked into what was really a large workshop. The walls were whitewashed breeze blocks, the floor was bare cement, and the ceiling was made from reinforced glass. A pair of security cameras watched our movements. At the far end of the room a technician was checking over the electric furnace. I could clearly see through his mask the beads of sweat joining up on his brow. He looked worried, but tried to maintain an air of professionalism. From twenty feet away I felt the heat. An extractor fan on the back wall seemed to be blowing the hot air towards us. It felt like the parched wind which rips across the Sahara in June. Wayne said things would get much hotter; and then they did. We dressed up in protective silver outfits, like astronauts, donning masks and gloves. Then we crowded round and winced as our bodies were washed in boiling sweat beneath the silver suits. The furnace was the shape of a very large barrel. It was tipped by a system of hand cranks. Gradually a steady semi-molten flow poured out that reminded me of lava spewing from a volcano. Then the flow changed to a stream of liquid gold. Wayne said that the slag ran off first, followed closely by the molten gold.

Five minutes later the ingots were thrown on to the concrete floor, and the bullion was knocked out like loaves of bread from their baking tins. Lega Dembi is considered a medium-sized plant, and it produces about three hundred and fifty gold bars a year. A single bar of the bullion weighs about 20lbs and is worth approximately $80,000. Given the extent of its reserves, Ethiopia could yield much more if international investors came forward. I found myself thinking about the gold and whether it might be the key to reviving Ethiopia's economy. As I pondered the question, the rough blackened ingots were whacked with a hammer. The surrounding crust of slag fell away, and for the first time I saw the glint of pure gold.

The next morning Samson and I huddled in a doorway out of the rain, waiting for the bus to Addis Ababa. An elderly man was crouched on a stool opposite. His trousers were too tight, and they were ripped at the knees, and his shirt was split. Every so often, his body trembled and his limbs twitched. Samson said he was called 'Old One' because he'd been an old man even in his youth. He had a penchant for whipping small boys with a long leather switch, and children would creep up from behind, baiting him. But now his eyesight was fading and his aim was less accurate than it had once been. Like an aged bulldog that's lost its teeth, Old One was a pathetic sight.

After four hours the bus arrived and we clambered on board. As we pulled out of town, I noticed a tall athletic man running alongside the bus. He was calling out a woman's name, and he had taken off his shoes so he could run faster.

'Who's he?'

Samson asked one of the other passengers.

'His wife is running away with another man,' he said.

The bus driver had a severe bladder disorder which forced him to stop and pee in the bushes every few minutes. His affliction, coupled with the low speed of the bus, made the vehicle the worst means of escape imaginable. The adulterous woman must have been cursing herself for ever having climbed aboard. At the third pee-stop her husband caught up with the bus and dragged her off by her hair.

That evening back in Addis Ababa, we went to the Sheraton to celebrate. The hotel was yet another of Mr Amoudi's investments and rumour had it that he'd paid $100 million to build the place. Now it was full of foreign aid workers, all on expense accounts and all earning magnificent tax-free salaries. They appeared especially keen on the French restaurant where they could dine on lobster thermidor, Scottish smoked salmon and *foie gras* imported from Fauchon in Paris. Ethiopians in the restaurants or bars were few and far between, but young courting couples liked to stroll along the hotel's palatial corridors and walk hand in hand in the gardens.

At the buffet Samson piled a spectacular amount of food on to a soup bowl. It was the first time he'd been in the Sheraton but, despite eating his body weight in cooked meat, he said the food wasn't anything special. In fact he had said very little since our incarceration in jail, though he thought our release was due to God answering his prayers. We were friends and would remain so, but I sensed he had lost faith in me.

Now that I'd seen an illegal mine in operation, I had some inkling of how gold must have been mined in Solomon's time. But I was captivated by the idea of Frank Hayter's lost mine-shafts on the remote mountain of Tullu Wallel in western Ethiopia. And besides, I still had to investigate the five spots on the map where I'd laid my pebbles – places which might yet yield answers to the riddle of Solomon's mines.

Over dessert I introduced the subject of continuing the search. Samson put down his spoon, covered his eyes with his hands, and sighed.

'We have been to the illegal gold mines,' he said.

'They're like Solomon's mines would have been, but they are working a new seam,' I explained. 'Ophir must have been further to the west.'

'How do you know?'

'We've still got five other places to visit,' I said, sidestepping the question. 'How can we stop now? We haven't even been to Frank Hayter's mine yet.'

Samson peeped through his fingers.

'*We?*' he asked.

The only way I could talk Samson into coming with me was by promising that I'd hire a vehicle for the rest of the trip. Local buses, said Samson, were hard on the buttocks and far too slow. My budget was limited, and I'd heard that renting a 4×4 in Ethiopia was fiendishly expensive, but Samson insisted that with his contacts we'd get a great deal. The next morning he set off to find a car while I went to meet a gold merchant in the Mercato area of town. The man who cleaned the lavatories in the Hotel Ghion had put the business card of the goldsmith on my bed. His name was Abdul Majeed, which means 'the Servant of the Glorious' in Arabic, and his shop was called 'Solomon's Gold'.

When I reached the goldsmith's street I found it was lined with dozens of small jewellery shops. In the gutters outside, men squatted over primitive stoves on which crucibles rested. The sight reminded me of the *ghamelawallas* in India who pay goldsmiths for the dust they sweep from their workshop floors. In Calcutta alone there are more than a hundred thousand men, women and children who work as *ghamelawallas*, all retrieving minuscule particles of gold from the dirt.

When I entered his shop, Abdul Majeed stood up, blew on his palm, and extended it for me to shake. His teeth were capped and his nostrils were flared, and he wore a skull-cap embroidered with tarnished gold thread. When he spoke, he leant forward until his mouth was no more than an inch from mine. Abdul Majeed had extremely bad breath.

Making it clear from the start that I hadn't come to buy, I asked what he knew about Solomon's mines. He invited me to sit, before sliding over a glass of weak tea.

'First the refreshment,' he said, 'and afterwards the chatter.'

We sat for a few minutes in silent contemplation, sipping our milky tea. I glanced around the small shop. A series of well-built mahogany display cases covered the back wall. Their shelves were lined with green velvet that had been faded by years of sunlight. Against an adjacent wall stood an elegant grandfather clock, made in Hamburg. Opposite that hung a calendar, illustrated with a picture of the Empire State Building and opened at the page for April 1993. When it comes to time, Ethiopia has its own rules which place it in a sort of parallel universe. Instead of following the Gregorian system, as we do in the West, Ethiopians use the Julian calendar, a system seven years and eight months behind us. In Ethiopia there are twelve months, each of thirty days, and a thirteenth month of just five days. Every year thousands of unsold Western calendars are shipped to Addis Ababa, stored for seven years, and then sold to people like Abdul Majeed.

The shopkeeper served me a second cup of tea and we continued to sit in silence. Then, the refreshment over, he began to speak.

'Gold,' he said pensively, 'I could talk on the subject for a lifetime and would still not have begun.'

'Do you have any advice for a seeker of Solomon's mines?'

'If you want an answer,' said Abdul Majeed, leaning towards me, 'you have to consider much more than Solomon. You have to think about the ancient trade routes, the politics, and the reasons why Solomon needed gold.'

'The great temple,' I said, leaning back in a hurry, 'I've been to Mount Moriah, where it supposedly stood.'

'That's a start, but what do you know of God's Land?'

I didn't know what he meant.

'I am talking about the ancient Egyptian Land of Punt,' he said.

Then he licked his finger and held it in the air.

'To understand the puzzle of Solomon's mines,' he said, 'you have to understand the riddle of Punt – the place from which Egypt once got its gold.'

'Do you think Ophir and Punt were the same place?'

The shopkeeper ignored my question.

'The Israelites' kingdom was destroyed after Solomon,' he said, 'and their records were lost with them. You will find no clues from Solomon's time, or from the centuries which followed. You have to go backwards, not forwards . . . back to the Egyptians.'

He got up to serve a customer and then returned to resume the conversation.

'What do you know about Queen Hatshepsut?'

I shrugged.

'There is a temple on the western side of Thebes called Deir el-Bahri. On its southern wall are hieroglyphs which I have seen with my own eyes! They show Queen Hatshepsut's fleet returning from Punt. The journey wasn't long before Solomon's reign!'

He thrust his face forward into mine, his eyes glittering with excitement. I tried not to flinch.

'Most people say that Punt was in Somalia. But now the scientists have changed their minds. Now they say Punt may have been here in Ethiopia.'

'When exactly did the Egyptians start going to Punt?'

The shopkeeper gazed into my eyes. I sensed that he had waited years for a customer to turn up with an interest in Punt. Now such a man had arrived he was eager to demonstrate his knowledge.

'The earliest record was in the Fifth Dynasty,' he said, 'when Pharaoh Sahure sent a fleet of ships down the Red Sea. They returned in triumph, the boats piled high with Puntian myrrh, ivory, ebony, electrum and gold.'

'Were Punt and Ophir connected in some way?'

'They may have been the same,' whispered Abdul Majeed. 'After all, the Israelites learned their skills of metal-working directly from the Egyptians. You must remember that until they arrived in the Promised Land, they'd been enslaved in Egypt.'

'So you think that Solomon's gold mines were really the mines of the pharaohs?'

'Imagine that *you* were Solomon,' he said. 'You wanted a huge amount of gold, and you knew that your neighbours obtained it from mines not so far away. Surely you'd send ships to that place rather than begin an entirely new and dangerous search of your own.'

The shopkeeper's theory certainly made sense. But before I could give it much thought, he stepped over to one of the display cases and pulled out a set of earrings. They were circular convex shields made of eighteen-carat gold, each about an inch and a half wide. I expected the sales patter to begin but he wasn't selling the jewellery.

'Look at these,' he said. 'They're worn all over Ethiopia, but you can't find them anywhere else in the world, except in Egypt. You can find identical jewellery in the Cairo Museum.'

Abdul Majeed, the Servant of the Glorious, blew on his palm and held it out for me to shake once again. He'd enjoyed talking to me about the past, he said, as he hardly dared to think about history these days.

'It's not like the old days,' he said, leaning forward for the last time. 'Ethiopians used to be proud of their traditions. They walked tall and had self-respect. Now all they care about is getting to America.'

7

The Emperor's Jeep

'Princes shall come forth out of Egypt, and Ethiopia shall
stretch forth her hands unto God.'

Marcus Mosiah Garvey

FRANCO SAID HE could not remember a time when he did not live
in Addis Ababa. He had survived the bad times and the even worse
times. He'd seen the capital set ablaze, and the gutters running with
young men's blood. Three generations of his family had lived and
died in Ethiopia and the last thing he was going to do was leave
now. When he had money he dined at Castelli, a plush Italian restaurant favoured by aid workers. In leaner times he sat on the porch
of his ramshackle shop and drank Bedeli beer from a bottle. Five
decades of the summer sun had seared lines into Franco's face. They
told his age like the rings of a tree.

Most of Franco's family possessions had passed through the shop
at one time or another. He'd sold his mother's wedding-gown, his
father's top hat, dozens of trinkets, even his grandmother's false
teeth. I poked about the shelves, admiring the merchandise, but
Franco wasn't really bothered whether I bought or not. His atti-
tude was much the same as that of Abdul Majeed, his friend of forty
years whose shop lay opposite, on the other side of the street.

Bric-à-brac shops containing anything of real value have all but
disappeared in the West. These days no one throws anything out
for fear that it might be worth something. But a browse through
Franco's shop told the recent history of Ethiopia. There were pictures of Haile Selassie as a young man in his imperial robes. There
were Fascist medals and rings made from Italian coins. On a hat-
stand hung a pair of moth-eaten uniforms along with a pith helmet
and a clutch of crumpled silk ties. There were dozens of Ge'ez

prayer books and Bibles as well, and scrolls from monasteries, silver crosses and ebony neck-rests. The back wall was covered in feathered masks and clay lip-plates from the Mursi tribe on the Omo River. Adjacent to them, in the shadow of a forlorn stuffed lion, hung half a dozen crocodile-skin shields, tribal spears and amulets on strings.

'That's quality stuff,' said Franco, leaning over my shoulder. 'You just can't get it any more. It's all from the Danakil.'

He held a bowl up to my nose. It was filled with what looked liked dirty shelled pistachio nuts.

'What d'you think these are?'

I had a sniff. They smelled of nothing at all.

'Don't know.'

Franco rolled back on his heels and grinned.

'They're testicles,' he said.

Back at the Hotel Ghion I thanked the hotel cleaner for his tip-off about Abdul Majeed's shop and showed him my bowl of Danakil testicles, which impressed him no end. I found out later that they were fakes, which saddened me greatly. The cleaner pointed out three businessmen from Shanghai sitting in the hotel's foyer. They were smoking cheap cigars and sharing a joke. Wiping his face with his rag, the cleaner said they wanted to meet me. The men were cement barons and they were eager to break into the European construction business. Shanghai cement, said my confidant in a whisper, is the best in the world. A man bright enough to buy Danakil testicles and other rare *objets* would, said the cleaner, surely see the value of an opening like this.

There was no time for cement barons, I explained. I had work to do and pieces of a puzzle to slot together. My quest for Solomon's mines was far from finished.

Over a pot of tar-like coffee, I thought about the goldsmith's advice. He was right: the best way to understand Ophir and Solomon was to look forward from the Egyptians, rather than back from the time of Christ.

Queen Hatshepsut was indeed a key. As Abdul Majeed had recounted, in about 1500 BC, a little over five centuries before the time of Solomon's reign, the Queen sent five great ships to Punt.

There, as the hieroglyphs which adorn the reliefs at Deir el-Bahri relate,

> We loaded our ships very heavily with marvels of the country of Punt, all goodly fragrant woods of God's Land, heaps of myrrh-resins, of fresh myrrh trees, with ebony and pure ivory, with green gold of Amu, with cinnamon-wood, with incense, eye cosmetic, with baboons, monkeys, dogs, with skins of the southern panther, with natives and their children. Never was the like of this brought for any king who has been since the beginning.

The reliefs at Deir el-Bahri clearly show the Queen's vessels piled high with exotic merchandise. This wasn't the first time an Egyptian ruler had sent an expedition to Punt, but it was probably the greatest and most successful of all the Puntian journeys, which explains why the Queen chose to immortalize the voyage in such an elaborate frieze.

The reliefs, which still bear traces of their original paint, show glimpses of Punt. There are beehive-shaped huts, similar to those still found in some parts of Ethiopia, and alongside them there are Hamitic figures with refined features, perhaps related to one of the Ethiopian tribes like the Oromo or the Tigray.

Scholars have pointed out other similarities between modern-day Ethiopia and ancient Egypt. Reed boats like those used in Pharaonic times still ply Lake Tana, and the traditional *sistra* instrument of Ethiopia is thought to be of Egyptian origin. Incense is still valued highly in Ethiopia, just as it was thousands of years ago in Egypt. Other experts have suggested etymological links between the two cultures. Graham Hancock, the celebrated hunter of the Ark of the Covenant, has spoken of the ancient Egyptian trade in dwarfs, who were needed to 'dance before the gods' – the Egyptian word *dink*, or dwarf, is found today in both the Hamitic and the Semitic languages of Ethiopia.

At the time of the great voyage, the Israelites were still an enslaved people, but they would have heard of the mysterious land of Punt, and of the pomp and ceremony that greeted Hatshepsut's fleet when it returned to Thebes. Such a voyage may well have passed into Israelite folklore, so providing Solomon with a source for the gold he required to build his temple.

I felt I was beginning to make progress, but only by covering more ground could I hope to tease out the clues which, I was sure, lay in the Ethiopian hinterland. Frank Hayter and his fabulous mine-shafts were never far from my thoughts, but first I wanted to go north.

While we were at the mines, Samson had left his taxi in the care of his youngest brother, Moses. The twenty-year-old Lada, which was rented for fifty *birr* a day, was Samson's pride and joy. He polished it constantly with a rag, and each morning the seats were dusted down, the windows wiped and the engine checked over. Samson said that if he didn't take pride in the car, he wouldn't take pride in the job, and he'd tried desperately to instill the same reasoning in his brother. But Moses was more interested in meeting girls than in eking out a living with the taxi.

The morning after our return from Kebra Mengist, Samson slunk into the Hotel Ghion. The bounce had gone out of him, and his conversation lacked its usual religious undertones. I wondered what had happened.

'The Devil is on my shoulders,' he said ominously.

He tapped a finger to his clavicle.

'There,' he said, 'can't you see him?'

'What's wrong?'

The first problem was that Moses had crashed the taxi. While it was being repaired, they would earn no income but would still have to pay the rental, not to mention the bill for the repair work. In addition the police had been called to the scene of the crash because the taxi's passenger had sustained injuries. Who knew what further bills would follow? But that was only the beginning. On our arrival back in Addis the night before, Samson had gone out to buy some food. In the few minutes he was gone, Moses had managed to burn down the one-room shack in which they lived, and most of their possessions had been incinerated in the blaze. It seemed amazing that Moses had survived to tell the tale.

'He put a candle on my radio,' said Samson, 'and then he fell asleep. The candle fell and set fire to the mat, and then the bed and all my books. I came back with lots of food, but our house was in flames!'

Samson stood tall and tried to hide the burns on his hands, but there were tears in his eyes.

'I'll never forgive him,' he said. 'There are some things so precious that they can never be replaced. You see, my Bible was destroyed in the fire.'

Together we went by taxi to look at what remained.

Samson's shack lay in a compound walled with a thorny hedge on the outskirts of Addis Ababa. As we neared the burned-out building, I could smell scorched plastic, and then I spotted a pile of charred belongings. Moses was sitting on a stool dolefully sorting through what was left. Samson gave him a poisonous glare and then led the way to the spot where their home had stood. It had been a rectangular mud-built structure, about the size of a family estate car. He had rented the room from a widow who lived opposite with her seven dogs, for 120 *birr*, ten pounds, a month. By Ethiopian standards, rents in the capital are extortionately high. The widow was sympathetic towards the brothers' plight, but she needed money to rebuild. In the meantime, Samson and his brother had nowhere to live.

That afternoon, I bought a few token objects and handed them over with a wad of low-denomination *birr* notes. Samson was bright and hardworking, and he had given himself an education but, like most Ethiopians, he lived on a knife-edge. Destitution was never far away, and a disaster such as this could ruin him.

Despite his troubles, Samson had managed to find a car for the next leg of our journey. It sounded exactly what we were looking for – a brand-new Toyota Landcruiser with air-conditioning, off-road tyres, a spare fuel tank and a skilled driver. When I asked the price, Samson said we'd have to negotiate, so we went to have a look at it and meet the owner.

I cannot remember when I last saw such an exemplary vehicle. It was exactly what I had had in mind. The bodywork was immaculate, the tyres had hardly ever been used, and the seats were upholstered in an attractive shade of lilac. My chest tightened in expectation.

Standing next to the car was a man whom we took to be the driver. I asked the price. Samson translated the question.

'How much did he say ?' I asked.

Samson shook his head.

'I've made a mistake,' he said, 'this is not the vehicle. It belongs to the French Ambassador. This man is his driver.'

'Then where's our car?'

Samson pointed to a second vehicle which was parked at an angle behind the first. My face fell. A much earlier model of Landcruiser, it had seen its fair share of Ethiopian roads. In fact it looked as if someone had taken a mallet and struck every inch of its off-white body. The tyres were balder than bald, and the back doors were welded shut. I peered through the cracked windscreen. A man was stretched out asleep on the back seat.

'That must be the driver,' said Samson.

I've never had much luck hiring vehicles for rough journeys. The last thing I rented was a rotting hulk of a riverboat in which I sailed up the Amazon. It looked like the *African Queen* shortly before she blew up. My Amazon trip had been fraught with incidents, many of them the result of the riverboat's condition. I'd also had problems with the crew. This time I was going to make sure that the vehicle and its driver were carefully vetted.

I clapped my hands to wake the driver up but he didn't stir. So I leant through the passenger window and yanked his big toe. The man sat up with a start and then peered out of the window. His eyes were bloodshot and a trail of spittle ran down his chin.

'What's his name?'

'Bahru.'

'Where does he come from?'

'He's a Somali,' said Samson, grimacing.

I said we were interested in hiring the vehicle. The driver got out of the car and did his best to stand to attention, though his gaze never strayed from my feet.

We weren't to be deceived by the rough condition of the vehicle, he said. Beneath the dents was a chassis of iron. We could search the whole of Addis Ababa and never find a car half as sturdy. Then Bahru lowered his voice.

'This Jeep used to be very important,' he whispered. 'It once led the imperial convoy of Haile Selassie.'

We negotiated over the price for an hour and ended with a figure twice my original budget. Bahru agreed not to drink and drive, and that he'd provide his services free of charge and find his own place to sleep at night. I stressed that I wouldn't pay for his food. It seemed miserly in the extreme, but through bitter experience I have learned that it is best to promise little and then to reward hard work with generosity. Finally, I gave him a list of repairs that I wanted carried out before we left Addis.

Bahru said the Emperor's Jeep wouldn't be available for two days. A feud had arisen between his family and another. He couldn't leave town until it was sorted out. Samson muttered that it was a mistake ever to use the services of a Somali, but I ignored him.

'Is two days enough time for the feud to end?' I asked.

Bahru rolled his bloodshot eyes. Then he licked his thumb and pressed it to his throat.

'What does that mean?'

'Some things cannot be translated,' said Samson.

In Addis Ababa I kept seeing Rastafarians. Most were from Jamaica, although some had come from Europe. They would stroll about the streets with an air of confidence which many Ethiopians lacked. Intrigued by the Rasta link with Haile Selassie, and in turn with the line of Solomon, I had started reading books on the movement.

As I understand it, the Rastafarians are concerned with the plight of black people. Yet they are not a political party nor a relig-ious sect. Instead, like the Israelites, they see themselves as a people waiting to be reunited with their Promised Land – Africa. They believe that Haile Selassie is their Messiah, their redeemer.

These days when we talk of Rastafarians, we think of their music, most notably the songs of Bob Marley, but the man who established the precursor of the modern Rastafarian movement, Marcus Mosiah Garvey, has all but been forgotten.

Garvey was a Jamaican, and in the 1920s he promoted the Universal Negro Improvement Association whose aim was to return all black people to Africa. Blacks had become 'mentally enslaved' by white people, he said. The only way to restore their dignity was to get them back to Africa. So Garvey used a black-owned steamship line to effect a mass migration to Liberia.

Garvey's work to repatriate African Americans failed, but his great interest in the continent survived. 'Look to Africa,' he said, 'when a black king shall be crowned, for the day of deliverance is near.' Soon after, in November 1930, Haile Selassie was crowned in

Addis Ababa, fulfilling Garvey's prophecy. Garvey himself died in 1940, and in the years that followed, his influence waned, but the Rastafarian movement has grown. A line from Leviticus ('They shall not make baldness upon their head') is taken to mean that Rastas should grow their hair, and another line from the Psalms ('He causeth the grass for the cattle, and the herb for the service of man') lies behind the Rastas' adoption of *ganja*, or marijuana.

At breakfast next morning I asked Samson what he thought of the Rastafarian movement. He screwed up his face and stuck out his tongue.

'They're not good people,' he said. 'They come in my taxi and order me around. They pretend to be Ethiopians, but they don't know anything about our country.'

'Where can I meet some?'

Samson seemed disappointed.

'They're a waste of time,' he said.

An hour later we arrived at a shanty town on the northern fringes of the city. The shacks were made from little more than cardboard, which was melting into the mud now. Here and there sheets of plastic sacking offered some protection from the rains. In the gaps between the buildings, raw sewage flowed, and the alleyways were full of vicious dogs and even wilder children. Women were washing clothes in buckets, struggling to achieve cleanliness, while their husbands and teenage sons sat about laughing and watching the women work. As we approached, we saw a snaking line of people walking slowly through the slum towards us. They were all dressed in simple white *shammas*, their faces solemn.

'It's a funeral,' said Samson. 'Someone important has died.'

Sure enough there was a body in the middle of the cortège. As we bowed our heads in respect, I wondered if our visit was appropriate.

One of Samson's contacts had said that a splinter Rasta group was living in the shanty town and that they were anxious to get back to the grassroots of the Rastafarian creed. When the funeral procession had passed us, Samson went in search of the leader of the group. A few minutes later he hurried back and led me to the hideaway. The headquarters of the Rastafarian New Order lay in a steep-sided house. The place was well swept and lit by natural light which flooded in through a pair of large windows adjacent to the door. A single figure was sitting at the back of the room. His name was Jah and it was he whom we had come to see.

Jah didn't get up, but even before I saw him walking, I knew he was the kind of man who walked with a sway of the hips. He wore a denim jacket torn at the collar, stone-washed Levis and a red mohair waistcoat, with no shirt underneath it.

'All white men are sinners,' he said in a thick Jamaican accent. 'The whiter you are, the more you have sinned.'

I thanked him for the information and introduced myself. I was pleased we'd managed to meet with so little trouble. I was looking forward to talking to him.

'I'll talk,' he said, 'but I need some cash for *ganj*. No cash, no *ganj*, no talk.'

It was a firm line to take, but I respect a man with principles, so I slipped him a torn fifty *birr* note. Jah stuffed it in his jacket pocket and pulled out a cigar-sized joint. Then he leaned back on a dilapidated couch, thrust back his mane of dreadlocks, lit the joint and inhaled.

'Welcome to the New Order,' he said.

'How are you different from other Rastafarians?'

He asked if I knew of the history of the movement. I said I'd read a certain amount. I knew about Garvey and the steamship plan. He nodded through a haze of smoke.

'That's good, man, that's good. You know about Garvey.'

'Yes, I do.'

'Then you know that the path strayed.'

'What do you mean?'

'Garvey had a goal: Africa. That's why I'm here,' he said. 'He knew the work can only start when we're on this *holy* ground. But Garvey got lost and Marley got found.'

'Great music,' I said limply.

'Screw the music, man. Bob Marley got it wrong. We are the new path . . . we're gonna retrace the steps . . .'

'From Garvey?'

'Yeah, man,' said Jah in a fog of smoke, 'we're gonna recraft the message. Black takes white.' He paused for effect. 'Checkmate.'

'What about Ras Tafari and his line, the line of Solomon?'

'Ras Tafari was a dude,' said Jah, 'so was Solomon. They understood about the Rasta Way . . . the Path. Yeah, man, those dudes were Rastas.'

When Jah had finished his joint he lit another. I asked him what he knew of Solomon.

'King Solomon was the wise king,' he said. 'Think about it. If you were as wise as he, wouldn't you line your pockets too?'

'But he needed the gold for the temple on Mount Moriah.'

'What are you on, man?' snapped Jah. 'Solomon just *said* he needed the gold for the temple.'

'You mean he was lying?'

'No way, man, he was the *wise* king.'

'So what happened to the gold?'

Jah inhaled until his lungs were bursting. His nostrils flared and his eyes widened so much I thought they'd fall out on to his lap.

'The Copper Scroll,' he choked, 'check out the Copper Scroll.'

Mariam was arthritic, had flat feet, and a taste for chewing chicken bones. He kept a plate of carcasses within easy reach and sucked on them between meals. Samson had taken me to the old prospector's shack which was lost in the sprawl of Addis Ababa's bustling Mercato area. Mariam, he said, was a regular in his taxi cab and had mined in the north of Ethiopia forty years ago. I wasn't sure why Samson hadn't mentioned the old man before.

Mariam must have been eighty though he didn't look it. The grease from the chicken bones had kept his skin soft and oiled. It was his speech that gave away his age. It was punctuated by wheezing, as if an enormous weight was pressing down on his chest. Even so, he spoke fluent English and Italian as well as four Ethiopian languages. He had never met Frank Hayter, but he remembered his friend, a cantankerous Irishman called Thaddeus Michael O'Shea.

'Everyone knew O'Shea,' he said, fumbling for another bone, 'he was a legend. He claimed to have found a cave full of gold . . .'

'At Tullu Wallel?'

'No, no, in the north, near Axum. Near the monastery of Debra Damo.'

'Another cave, another treasure?'

Mariam nodded and rubbed a sleeve across his mouth.

'There's more than one treasure all right,' he said. 'O'Shea found the cave while prospecting. But he never mined any gold there. He was terrified by the curse.'

'What curse?'

'Anyone who mined gold in the cave would have their body ripped limb from limb by wolves. Then the wolves would hunt down the victim's family and eat them as well.'

The curse reminded me of the hyenas in Harar. I wondered if there was a link. The stories credited to Hayter and O'Shea spoke of caverns filled with gold. No one seemed to know for certain whether they were the entrances to mine-shafts or simply caves in which treasure had been stashed. If they were old mines, then it was more than likely they'd been mined out in ancient times.

I told Mariam that we were planning to follow Hayter's trail to Tullu Wallel after we had been north.

'Tullu Wallel is a savage place,' he said. 'Only a fool would head that way, especially now the rains are here. The mud will be three feet deep, and four feet in places. You'll need a great many mules and ropes, and some good men.'

'I've hired a Jeep,' I said, gloating. 'It used to be in the imperial motorcade.'

Mariam narrowed his eyes and threw down the chicken bone.

'It won't get anywhere near the mountain,' he said.

Later, at lunch, Samson picked at a bowl of spaghetti without speaking. I knew his thoughts were on his taxi repair bills and his burnt-out house. As his employer I felt it was my responsibility to weigh in and help get him out of the quagmire of debt. So, overcome with weakness, I doubled his salary and slid another wad of cash across the table. A faint glimmer of a smile appeared. I asked him what he thought about the story of Thaddeus O'Shea and the cave filled with gold.

'I think Ethiopia is different from your country or America,' he said. 'People here cannot afford to go around looking for treasure in caves. That would take time, and they need their time to earn money. If they don't earn, they starve.'

'But why hasn't the government searched for the caves?'

'Perhaps they already have.'

The Emperor's Jeep lurched up the hill to the Hotel Ghion at six o'clock the next morning. Only three cylinders were functioning, and none of the repair work had been carried out. Bahru shook my hand violently. The car might look in bad shape, he said, but it was as strong as an elephant. I was so pleased he'd actually turned up that I decided to believe him. We loaded the bags, some sturdy three-ply rope that I'd bought in the market, a pair of Chinese-made jerry cans, a charcoal brazier and forty square feet of tarpaulin. Bahru had left the vehicle running and was forced to admit that the starter motor didn't work. The engine could only be turned off if the Jeep was pointing downhill.

When everything was aboard, Samson climbed into the front seat and I got in the back. Our first destination was to be Lalibela, where the 'Gold of Sheba' was supposedly kept in the treasury of a church. Looking at my Michelin map I judged the distance from Addis Ababa to be about four hundred miles. I asked Bahru how long it would take to get there, but he refused to say. Samson had no idea either. In the end it turned out that neither of them had ever been north of the capital.

On hiring the vehicle I had given Bahru seven hundred *birr* to fill up with petrol and to change the tyres. After that he would be responsible for all breakdowns and punctures. Now the tyres were as bald as ever and the tank was almost dry. I kicked myself for having believed that the money would ever be used for the correct purpose. As I'd discovered in Peru, when people are living hand-to-mouth, funds are spent on necessities, though in Bahru's case I suspected he'd had a night on the town instead.

Before setting out on the Amazonian riverboat journey, I'd watched my guide, a Vietnam veteran called Richard Fowler, publicly humiliate and then fire one of the employees. He told me later that he'd done it as a warning to the rest of the crew. Fowler said you had to be cruel to be kind. Following his example, I launched into Samson and Bahru. If I had any trouble from either of them, I said, they'd be returning to Addis on the bus. They looked at me with long faces. The journey north had begun on a sour note.

We drove out of Addis Ababa at low speed. The Emperor's Jeep wasn't a patch on the French Ambassador's car but it was a great improvement on the local bus. Although it was still early, hundreds of people were walking into the city through the platinum light. Most Ethiopians living in rural areas have no choice but to walk. Some of them were herding flocks of animals down the main road and must have come from far away. Long-horned cattle were goaded forward with the swish of a cane, their backs steaming, their heads bent low. There were donkeys as well, all laden with merchandise: sacks of coffee, baskets and firewood, earthenware pots and pans, scrap metal and hides. And on the edge of the road hundreds of barefoot children staggered along beneath piles of sticks.

We passed through the first of many small towns. The street-sellers were getting ready, placing potatoes and dung patties in neat clusters on their pavement stalls. Others were laying out fresh animal hides to dry in the sun, or slaughtering chickens and draining their blood. Morning in Africa is the most peaceful time and place I know. There's a gentleness about it which is hard to describe, except to say that it's framed in a naturalness which has been knocked out of our own world.

We drove through forests of eucalyptus and out over a pancake-flat plateau. We passed a church, at the steps of which a pair of elderly women were kneeling while the priest beat a row of carpets with a baton. The rough fields were awash with children dressed in rags, many no older than four or five. Most of them had been out all night tending the goats. Their noses were streaming and their faces pale with cold.

The Emperor's Jeep ground along in fourth gear at fifteen miles an hour. Bahru had already demonstrated an alarming habit of waiting until he was on a blind bend before overtaking. Most of the vehicles on Ethiopian roads were gargantuan trucks, overladen with goods. Private cars were almost non-existent, except for those owned by aid organizations. Samson said that people in Addis preferred to stay there. The roads were too dangerous and besides, once you'd tasted life in the big city, village life seemed dull.

Outside a hamlet Bahru slammed on the brakes. He'd spotted a man selling some *qat* by the side of the road. The Jeep took a hundred yards to stop. I made a mental note to get the brake-pads seen to.

The *qat*-seller had a strand of turquoise cloth wound in a crude turban around his head. He pointed to a pit which could only be seen by leaning over a craggy stone outcrop. The Italians, he said, had once killed seventy children and hurled their bodies into the pit. If we looked hard we'd see their bones.

Gradually the round huts were replaced with square ones that had tall thatched roofs. Wood smoke spiralled up from fires in the forest, and dry stone walls divided the fields. Then we came to meadows and terraced hillsides where nothing but tiny purple flowers grew; and we passed through a series of tunnels hewn out of the rock, their rough sides glistening like cut glass. Further on we passed camels chewing listlessly at the cacti that grew along the road. High above, rain clouds threatened a monsoon downpour.

The road was not good, but it was far superior to the others I'd seen in Ethiopia, though every mile of it was dotted with the rusting chassis of wrecks. In the West we hold roads in high esteem. They lead us from one place to the next. We care about their condition and their straightness. But in a land where most people travel by foot, and where so many road journeys end in fatalities, roads are not held in high regard at all.

Samson hadn't forgiven me for berating him before setting out. His taxi had crashed, his house had burnt down, and on top of all that, I'd yelled at him for the sake of it. At the third stop for *qat* I took him aside and apologized. I'd shouted, I said, to make sure Bahru didn't take advantage of us. It had been nothing more than an ingenious ploy. Samson's expression warmed, and the dimples returned to his cheeks. He rummaged in his tartan bag and took out a large brown manila envelope. It was a gift, he said.

'What is it?'

'Some research.'

I broke the seal and took out several sheets of paper. Samson had found an article on the Copper Scroll, the one which Jah had spoken about. Though I'd actually seen the Copper Scroll in Amman's National Museum a few years before, I hadn't understood its importance at the time.

The Copper Scroll was found along with the other Dead Sea Scrolls at Qumran in 1952. While most were written on papyrus, the Copper Scroll's text was, as its name suggests, etched on a sheet of beaten copper eight feet long but less than one-twentieth of an inch thick. The text listed sixty-four locations in the Holy Land where an enormous quantity of gold and other treasure acquired from a great temple was hidden. Scholars have postulated that the temple could have been that of Solomon.

Copper was an expensive metal in ancient times, and writing on it an extremely slow business. It is hard to believe that anyone going to the trouble of writing on such a rare medium would have made it up, and it is clear that the Essene priests at Qumran used copper because they didn't want the text to deteriorate. Biblical scholars agree that the text speaks of a monumental hoard of gold and silver but, depending on the translation, the weight of the gold varies from twenty-six tonnes to forty-four tonnes. More aggravating still is the fact that no one has determined exactly where the treasure is buried.

That evening we slept at a roadside bar in a village of uncertain name, perched on a steep hill. Night fell after a thunderstorm of astonishing force. The Emperor's Jeep had overheated, requiring us to stop. Bahru promised that he'd fix the car's leaking radiator by dawn and, since morale was low, I decided to treat him and Samson to a dish of *injera*, fermented Ethiopian bread, and a mutton stew.

As we ate a teenage boy hobbled over, his weight supported by a pole. His right leg was wasted and bent sharply at the knee. The foot beneath it was curled and withered. Ethiopia's villages are full of such people whose dreadful deformities could have been prevented with a single dose of polio vaccine. He was too proud to ask for food but we could see his ribs and knew he must be desperately hungry. Samson asked him to join us. The invalid refused politely, as if he had a better invitation elsewhere. Again, Samson asked, and again the boy refused. Only when Samson stood up and led him to our table did he give way. Then Samson selected the best pieces from the stew and made sure our guest ate them all.

As I sat there after the meal, touched by Samson's thoughtfulness, I reflected on Ethiopia. The country was once occupied by the Italians but it was never colonized. As a result it has retained its own very distinctive identity and sense of pride. Ethiopians listen to Ethiopian music, they wear Ethiopian dress and they eat their own traditional food. Though many want to emigrate to America, they know very little about Western society. The only flaw in this cultural homogeneity is the absence of an awareness of their past. The more time I spent in Ethiopia, the more I came to understand how incongruous this was. There is no other sub-Saharan country with such a rich cultural heritage and it seemed extraordinary that the wealth of its history was not being harnessed.

Unlike most of his countrymen, Samson had studied the nation's history. He was a self-schooled expert on the *Kebra Negast* and the other important Ge'ez texts. His strength was founded in his knowledge of Ethiopian history. It seemed a terrible waste that such a solid member of society should be so desperate to leave, to go to America.

'There is no future here,' said Samson after the meal. 'You come from a country where people have choices, even though they may be unaware of the fact. We're looking for Solomon's gold mines because we have food on our plates and we're healthy. We can wake up in the morning and not have to worry about getting enough money to eat. But put yourself in the place of the boy who was our guest tonight. Most Ethiopians are like him. A few *birr* in his pocket and a little education would allow him to think of the future. But that boy and millions like him don't have that layer of fat to support them . . .'

Samson stopped mid-sentence and then took off his wristwatch and put it on the table.

'They live second by second, minute by minute, hour by hour until . . .'

'Until what?'

'Until their time runs out.'

In his youth Samson worked as a gold miner in southern Ethiopia's illegal mines. Realizing he was wasting his life, he turned to God, and to the enormous Bible which was never far from his side

Harar's hyena-man, Yusuf, slaughters a cow outside his family home, in preparation for the night's feeding frenzy. A local legend says that the town's hyenas guard Solomon's treasure

Each night Yusuf feeds the pack of wild hyenas which come out of the darkness, lured by the smell of fresh blood. Like all Harar's people Yusuf believes that if he stops feeding the animals, they will descend on the town and eat all the children

Travelling by local bus in Ethiopia is a very slow business. No one seems fazed when, every few miles, the bus breaks down

The illegal gold mine at Bedakaysa was like something out of the pages of the Old Testament: hundreds of men, women and children digging the ground with their hands

Around each miner's neck hangs a pouch for storing the precious gold dust. In this case it is made from a miniature gourd with an amulet attached to the same string

Noah takes a break from digging in a mine-shaft at Bedakaysa

Molten gold cascades from the furnace into ingots at Lega Dembi, Ethiopia's only
licensed gold mine, which produces about 350 gold bars a year

The author straining under the weight of three newly made bars of pure Ethiopian gold

A priest sits in the doorway of one of Lalibela's fabulous churches, all twelve of which were carved from a volcanic plateau in the twelfth century

At Bet Giyorgis, the Church of St George, a priest holds up two ancient Ethiopian crosses. The one on the left is known as 'The Gold of Sheba'

Kefla Mohammed, leader of the salt caravan, poses with a pair of his camels on the road to Mekele. Both animals are laden with blocks of salt

A typical Ethiopian depiction of religious events, including Christ teaching and being crucified. The image in the bottom left-hand corner shows Abba Aregawi being pulled up the Debra Damo mountain by a serpent

The flat-topped mountain of Debra Damo is home to the oldest monastery in Ethiopia. No women or female animals of any kind are permitted to ascend the sheer cliff face to visit the monastery

The apprentice priest, Eyba, standing outside the main monastery building at Debra Damo

A priest at Debra Damo shows the *Kebra Negast*, an ancient Ethiopian text that tells the tale of Solomon and Sheba

Beside the shrine in Axum where the Ark of the Covenant is supposedly housed, a priest shows off a collection of Ethiopian crowns and crosses, some of which are said to be more than 1,600 years old

Berehane with a picture of his Italian-born grandfather, Antillio Zappa, who was a friend of Frank Hayter and mined gold near Nejo during the 1920s

The indomitable English adventurer Frank Hayter, who claimed to have discovered a treasure cave on the mysterious mountain of Tullu Wallel in western Ethiopia. He was convinced that the gold and precious gems he found were part of Solomon's treasure

8

Sheba's Gold

'Our excitement was so intense, as we saw the way to Solomon's treasure chamber at last thrown open, that I for one began to tremble and shake.'

Henry Rider Haggard, *King Solomon's Mines*

EARLY NEXT MORNING at the roadside bar, a group of six Tigrayan girls sat at the back, preening themselves and spreading their legs as widely as they could. They were improbably dressed in white coats, the kind which doctors wear in hospitals, and their feet were strapped into high heels. It was five o'clock but as far as they were concerned the night shift hadn't ended. I glanced over at them as I sat waiting for Bahru to get the Emperor's Jeep warmed up. The girls looked away, pretending to be coy, though they knew better than I that coyness was a quality incompatible with their trade.

I watched as a truck driver staggered over to one of them. His shirt-front was spattered with dried vomit and his waxy face was peppered with sores. The Tigrayan woman didn't seem put off by her customer's appearance. First he flirted and she bargained, and then he bargained and she flirted. Eventually they struck a deal. The client handed over his cash, bought a bottle of Coca Cola, and followed the girl into a back room. I asked Samson why a man with an obvious taste for stronger liquor would have wasted his money on Coke.

'In the countryside,' he said, 'some people believe that if you wash your groin with Coca Cola you won't get Aids. The prostitutes insist on it.'

The night before, the bedbugs had been ferocious. My face and shoulders were so badly bitten that I looked as if I had a chronic skin disease. Samson had been attacked by insects as well, but he didn't complain. We needed hardening up, he said sternly, if we were ever to make it to Tullu Wallel and Frank Hayter's mine-shafts. As we spent more time together, Samson and I developed a curious relationship. Each of us saw it as his mission to force discomfort on the other. Rather like Inspector Clouseau's manservant, Kato, Samson knew he was making me stronger by causing me pain. I never quite knew if he was doing it out of loyalty or cruelty. For my part I felt a deep sadistic urge come over me whenever I saw Samson flagging. I couldn't help it. If he suggested we rest at seven, I insisted we continue until ten; and each morning I forced him to take a freezing cold shower before the day's start. He had stopped complaining long ago, well aware that a sadist is empowered by the slightest hint of victory.

We left the white-coated whores to their business and drove out of the village. The sun would soon be rising, forcing the girls back into the shadows. It was good to be moving again. Bahru shifted the gears restlessly, coaxing the vehicle west towards Lalibela. As the Emperor's Jeep ground its way around the potholes, I lay stretched out in the back watching the green landscape unfold. The road wound its way upwards, round one hairpin bend after another. Most of the hillsides were cultivated, their reddish-brown soil sprouting with thick crops of maize and wheat. The more I saw of Ethiopia's rural areas, the more confused I became about the country's image. In the West everyone thinks of Ethiopia as a place of starvation and famine, but although there are isolated pockets of desert, most of the country is lush.

We stopped at the town of Dilbe. Bahru was urgently in need of some *qat*. As he tottered off towards the market Samson and I got out of the Jeep to stretch our legs. Nearby stood a bar, little more than a lean-to, that served thimble-sized cups of coffee made with an Italian espresso machine. Mussolini's invasion in 1935 had brought nothing but misery to Ethiopia, nothing that is, except for espresso machines. They can be found even in the smallest towns and they are the only pieces of machinery in the country which never break down.

As the *qat* began to take effect, Bahru's foot grew heavier on the accelerator. Despite the terrible road surface we raced along at an impressive speed. Chewing furiously at the dark green leaves, his pupils dilating, Bahru bragged that the engine had been overhauled during the night. Samson said that Bahru hadn't wanted to ask me for money so he'd paid for the overhaul himself. I checked my bags to see that they were all still there.

'What exactly did he sell?'

Samson translated the question into Amharic, and Bahru spat out an answer.

'What did he say?'

'He said he sold three of the brake-pads,' replied Samson.

A pair of white girls were sitting by the side of the road. They were in their early twenties and their hair was matted and their skin grimed with dirt. They had spent the night in the open. At twilight the day before, the bus they were taking had swerved to miss another. Luck had been on their side – it was the oncoming bus, not theirs, that had gone over the cliff. When the Emperor's Jeep rolled to a stop, one of the girls pointed to the wreckage in the ravine below.

'It was like a horror film,' she said. 'The other bus had no choice but to go off the road. When our driver realized he was still alive, he burst out laughing and honked the horn. He drove on, but we wanted to stay and help the injured and the dying. So he left us here.'

'Dead bodies were strewn everywhere,' added the other girl. 'Some of the survivors were lying face down, praying to God. Dozens of them were screaming. One woman had lost all the fingers from her right hand and she couldn't speak. She was in shock. We didn't have any medical supplies, and even if we had had some there wasn't much we could do. Still we did our best to comfort the injured, until help arrived.' She paused and stared at the ground. 'But no one ever came.'

Samson and I got out of the car and looked over the edge of the cliff. Fifty feet below, the mangled white shell of a bus lay in a ditch. There were seven or eight bodies scattered on the ground near the vehicle, and I could make out several survivors huddled together under a tree.

'We have to get word to Lalibela,' said the first girl. 'Someone there will come and help.'

We told the girls to get in. Then Samson and I exchanged a

worried glance. We both knew that the chance of anyone in Lalibela volunteering to help was remote, and that it wouldn't be long before the local villagers descended to strip what they could from the wreckage.

The first thing we noticed in Lalibela were the flies. They swarmed over us like locusts, getting in our ears, up our nostrils and in our mouths. For once, I kept my mouth shut. Samson said he'd go and find an aid organization with medical supplies and he got out of the car. Within seconds, he disappeared in a cloud of flies. I told him to hurry. I was impatient to locate the Gold of Sheba.

Lalibela contains twelve churches hewn from the living rock. They may not be as grand as the monuments of the Nabateans at Petra, or on such a scale as the Pyramids, but they are equally mysterious and very beautiful. Were it not for its location, Lalibela would be swamped with tourists.

The story goes that in the twelfth century, during the rule of the Zagwe dynasty, a male child was born to the Queen. The King had died, and the boy's elder brother ruled as regent. Soon after the birth of her second son, the Queen noticed that his cradle was infested with a swarm of bees. She recalled an ancient Ethiopian belief which says that the animal world can foretell the arrival of true nobility. In Ethiopia children are generally named some days after their birth, once their character has shown itself. The Queen thought that the bees were a sign, and so she named her second son Lalibela, 'the man whose sovereignty is recognized by bees'.

Years passed, and Lalibela's brother grew jealous. Fearing that his younger brother would usurp him, he had him poisoned. Lalibela drank the poison and fell into a deep sleep. As he slept, he dreamed that he was taken by angels to the first, second and third heavens. Then God spoke, telling Lalibela to return to earth and to build fabulous churches, the like of which the world had never seen before. When Lalibela awoke, his brother paid homage to him, declaring him to be the true king. Then Lalibela gathered together stonemasons and craftsmen, and ordered them to start carving the rock. During the day they worked with great speed, and during the night the work was carried on by angels.

The twelve churches that Lalibela created are laid out in two main clusters. Each building is unique and can only be appreciated by looking at the space around it. Where there is empty space there was once rock. All the churches were carved out of the surrounding red volcanic tuff.

After an hour of waiting for Samson to reappear, I decided to continue the search for the Gold of Sheba alone. Leaving Bahru to chew *qat* in the shade, I began to make my way to the northern cluster of churches. Within five strides of the Jeep, I was surrounded by a gaggle of boys. They spoke good English, which is rare in Ethiopia, and all of them wanted to be my guide. I said that I wanted to see the Gold of Sheba. I expected blank looks, but to my surprise they all nodded keenly. Then a boy of about eight with bloodied knees spoke for the rest:

'The Gold of Sheba is kept in a big box, which King Lalibela himself made. It's locked and guarded by the priest at Bet Giyorgis.'

The children were adamant that only one of them could be my guide. That was the rule. They could decide amongst themselves by fighting, one said, but it would take time and cause them pain. It was better that I choose my guide as quickly as I could. A small boy stood a little apart from the group, clearly afraid that he would be beaten by the others. Darker-skinned than the rest, he was also the weakest. I chose him, and the others scowled.

I asked the boy his name. He had a high-pitched voice and a cheeky smile. He said he was called Amaya, and that his mother and father were dead, so now he lived with his grandmother who was blind.

We set off down the narrow path which led through tall, lush elephant grass towards the northern churches. Amaya rambled on in English, telling me about life in Lalibela and skipping to keep up. He took me first to the biggest church, Bet Medhane Alem, 'Saviour of the World'. The church stands in a great courtyard carved out of the volcanic rock, and the building itself is encircled by columns, with many more inside its carved interior.

In 1521, a Portuguese priest, Francisco Alvares, arrived in Lalibela and was astonished by what he saw. Yet when he came to write his journals, he was convinced that no one would believe his description. In *A True Relation of the Lands of Prester John*, he explains: 'It wearied me to write more of these works, because it seemed to me that they will accuse me of untruth . . . there is much more than I have already written, and I have left it that they may not tax me with it being falsehood.'

A few minutes from Bet Medhane we came to the church of Bet Maryam. Each of the churches has its own sacred well. That at Bet Maryam is said to contain healing water which has the power to make barren women fertile. Inside, the arches are adorned with carvings and fabulous frescoes, some of which bear the Star of David. Elsewhere I saw ventilation holes carved in the shape of swastikas, evidence of ancient trade routes between Africa and the Indian subcontinent.

On the southern side of Bet Maryam a tunnel led us to more churches. Among them is the most sacred chapel of all, the Selassie Chapel, reputedly the resting-place of King Lalibela himself. Then Amaya led the way to Bet Giyorgis.

Lalibela's Church of St George is one of the true wonders of the world. If it were in any other country, it would be surrounded by curio-sellers and hot-dog stalls. Guided tours would be conducted, and a five-star hotel erected to overlook it. Thankfully, it's in the middle of nowhere and so has been left alone. Bet Giyorgis is carved in the shape of a Greek cross, and it stands on a three-tiered plinth. Legend has it that when King Lalibela had completed his churches St George galloped up on a magnificent white steed. He was furious with the king for not dedicating a church to him. And so King Lalibela ordered one more church to be built in honour of Ethiopia's patron saint.

As he led me through a tunnel to the church's entrance, Amaya tugged at my shirt sleeve.

'This is where the Gold of Sheba is kept,' he whispered.

We ascended a flight of broad steps, removed our shoes and called out for the priest. The ceiling of the church was about twenty feet high, its interior square chamber carved out from the rock, with a shrouded cube – the Holy of Holies – in the centre of the room. As my eyes adjusted to the dim light, a man in deep purple robes stepped from the shadows. He had dark, sorrowful eyes and his beard was flecked with grey. I asked Amaya to translate, but the priest butted in, saying he understood English. There was no need for the boy, he said.

'I have come on a long journey from America,' I replied, as no one in Ethiopia ever seemed very impressed by a journey begun in England.

The priest's eyes widened.

'Ah,' he said, 'America. America is good.'

'I've come to Lalibela to see a precious treasure. I've heard you have that treasure here.'

He nodded.

'I am looking for the Gold of Sheba.'

The priest turned and motioned to a dark wooden coffer, sealed with an unusual lock which seemed to be fastened with a system of wooden levers and bolts.

'The Gold of Sheba is kept in there,' he said. 'The box was made by King Lalibela. It is sacred and cannot be seen by anyone.'

I had come a long way to see the Gold of Sheba and I was not going to be thwarted by religious bureaucracy. I looked down at Amaya and saw him rubbing his fingers together. I fumbled in my jacket pocket. The priest's tongue probed the hairs around his mouth, like that of a snake testing the air.

'I'd be willing to make a suitable donation,' I said obsequiously.

A moment later, the priest was opening the lock. He began by loosening a pair of large wooden screws. I leant forward to get a better look, but he turned his back to me and blocked my view. Minutes later he stepped back. In his hand was an Ethiopian cross intricately worked in gold.

'*This* is the Gold of Sheba.'

Holding the crucifix high above his head like a battle standard, the priest tilted it to catch the shaft of sun coming through the doorway. Amaya and I stumbled backwards as the bolt of light dazzled us. Although not as large as some other Ethiopian crosses, the Gold of Sheba was magnificent. The priest deciphered its complex design. An intricate cross lay at its centre, surrounded by twelve bosses that represented the Apostles of Christ. On the outer edge were a pair of birds that looked like hoopoes. The priest explained that they were doves from Noah's Ark.

'You are the first foreigner ever to set eyes on this sacred cross,' said the priest untruthfully. 'A man whose genius shines as brightly as yours, as brightly as the Gold of Sheba itself, is the kind of man who rewards true beauty when he sees it.'

'Where is the cross from?'

'It was crafted in the highlands.'

'By King Lalibela?'

'No, no,' said the priest, 'long before Lalibela. The gold was brought from Judah. The gold in the cross came from the Great Temple in Judah.'

'The Temple of Solomon, in Jerusalem?'

'Yes, that is right,' he replied, twisting the shaft of the cross in his fingers. 'An Ethiopian went to Judah after Solomon's death and brought back three of the gold treasures.'

'The hoards mentioned in the Copper Scroll?'

The priest said nothing, but he smiled.

I had listened to him with mounting suspicion. How tempting it was to believe his tale. The idea of Solomon's gold returning from the land of the Israelites to Ethiopia was wonderful – a completed circle. But it was implausible, and I had found no mention of the legend elsewhere. I asked the priest where he thought the gold for the temple in Jerusalem had been mined. He shook his head.

'What does it matter where the gold came from? More important is what happened to it when the Temple of Solomon was destroyed.'

Saying this, he laid the Gold of Sheba back in its box and fastened the lock.

'There are thieves,' he said furtively. '*Foreign* thieves!'

Amaya tugged at my sleeve. There had been a terrible theft in Lalibela, he said. Then the priest took up the story. In 1997, an 800-year-old solid gold cross that was kept in the Church of Bet Medhane Alem went missing. It weighed more than fourteen pounds, and was one of the greatest Ethiopian treasures. When the theft was discovered, the small community was plunged into mourning. Lalibela's people whipped themselves into a frenzy of grief, pleading with God to help them. Suspicion fell on the head priest, who was arrested and taken away. Some said he was tortured; everyone believed he was involved. Months went by and there was no word, no sight of the cross. The priest had not confessed. Then news came when it was least expected. The cross was discovered being smuggled into Belgium, where it had been sold to an unsuspecting purchaser. The Ethiopian government had to pay $25,000 to get it back.

Before we could leave the church, the priest fished out a collection tin from the folds of his robes and looked at me expectantly. I folded a fifty *birr* note and stuffed it through the slot in the lid of the tin. The priest smiled in gratitude and then he was gone.

A horde of beggars shuffled towards us as we walked out of the church. Like Lalibela's flies, they longed for sustenance. At the back of the pack was a very old woman. She was stooped low, her spine twisted and bent, and her body was shrouded in rags. Around her neck there hung an enormous growth, the size and shape of a coconut.

'The others say she's a witch,' said Amaya, 'that she talks to the Devil at night.'

'What do you think?'

Amaya smiled at the woman.

'I think her back hurts,' he said gently, 'but I don't think she's a witch.'

The desk clerk of Lalibela's Sheba Hotel cursed the government for driving the tourists away.

'We used to get pretty women coming here,' he said, staring into space. 'They had nice pink lipstick and jewellery that rattled when they laughed. But our leaders don't want the world to see the mess the country's in. They're greedy for the money the aid companies bring. The worse the situation sounds, the more money the United Nations sends. So of course they don't want the place to be stable.'

For a man working as a desk clerk in a small hotel, he seemed unusually well-informed. I asked if he expected tourism to pick up again.

'Hah!' he jeered. 'Only when the government falls.'

'When will that be?'

The clerk looked at his watch.

'It could happen any minute.'

Amaya had recommended that we spend the night at the Sheba Hotel and I had sent him off to find Samson. When I asked the clerk for my room key, he toyed with it, unwilling to end our conversation.

'I see from the register you're from America,' he said.

I replied that I was.

'Ah, I am going to America.'

'Oh, when?'

'When beautiful Ursula sends me the ticket and the visa.'

'Who's Ursula?'

The clerk leant over the counter and his eyes lit up.

'Ursula, *beautiful* Ursula!'

'Yes, but who *is* she?'

'She came here, from Texas,' he said. 'She has white skin, like the shell of a goose egg, and soft hair. When she came to Sheba Hotel we talked for hours. She said she wanted me to see America with my own eyes. She promised me that one day I would be a guest, and I promised to wait for her letter . . . the one with the ticket and the visa.'

'When was Ursula here?'

'Eleven years ago.'

Lalibela's buildings are unlike those in any other part of Ethiopia. The houses are circular with two storeys and are built of loose-fitting stones. The town's inhabitants eke out a living by keeping a few animals and tending their meagre crops of maize and *teff*. Around Petra or the Pyramids money from tourism trickles down into the local economy, and there's a hustle and bustle in the air. But at Lalibela what little money there is from tourism goes straight into the priests' pockets. The local people are ruinously poor and like all Christians in the country, they stand in awe of the priesthood.

Shortly before sunset, Samson turned up at the hotel. He'd spoken to some Danish aid workers about the bus crash and said they would go and have a look in the morning. I wondered how many more of the injured would have died by then, and cursed myself for not having ferried them to Lalibela myself.

'There's no hospital in Lalibela,' said Samson, reading my thoughts. 'And even if we did go and get them we'd run out of petrol. There's none of that here either.' He was right. Lalibela had a severe petrol shortage, and the town was littered with cars that had been abandoned when their tanks ran dry.

The Emperor's Jeep had an engine with an insatiable thirst, made worse by the fact that we could never turn it off. Our expedition was on a tight budget, but our transport had been constructed for an emperor who had had access to plentiful funds. Bahru had promised that the more distance we put between us and the capital, the cheaper petrol would become. By the time we were on the Eritrean border, he said, we'd find fuel was virtually given away. As a result, he had refused to fill up at any of the petrol stations *en route* and now we were running dangerously low.

Early next morning I told Samson to go and find some petrol. If he couldn't find any, he was to look for high-octane aviation fuel. He ambled away in the direction of the market with a one-gallon bottle under his arm. He hadn't quite understood the extent of the Jeep's thirst.

An aid worker in Addis Ababa had told me to be careful when buying fuel in rural Ethiopia. Much of the stuff on sale is diluted with kerosene or even with water. The best way to test its quality is to offer a little fuel to the person you are buying from. If he jumps at the idea you know he's hawking the real thing.

The only man in town with petrol for sale looked surprisingly gloomy given that he had a monopoloy on all the fuel.

Samson checked the price and was quoted four times the usual rate.

'That's scandalous!' I shouted. 'But we're desperate, so tell him that we'll buy all the petrol he's got – so long as he puts some in his own tank first.'

The petrol-seller's face froze as Samson translated my words. Then he grew very angry and threatened to call the police. While he was shouting, Samson took a sniff at the fuel he was touting.

'This isn't petrol,' he said, 'it smells like horse urine.'

For the next two days we waited for a petrol tanker to arrive. The two girls we'd picked up had wisely decided to catch a lift westwards to Gondar on a truck piled high with crates of ouzo. Like the espresso machines, ouzo had been introduced by the Italians, and the Ethiopians had developed a taste for it. As a result, there was a distinct correlation between wrecked trucks and the contents that they were carrying at the time of the crash. Many of the vehicles we saw that had plunged into ravines seemed to have been carrying ouzo or beer or vodka, or in some cases all three.

The problem with having your own transport is that it limits your movements. All I could do was force Samson and Bahru to stand by the roadside and flag down vehicles to ask if we could buy any of their fuel. On the first day only one truck passed, and it ran on diesel. On the second day they were a little luckier: a government jeep rolled into Lalibela. Samson begged the driver to sell us some precious fuel, but the man jeered at him and drove off.

I was secretly pleased to have been marooned in Lalibela and spent the first two days exploring the town and its churches with Amaya. But then, having seen all there was to see, I grew impatient.

By the third day, Samson and Bahru had still had no luck and I retreated to the Sheba Hotel. The desk clerk was also tired of waiting, in his case for non-existent guests. He asked me if I'd man the front desk while he took the afternoon off. What if a tidal wave of tourists flooded in? His face lit up for a second and then fell.

'This is Lalibela,' he said, 'not Las Vegas.'

So I sat behind the front desk and re-read Frank Hayter's account of his discovery of the mine-shafts at Tullu Wallel:

It was not until I was within a few yards that I realized what the patches of darker stone were – the entrance to underground caves; and not natural entrances either, for the stone uprights and heavy lintels that squared the openings had been fashioned by the hand of man.

Switching on my torch I stepped between the massive uprights. Ahead loomed a narrow passage which at some remote age had been hewn through the rock. I glanced at the walls and saw that they had been roughly chiselled. Here and there various-sized bosses of darker stone had been left protruding from the wall's surface, giving the impression that the workmen had found the task of cutting through them an impossible one. Advancing step by step I penetrated some forty feet and was wondering how much farther I could go before the passage ended, when the torch-light illuminated the far wall of a huge cave.

After reading Hayter's words, I took another look at the photograph of the mine opening in Captain Bartleet's book. The dressed stone doorway near the rough cave entrance looked convincing, but I knew that the only way to solve the matter was to make for the mountain myself.

When I am about to embark on a difficult journey, I comfort

myself by reading the accounts of the great nineteenth-century travellers, men like Stanley, Burton, Speke, Burckhardt and Barth. They are towering figures who persevered through the most brutal circumstances imaginable, often in disguise, though today their methods seem rather savage. If any of Stanley's team gave him trouble, he had them put in chains.

Of them all my favourite is Samuel White Baker. He travelled throughout Abyssinia, as Ethiopia was then known, and he was instrumental in locating the source of the Nile. Baker was a man of overwhelming ambition who thrived on adversity. When the chips are down and I'm wondering how best to proceed, I turn to him.

Samuel Baker was the only Victorian ennobled directly as a result of his explorations. He was also the only adventurer of his era who travelled with his wife, Florence. Baker had purchased her at a Bulgarian slave market, and they became inseparable. The journey on which they met was typical of a time which, sadly, no longer exists.

Baker had agreed to take a young Indian Maharaja, Duleep Singh, on a bear-hunting trip to Transylvania. Duleep Singh divided his time between Claridges Hotel in London and a Scottish castle in the Highlands, where he pursued his passion for hunting. On the journey to Transylvania he travelled under the pseudonym of Captain Robert Melville. He also insisted on bringing his three English servants with him, including his butler. Most of his voluminous luggage seemed to consist of crates of vintage champagne. The party reached Budapest by train, and then Baker bundled the Maharaja and his entourage aboard a corn barge which was heading down the Danube.

While sailing downriver, the corn barge collided with an ice-floe near the Ottoman-controlled town of Widdin, in what is now Bulgaria, and the Maharaja and his retinue were forced ashore. Widdin was as sordid a place as one could imagine, its only business the sale of black, white and Chinese slaves. While waiting for the corn barge to be repaired Baker and the Maharaja went to look at the slave market, It was there that Baker first set eyes on Florence, with whom he fell in love instantly. He haggled furiously for her, but he never disclosed how much he had paid.

Four days after our arrival at Lalibela, Samson flagged down a jeep. In the back there were seven jerry-cans that belonged to a local businessman. Even before I saw the driver's face, I knew the negotiations would be hard. I stood out of the way, for the appearance of a foreigner tends to quadruple the going price. Samson put on his most courteous voice and smiled so much that his eyes disappeared in creases. He motioned a finger to the cans. The driver nodded. Samson smiled again. I could tell money was being discussed. The driver kept nodding. The bargaining continued for about half an hour, with the driver nodding and Samson smiling. By the end of it Samson was no longer smiling, he was chewing his upper lip.

'How much?' I asked.

'A lot.'

I handed over all the money in my wallet.

'We're going to need more than this,' said Samson nervously, 'we're going to need the money in your shoe as well.'

Before we left Lalibela I gave Amaya a selection of old clothes. He'd asked if I had a dress in his size. He'd always wanted a dress, he said. I was confused and rather concerned that a small boy wanted to dress up as a girl. I asked Samson to have a chat with him and explain that dresses are for little girls, not little boys. Amaya started to grin and then burst out laughing. Then Samson started to laugh.

'Amaya *is* a little girl!' he said.

Ten minutes later we were on the road again with Bahru crunching the gears and jerking the wheel as usual, an enormous quid of *qat* stuck in his cheek. The scenes we passed were now familiar: children with huge piles of sticks on their backs, goats being herded along the road, people trudging to distant destinations, solemn funeral processions of elders wrapped in white, making their way down mountain trails, walking in silence towards a burial ground. I asked Samson why so many people were dying.

'Life in the country is hard,' he replied. 'If you fall sick you get sicker and then you die. People with a little money use it to buy food, not medicine.'

The contrast between village life and a small town in Ethiopia is astonishing. Small Ethiopian towns are vibrant places, full of bustle. Cluttered shops sell a colourful display of goods imported from China. Boys play table tennis on the pavements. The bars are alive with deafening music, the flow of warm bottled beer and the lascivious solicitations of whores. And all the while, there is a constant flow of people arriving from the villages to barter and to buy basic necessities. In a remote village or hamlet, days from the nearest road, there are no paraffin lamps or electricity, only candles; no running water either, or shops, or the noise of an ill-tuned transistor radio. I am not new to Africa or to lands where good, innocent people are struggling to survive. Even so I found myself reeling at the extraordinary level of hardship that rural Ethiopians endure.

Ask me to list all the things which I own and I wouldn't know where to start. I have rooms filled with possessions I never use. Our attic is packed to bursting with objects I've collected and forgotten about. But ask a villager in the Ethiopian highlands what he has in his *tukul* and the list will be precise and short. Everything is functional and has ten uses. There's a knife, perhaps an axe, a candle or two, or a lamp made from the bottom of a tin can, a blanket and hides, a bucket, a pot, a sheet of polythene, a few old clothes, some flour and a pile of sticks. That is all.

9

The Jinn of Suleiman

'It is better to die than to live without killing.'

Danakil proverb

FIVE HOURS OUT of Lalibela we passed a terrible accident on what was surely the world's roughest road. A truck had somehow toppled over on a flat stretch, and its cargo of ouzo had shattered. The driver was dead. So was his companion. The bodies had been pulled out of the cab and were lying on the side of the road. The fact that there was so little blood indicated that they'd probably died instantly. To my relief there was no sign of the two Dutch girls. They had been travelling west. This road led north.

A few miles further on Bahru sped through a village and hit a dog. He burst out laughing and clapped his hands. I turned round and through the rear window saw the poor creature writhing in its death throes. I shouted at Bahru, but he didn't understand why I was so angry. As far as he was concerned stray animals on the road were fair game, something to enliven the tedium of the job.

By now, the deficiencies of the Emperor's Jeep were becoming apparent. The worst problem was the tyres. On a good day we would have only a couple of punctures. On bad days the number would rise to seven or eight. The reason was blatantly clear. The tyres had gaping holes in them. At first I found myself yelling at Bahru. Why didn't he get the tyres properly repaired? But eventually I came to see his point of view. In Addis Ababa I had insisted that Bahru be responsible for all punctures and breakdowns. As far as he was concerned, the less money he laid out on tyres, the more he had to spend on *qat*. If your life revolves around chewing an intoxicating leaf, it makes perfect sense.

Though Ethiopian villages have very little in the way of merchandise to offer, they do usually contain at least one shop selling a selection of worn and lacerated tyres at highly inflated prices. At Sekota, Bahru was finally persuaded to buy ten tyres. Though we all knew they probably wouldn't get us through the day, I felt I'd achieved a minor victory.

While we were at the tyre stall I got chatting to a frail balding man who smelt strongly of sulphur. Every few minutes he'd pull up his shirt and apply a layer of Indian-made ointment to a suppurating wound on his chest. He was old and underfed, and it was clear that the injury wasn't healing. I had a look at the instructions on the tube. The ointment was supposed to ease back pain.

'Strong medicine,' said the man.

'Does it help?'

'Oh yes,' he said, 'it's *imported* medicine.'

'Where did you get it?'

'I bought it at the market. It was expensive.'

'But it says you must not put it on an open wound.'

The man looked confused but then he raised his shirt and massaged more ointment into the lesion. He grimaced with pain. In the Ethiopian highlands there's an enduring trust in foreign-made goods. Local markets are flooded with cheap Indian medicines which are regarded as the height of sophistication. Imported drugs are seen as panaceas: a randomly selected cream, lotion or tablet is used to cure any illness.

Samson said that when he was a teenager his parents thought he had meningitis, so they went to the market to buy some medicine. The stallholder there weighed out a few handfuls of unlabelled tablets and prescribed them to be taken with chicken broth.

I asked Samson if he'd had seizures as a result.

'No, no,' he replied, 'I got better with a little time, although my sweat turned brown.'

My geologist friend in London had looked at the map of Ethiopia and had said that he'd put money on Afar being the ancient Ophir. He had pointed to a ridge of low mountains that rise up along the Red Sea coast. They were the place he'd head for. I had scoured dozens of geological reports, but none of them mentioned there being any gold in Afar, though there were gold prospectors' reports on just about every other corner of the country. Still, I knew I had to go and see for myself. And if Afar wasn't Ophir, it had other attractions.

The north-eastern region of Afar is a desolate expanse of desert peopled by one of the most ferocious tribes imaginable – the Danakil.

I have always been fascinated by the curious habit of taking human body parts as trophies. Most cultures have at one time or another slain their foes, lopped off their heads and paraded around with them. But the Danakil developed a reputation for taking quite a different kind of trophy. Their predilection was for testicles. A warrior hadn't proved himself as a man until he'd spilt his enemy's blood and had the man's genitals hanging round his neck. A search through Ethiopia for Solomon's mines wouldn't have been complete without a journey to Afar.

Once we were on the main road I told Bahru to start heading east rather than north. He continued to chew his *qat* and didn't blink. I was pleased he hadn't objected, so I added that we would be going to Afar in search of the Danakil. I watched Bahru's face in the rear-view mirror as we bumped along. It contorted and then froze in paralysis, as if his *qat*-chewing jaw had at last seized up. Samson was equally horrified. He said that the Danakil were a brutal people who only had one thing on their minds.

'What's that, then?'

'Testicles!'

'But we're driving in the Emperor's Jeep,' I exclaimed, 'no one's going to mess with us.'

Bahru's jaw suddenly loosened in a torrent of Amharic.

'What's the problem?'

'Bahru says he's not going to drive to Afar. If you want to go there you'll have to go on foot.'

I tried everything I could think of, but Bahru wouldn't budge. He was a man with no fear, he explained, but he was more attached to his testicles than he could say. Wild horses wouldn't drag him into the Danakil Desert. Bahru's own tribe, the Somalis, have a formidable reputation for courage in battle, so I was surprised by his refusal to continue. Maybe going to Afar *was* too dangerous.

'Samson, what do you think?'

The indefatigable fixer wiped his face with his hand.

'They're heathens,' he said.

'Then look on our journey as a missionary expedition to preach the Word of the Lord.'

At that Samson seemed to perk up and I caught the glint of missionary zeal in his eye. He fished out a newly acquired Bible from his disintegrating tartan case. It was much smaller than the one he had lost in the fire, but the Word of the Lord takes many forms.

'We will go to Afar,' he said boldly, 'and we will spread the Word.'

After a great deal of coaxing, Bahru agreed to take us as far as Didigsala on the edge of the Danakil Desert. He would leave us there and beat a hasty retreat, meeting us later at Mekele, the capital of Tigray. I'd heard that in Didigsala we could join one of the salt caravans that make their way through the desert to the market at Mekele.

On my recent journey up the Amazon to the Shuar people, my companions and I had been terrified that we might have our heads chopped off and dramatically reduced in size. The very thought had had a dire effect on the morale of the expedition. But modern times have brought change, and missionaries have now replaced Shuar blowpipes with tambourines. The destruction of ancient customs in a matter of years angers me, but I suspected that the testicle-lopping days of the Danakil had probably come to an end. I informed Samson that Alabama missionaries had probably beaten us to the Danakil. He smiled widely. He looked forward to talking to them about Jesus.

Wilfred Thesiger is one of the few to have written about the proud traditions of the Danakil. He was born at the British Legation in Addis Ababa in 1910. The capital was then still young, and until Thesiger was sent to boarding school in England at the age of eight, he'd never seen a car. His father, a high-ranking diplomat, was instrumental in helping Ras Tafari accede to the Ethiopian throne, but before the prince could be crowned as Emperor, Thesiger's father died quite suddenly of a heart attack. Wishing to acknowledge his gratitude to the family, the Emperor extended a personal invitation to Wilfred Thesiger to attend his coronation in his father's place.

In November 1930, when the festivities came to an end, Thesiger embarked on his first true expedition. He had heard that the land of the Danakil had good hunting, so he set off for the desert, writing later that 'The whole course of my life was to be permanently affected by that month.'

Thesiger has often told me of that, his earliest, African expedition and he recounts the tale with characteristic animation. He was aware that the Danakil were ferocious, but he had little idea quite how dangerous. The more officials pleaded with him not to go, the more determined he became. Almost every foreign expedition that had headed into the Danakil Desert in the past had been wiped out, the testicles of every participant seized as trophies. When, therefore, Thesiger returned in one piece, he became something of a hero. He was just twenty years old.

At virtually the same time that the young Wilfred Thesiger was rounding up pack animals for his journey, another European was returning from the Danakil Depression. L. M. Nesbitt was a prospector and the foreman of a gold mine in western Ethiopia. He believed he might find gold in Afar, though in his book *Desert and Forest*, he hardly mentions the subject – serious prospectors always keep their cards close to the chest. Still, the fact that Nesbitt, a seasoned prospector, made such a perilous journey was encouraging. There might well be gold in Afar after all.

I rallied Samson and Bahru, telling them that Nesbitt's expedition proved there was the possibility of finding gold, or even ancient mines, in the Danakil region. I decided not to relate the details of Nesbitt's trip or tell them exactly how many of his men lost their genitalia.

The road to Didigsala was the greatest challenge that the Emperor's Jeep had faced so far. The dilapidated vehicle rattled at every joint, as if it shared its driver's fear of Danakil bandits. Thorn trees and eucalyptus gave way to low rocky hills and patchy scrub. We saw camels grazing, the odd shepherd with his flock of goats, and a smattering of huts nestling in the shadows between the hills. Samson took out his Bible and started selecting appropriate passages with which to convert.

Before veering off the main road towards Didigsala, Bahru

swapped the car's jack for a bale of *qat* at a small hamlet. I would
have stopped the unwise trade but we didn't have a spare tyre left,
and there was little hope of getting one now. Bahru chewed so
feverishly that his mouth foamed, and his eyes seemed to start from
his head like those of a man being electrocuted. Four hours later,
I spotted a cluster of low huts. We had reached the outskirts of
Didigsala.

Samson got down and asked the first man he saw when the next
salt caravan would be leaving for Mekele. I watched as, ever polite
and respectful of others, he posed the question only after lengthy
salutations. The local man waved his hands frantically, motioned
sideways and pointed at the sky. Then he bent down and put his
palms on the ground, did five press-ups, jumped up again, pulled
down his shorts and waved his genitalia about. Samson looked back
at me despondently.

'He's a lunatic,' he said.

Most small Ethiopian towns seemed to have a token madman,
and in rural areas people seemed to delight in throwing stones at
them. Samson passed a crust of bread to our madman, who whimpered with satisfaction. He was very thin, and the lines of his ribs
showed through his shirt. As he choked down the bread, a middle-
aged man dressed in a brilliant white *shamma* swept out of his
house. He picked up a large stone, and flung it at the maniac,
hitting him on the backside with considerable force. At that, the
madman fled.

A minute later a crowd had gathered round the Jeep. Thirty or
forty old men clutching grey blankets had stumbled over and now
they were peering in through the windows of the vehicle. Clearly
visitors were rare.

One of our new companions placed a hand on the Jeep's bonnet
and closed his eyes.

'You have come far,' he said.

I nodded.

'We have come to meet the salt caravan which goes to Mekele.'

'Ah, Mekele, very far.'

'How far?'

'Ah, very very far.'

Samson translated and winced with worry.

'When will the next salt caravan come from Afar?'

The old man pulled his blanket more tightly around him and then, lifting up his walking cane, he swung it in an arc toward the horizon.

'There they are now,' he said.

We shaded our eyes to follow the line of the stick. I could see nothing.

'He is right,' said Samson. 'I can make out people and camels. Dots. Many dots.'

'They will not reach here until morning,' said the man. 'You will stay the night with me.'

He led the way to his hut. Bahru needed no cue to unload our belongings. They were piled up on the sand before I'd said a word. Then he leapt back into the Jeep and said he'd meet us in Mekele.

'When? When will you get there?'

Bahru spat on his hands and revved the engine.

'The question is when will *you* get there,' he replied.

Then he was gone in a swirl of dust.

'He is a coward,' said Samson. 'Bahru is a disgrace to his tribe.'

The man with the stick called the others to leave us alone and lashed out at them with his cane. We were his property. As he led the way to his hut he said his name was Adugna. His wife was dead, he explained, and so he lived with his son's family. They were poor, but they were honoured to accept us into their home. I inquired about the camel train to Mekele.

'You will need strong legs,' he said. 'It is very far.'

'A week's walk?'

Adugna blinked his frosted eyes.

'Many days.'

Samson, who was brimming over with unexpected enthusiasm, comforted me.

'We are in God's hands,' he said. 'We are the Israelites in the desert. The only thing we should fear is the Devil.'

Adugna led the way through a ring of thorns that encircled his son's home. A hunting dog sprang at us from the shadow of the hut, but Adugna lunged at it with his stick. In the dark, smoky atmosphere of the one-room hut, a dozen eyes widened as we entered. I couldn't make out the features of faces at first, just eyes, all winking like owls in the trees. Adugna swung his cane to make space for us, then clapped his hands and barked orders. His family members hurried out into the sunshine and sought refuge behind the hut.

'You will stay with me for a month!' said Adugna. 'This is your home. We are brothers.'

'But we want to go to Mekele with the caravan,' I said.

The old man laughed a deep and sinister laugh.

'They will kill you and take your money,' he replied. 'They are bad men. The salt traders are greedy. Not like us. We have no money. We have no use for it. Money is the Devil's currency.'

The old man's son returned, stooping respectfully, and asked what we would like to drink. Without thinking, I said that tea would be very welcome. He stooped again, clasped my hand in his, thanked me, and left.

An hour passed. Samson asked Adugna about life in the desert.

'It's very hard, very hot, very dusty,' said our host. 'I was born at Lake Afrera in Afar. It's even hotter there.'

'How old are you?'

Adugna scrunched up his face and wiped it with the corner of his shawl.

'Oh, I must be very old,' he said. 'Maybe seventy by now, or eighty. Maybe even older. I remember the days when the Italians were here. I was a young man then. There were other *faranji* as well. They were looking for gold.'

'*Gold?* Did they find any?'

'There is no gold here any more,' he replied.

'Did there used to be gold, though?'

'Oh, yes, there used to be. Afar was richer in gold than any other place on earth. There was so much gold that our people were rich like kings. Gold was the only metal we had.'

'When was that? When was there gold?'

'A long time ago.'

'How long – a hundred years, a thousand years?'

'Oh, yes,' said Adugna. 'That long.'

'Which? A thousand years?'

'Yes, a long time ago.'

'What happened to the gold? Was it mined out?'

'No, it was not all mined,' said our host. 'There was too much ever to be mined. There was so much, I tell you, so much gold!'

'So it's still here, still in the ground?'

Again Adugna wiped his face with his shawl.

'It is here, but at the same time it is not here,' he said.

'How can that be?'

'Well, I will tell you. God got very angry with our people. He told them they were greedy, that they thought of nothing but themselves. So he punished them. He waved his cloak over the desert and turned all the gold into salt. But one day,' Adugna continued, 'when our people are no longer greedy, he will pull his cloak away and reveal the gold. That is why we stay here. We are waiting.'

Adugna called out to his daughter-in-law, telling her to bring the tea, which still hadn't arrived.

'Stay here with me,' he said. 'Be my guest and stay here. We will sit together and wait for God to pull away his cloak, to show us the fields of gold.'

Night had fallen by the time the tea finally arrived. Adugna's son and daughter-in-law slipped into the hut with a pair of steaming cups. They presented one to me and the other to Samson. We breathed in the steam and thanked them for their hospitality. The family clustered around and watched us. I took a sip of the boiling liquid. It tasted earthy and weak. I assumed it was some blend of local tea.

'Have another sip,' said Adugna's son anxiously.

So I did.

'Delicious.'

'*Is* it?' he asked earnestly. 'Are you sure it is delicious?'

'Yes, yes, quite delicious,' said Samson and I at the same time.

The air of anxiety seemed to lift.

'Can I tell you something?' asked Adugna's son.

'Of course.'

He touched his hand to his heart.

'Well, we did not have any tea,' he said. 'But it is our custom to give an honoured guest whatever he asks for. You asked us for tea. We did not know what to do. None of our neighbours had any tea either. Then someone found an old sack which had once had some tea in it. So we boiled up the sack. And we made tea from it.'

As I stretched out in the *tukul* waiting for sleep that night, I thought of Adugna's story of the gold. Throughout Ethiopia, gold and folklore seemed to be closely connected. Where you found one, you found the other. Many people knew of the legend of God punishing the Danakil for being greedy – I was to hear the tale a dozen times in different parts of the country. When other tribes recounted it, they did so with scorn, doubtless because the Danakil are feared and disliked. The Danakil themselves sincerely believed the legend: one day, God will transform the salt back into gold.

Adugna was an old man, but possibly not old enough to remember Nesbitt's expedition, though he must have heard of others with the same ambition. Before the Second World War, Ethiopia was a magnet for those wishing to seek their fame and fortune. Nesbitt himself described the European population of Addis Ababa in the late 1920s as 'always a mob of disillusioned, broken-down vagrants, meddlers, spies, sharpers – adventurers all. All are adept at something: some of them have academic titles, probably self-conferred . . . they are stayers-behind, dressed in ill-fitting threadbare clothes with untrimmed hair.'

But Nesbitt was different. He was educated and well-organized, and he knew the dangers of travelling among the Danakil. Three Italian expeditions in the 1880s had ended with the entire party being butchered in Afar. The focus of life for any young Danakil man was to kill. A man who had not slain another would never be accepted as a husband and would be called a woman by his peers.

The Danakil passion for killing is from another time, when slaying one's enemies brought honour and respect. My own ancestors in the Hindu Kush thrived on a culture where killing was respectable. They would dress their womenfolk up in red clothing so they wouldn't be killed in the crossfire.

That night Adugna slept outside the hut with his family, leaving Samson and me alone. I began to imagine a midnight assassination, but Samson seemed untroubled.

'Adugna's parents were wild people,' he said, 'but he and the others have kindness in their eyes.'

He was right. While we slept, the old man's daughter-in-law took our clothes and washed them. Her husband cleaned my shoes, and their children sprinkled the petals of fragrant flowers over us. I was grateful for their hospitality but saddened at the same time.

It seemed as if the Danakil had been called into line, like the Shuar and so many other once proud tribes.

Next morning, before the first light of dawn cut across the horizon, the salt caravan arrived. Forty camels and ten men walked briskly into the settlement. The camels were laden with what seemed to be large grey slabs of stone. Like every camel on earth, they resented being enslaved by man, but they were energetic, for their day had just begun. Their leader gave the order for the beasts to be given water and he checked the bindings of their loads. Then he came over to where we were standing.

Adugna introduced us. Kefla Mohammed was a slender man with skinny legs, calloused hands and an occasional squint. He walked with a limp, plunging his long stick into the sand as he went, like a gondolier. He must have been the same age as me, but he looked much older, his skin roughened by decades of desert sun.

When Adugna had introduced us, Kefla pressed his shoulders to mine in greeting.

'We will be friends for a thousand years,' he said.

'We wish to journey to Mekele.'

The leader stood tall, pushing himself up on his stick.

'You will walk with us and share our food,' he replied, 'for we are brothers.'

I thanked him.

'How many days' trek is it?'

Kefla took a step back.

'Far,' he said. 'It is very far.'

'Two days?'

'Perhaps.'

'More than that?'

Again he stepped back. Then he glanced at the fine sand which covered his feet.

'Perhaps.'

Two hours later our bags and our water-bottles were strapped on the strongest of the she-camels, and we took our positions at the rear of the caravan. Adugna and his family stood to attention and wished us good fortune. Other villagers came to bid us farewell too, but Adugna fought them away with his stick. This was his moment. I promised to return when I had visited Mekele, when I had found the gold of Solomon.

'I have told you,' he called as we left, 'come and stay here with me and we shall wait together for God's cloak to lift.'

Setting out on a journey of uncertain length in an unknown land is a thrilling prospect. I asked Samson if Kefla and his troop seemed trustworthy. He hugged his Bible close to his chest and hinted that they were good people but that they needed his Christian counsel. Only then, he said, would God raise his veil and restore the fortunes of the Danakil.

'Do you really believe the legend?' I asked.

Samson looked up at the sun blazing overhead.

'The Lord is wonderful and mysterious,' he said.

We trekked over parched ground, heading north-west. There was no tree cover and only a smattering of cacti and scrub. Whenever the camels spotted any vegetation, they would stop and graze. They were roped together like mountaineers and didn't seem in the least affected by the great weight of their loads.

The salt they carried had been carved from the dry bed of Lake Karum and from the salt flats around it in Afar. Long wooden poles are used to prize the blocks loose, and then the blocks are sawn into smaller pieces of a uniform size.

Kefla called us to the front and offered us some cooked meat and water from his bottle. He was eager to tell us about his life. Fortunately, like Adugna, he spoke some Amharic, and so Samson could translate.

'I have walked this route a thousand times,' he said, 'since I was a child. Before me, my father walked with the camels, as his own father did before him.'

'What of the dangers, the fear of *shiftas*?'

'These days there's no danger,' he said, 'except from scorpions and snakes. Our people used to enjoy killing foreigners but now we have come to trust them.'

Kefla glanced over at me as we walked. I knew what he was thinking. He was wondering if I'd heard of the Danakil's preoccupation with testicles.

'I have read of the proud traditions of the Danakil,' I said. 'It is sad that they have disappeared.'

'We are still proud,' he replied. 'We are Danakil. But we no longer kill every man whose face is unknown to us. That was the old way. It was a good way, but now it has passed.'

Most of the men in the party were related to Kefla, brothers or sons, nephews or cousins. They formed a strong unit, he said, each man trusting the others with his life. The salt caravan was no place for women. Kefla's wife, his third, was with the clan in the Danakil desert. They had been married the previous year, after his second wife had died in childbirth.

'What about your first wife?'

The leader thrust his stick in the sand, his gaze fixed on the ground.

'She died as well,' he said, 'of malaria.'

I changed the subject and asked about the legend of the gold.

'Ah, yes, the gold,' he said, almost as if he had anticipated my question. 'It has been turned into salt by God.'

'Do you think He will ever turn it back into gold again?'

'Perhaps,' said Kefla, 'and that would be good, as you can sell gold for a lot at Mekele. But I get angry when I hear my friends and clansmen cursing that the gold has gone. You see, God changed a useless metal into salt – and no man or camel can live without salt, but we can all live without gold.'

Nesbitt had warned of the danger of trekking with camels. He had written of the constant worry that they would catch a foot in a crack in the ground. Kefla and the others were alert for such clefts and, if there was any doubt, they would halt the caravan and probe the earth with their sticks before carrying on. Another problem was the stifling heat. I found myself drinking water incessantly. Kefla told me to be careful. Too much water, he said, was as bad as none at all. I doused a shirt in water and wrapped it around my head like a turban, and Samson did the same.

From time to time a block of salt was unstrapped from one of the camels and given to them to lick. At other times, Kefla would feel the sand with his hand. If it were too hot, the camels' feet would burn. Nothing was as important as the well-being of the camels.

Nesbitt wrote that he preferred to travel with human porters rather than with pack animals. Humans, he said, can take short cuts, negotiate precipitous slopes and cross torrents by jumping from rock to rock. More to the point, fresh porters can be hired when necessary. But then again, no man could heave blocks of salt such a great distance.

In the late afternoon, camp was pitched near a thicket of thorn trees. Samson had been keen to spread the Word of God to the Danakil, most of whom were Muslims. But now that he had a captive audience, he hadn't the strength. We sat in a heap on the ground: I was too exhausted to write my journal, and he was too tired to preach. Around us, the camels were being unloaded and watered, a fire was built and some scraps of meat were roasted. I asked Samson to find out how much further we had to go.

'Please do not make me ask that question,' he said. 'I cannot bear to hear the answer.'

So we lay there, waiting for the night, and I thought longingly of the Emperor's Jeep. I even began to think of Bahru with some affection.

Kefla told his eldest son to keep guard. He was a boy of about twelve.

'He's as wise as Suleiman,' he said, 'like his grandfather. Many girls already want to marry him. But there is time for that.'

'You know of Suleiman?'

'Of course,' responded the leader, 'all Danakil know how he came here himself searching for ivory and gold.'

'Did he find them?'

'Yes, yes, he did. I told you, there used to be gold here. There was much gold in the time of Suleiman.'

'Did he mine it?'

Kefla stoked the fire with his stick.

'His men cut the gold from the ground in slabs,' he said. 'Then it was loaded on to ships and taken back to the land of Suleiman.'

'How did they carry the gold to the ships?'

'Suleiman's army of jinn carried it, of course.'

The camels had been fed and were now sitting, chewing the cud. The sky was lit by a crescent moon and speckled with stars, and the air was cool, chilled by a light breeze from the east. Kefla's eldest son was called Yehia. He patrolled the camp with a Lee Enfield .303. He was close to puberty, the time when his forebears would have started to prepare for their first kill. The boy's finger never left the trigger; he was clearly itching to pull back the curved sliver of steel. But he had been born too late. Deaths are still a frequent occurrence among the Danakil, but now they are put down to self-defence rather than cold-blooded murder. These days when they kill, the Danakil don't bother to rip off testicles. Although Kefla and the others didn't say so, it was quite clear that they thought killing wasn't the same if you couldn't hack off your enemy's private parts.

When he passed me, Yehia clenched his jaw and swung the rifle to his shoulder in a practised movement. As a foreigner my kind had been fair game since the beginning of time. Only now had the rules changed, and the young warrior felt cheated. I smiled at him, but his mask of rage didn't break. His uncle Abdullah invited us to sit with him on a coarse goat-hair mat. He was taller than the others, with a slim neck, and he wore a pair of bandoliers strapped across his chest. He cut a piece of dried meat from a carcass in his lap and held it to my lips.

I was about to ask how much further we had to travel, but I knew Samson would be reluctant to translate the question. Instead I asked Abdullah about Mekele.

He frowned so hard that his brow rippled like corrugated iron.

'It is a very big city,' he said. 'Too many men, too many cars, too much noise!'

'So you don't like it?'

'Ah!' he said. 'Walk in the city and you see the worst side of man. People forget where they have come from when they reach such a place. They grow lazy and drink beer, and they waste their money. That is not the real world.'

'Then what is the real world?'

Abdullah loosened the bandoliers and then slapped his hands together and held them out like scales.

'*This* is the real world,' he said. 'Look at it! Smell it! Taste it! Listen to it!'

Kefla came over to where we were sitting and crouched on the ground. It was dark, but I could see he was tired. He said that Yehia would protect us in the night. If there was any trouble the camels would be sure to sound the alarm. They could smell a thief from a great distance.

'I hope we are left alone,' I said feebly.

Kefla smiled, and leant back on his heels.

'You may be wishing that,' he said, 'but Yehia is praying that we will be disturbed. He is ready to pull the trigger, to prove himself a man.'

All of the next day we marched, one foot ahead of the next, as the sun rose from a faint pink glimmer of light to a raging ball of fire above the desert. I found the going hard. By early afternoon it was so hot that my spit sizzled on a rock. My mind kept flashing back to the jungle. The desert was bad, but nothing could compare with the horrors of a tropical rain forest. As I staggered on, I thanked God that we were far from the jungle. We had seen no insects or reptiles, and we could walk freely, unhindered by low vines, fallen tree trunks and the press of undergrowth. Samson had never been in the jungle, so he didn't know how lucky he was. He started moaning about missing Addis Ababa, saying that his girlfriend would be longing for him, and that he had to get back to urgent commitments. His misery gave me new strength. I found myself sympathizing with Henry Stanley and his habit of throwing men in irons at the slightest whisper of dissent.

The camels were unloaded every three hours and their bindings were constantly checked. Rubbing would lead to sores. The only journey I had ever made with camels was in India's Thar Desert years before. On that trip we had actually ridden the camels, rather than walking alongside. But I'd soon come to appreciate the unique relationship between man and camel. The animals look at their masters with loathing. But the men in a caravan regard the camels with silent wonder. They would never admit it, but you can see that they value the beasts as highly as their closest friends. This was never more apparent than when one of Kefla's camels went lame.

It was the late afternoon of the third day and Kefla was leading the caravan through a series of low barren hills. We were all exhausted. The camels were about to rest and be watered. We had grown used to being blinded by light so dazzling that it scorched our retinal nerves and made our eyes stream with tears. Somehow, the Danakil coped with the brightness and remained alert to the camels' every move. They needed to: a single misplaced step could spell disaster. Then, suddenly, one of the smaller she-camels plunged to the ground and let out a truly terrible bellow of pain.

Without wasting a second, Kefla took a knife from beneath his shawl and sliced away the straps which held the slabs of salt. The animal thrashed in agony and her bellows turned to a high-pitched shriek. With the others struggling to keep her still, Kefla made a quick inspection. It was obvious that her right foreleg had shattered. Then the caravan's leader picked up his knife and pressed it against the camel's neck. '*Bismillah ar-rahman ar-rahim*, In the name of Allah, the Beneficent, the Merciful,' he cried.

With a whack of the blade, the animal's jugular was severed. Blood gushed out of the wound as the camel kicked in a last frenzied gallop, her eyes rolling, her mouth wide open. A few moments later she was dead.

Kefla stood over the carcass, his knife still wet with blood. There were tears in his eyes. He covered his face with his hand and then wiped it with the edge of his shawl. I was not surprised that a Danakil was weeping. His friend was dead. While the other men unloaded the rest of the camels, Kefla walked away into the distance to be alone.

10

The Place of Gold

'The Desert of the Danakil is a part of the world that the
Creator must have fashioned when he was in a bad mood.'

Ladislas Farago, *Abyssinia Stop Press*

IT TOOK ALL evening to dismember the dead she-camel. The men
worked together, cutting the flesh from the carcass, draining the
hump of its liquid, removing the entrails and cooking the bones for
their marrow. For once Kefla stood back and let the others do the
work. The dead camel was his favourite. He had bought her as a
calf and they must have travelled the route together hundreds of
times. The rest of the party were sensitive to their leader's loss. One
of them put out a mat for him to sleep. He crouched on it but
refused to lie down. The air was heavy with the smell of his beloved
camel roasting.

The last time I'd eaten camel was in the Jordanian desert where
it was made into *mensaf*, cooked in milk and served in a rich *pilau*.
The Bedu had prepared the dish during Ramadan, the holy month
of fasting. Each evening when the fast breaks, a feast is held. Then
the meat had been succulent and tender. The she-camel's flesh in
Afar couldn't have been more different. It was tough and sinewy,
as if the long treks across the desert laden with salt had drained it
of all moisture.

We did not sleep until late that night. All the meat and the
entrails were cooked, and much was eaten. What was left over was
packed up in sackcloth next morning and stowed on the back of
the last camel. The blocks of salt were then redistributed, all the
animals sharing the load of their dead sister.

Samson rose early that morning to read the Bible. Like me, he'd
been touched by the camel's death and its effect on Kefla

Mohammed. I watched from a distance as he tied two sticks together and planted them in the cleft where the camel had caught her foot. It was a marker to warn others of the danger, as well as a tribute to the dead animal.

The morning's departure was delayed, and we didn't start walking until some time after eight. Sensing a slackening of the pace, I asked Samson if he thought we were nearing our destination. He was reluctant to find out, but he winked at me. He could smell civilization, he said.

Four hours later, after crossing a ridge of hills, we saw a cluster of houses on the horizon. As we drew nearer we made out people, goats and a few cars. Kefla pointed to the distant settlement.

'That is Kwiha. We will be in Mekele this evening.'

Inside I was jumping for joy. The novelty of trekking through Afar had long since worn off. I slapped Samson on the back and promised to treat him to the softest bed and the biggest meal the Tigrayan capital had to offer. He smiled, his cheeks dimpling, but before he could reply, Kefla came over.

'We will sell some of the salt in Kwiha,' he said. 'The market there is good.'

Soon the caravan was making its way through the dusty lanes of the small town. The camels seemed awkward now that we'd escaped the desert. They did not belong in a town, just as cars don't belong in the desert of the Danakil.

We made a beeline for the market which was in full swing. There was the usual assortment of green plastic buckets, piles of dirty bottles, polythene bags, old clothes, worn-out tools, grain and butchered meat on sale. Women haggled for food, and their children rummaged through the heaps of old clothes in the local equivalent of window-shopping.

The camels were led to one side and relieved of their loads. About a third of the salt was taken off to be sold, and what was left was then redistributed.

Danakil traders such as Kefla sell their salt to a central dealer. He in turn sells slabs to middlemen who saw it up into smaller blocks. Individual customers buy only a small block, a few inches square.

These days salt is brought from Afar to be eaten. But in more ancient times the salt bars, called *amole*, were also used as currency. The Egyptian monk Cosmos recorded their use in about AD 525, and a thousand years later the Portuguese priest Francisco Alvares said he saw salt being used as money throughout Ethiopia: 'He who carries salt finds all that he requires.' Even as late as the 1960s travellers to Tigray reported seeing salt being used for trade.

As I stood there in the market, listening to the rhythmic sound of salt slabs being sawn, it began to rain in great splattering drops. Rain is generally welcomed in the north of Ethiopia, but it is the curse of the salt business. The sellers scurried away to borrow plastic sheets from their neighbours to protect their precious inventory.

Within an hour we were ready to press on to Mekele. Somehow the camels knew we were close to our destination and the pace quickened. Kefla was pleased with the money he'd made from the sale at Kwiha and he stuffed a great wad of bills under his shawl. Before we started the last leg to Mekele, he had ordered Yehia to untie all the camel meat which was still uneaten. He had then approached a group of beggars dressed in rags, and offered them the food. Samson was touched by his generosity.

'Kefla is a good man,' he said. 'He may not be a Christian yet, but I think he will go to Heaven.'

From the moment we crossed Mekele's city line, it was obvious that the place was going to be different. Not just different from the desert, but different from every other town and city in Ethiopia. Mekele was inexplicably modern. The tarmac under the camels' feet was newly laid and as smooth as patted butter, with cats' eyes in the middle, and gutters along the sides of the road. The houses were large and imposing, with imported tiles on their roofs and satellite dishes the size of fish ponds in their backyards. There were large hotels and restaurants, and petrol stations where fuel was actually on sale. All the vehicles were brand-new, running on flawless tyres.

Samson looked astonished at his first sight of Mekele.

'I have heard of this place,' he said. 'People talk about it in the bars in Addis. They are usually laughed at, though, because no one believes them.'

'Why is it so prosperous?'

'The President,' said Samson. 'The President's from here.'

Kefla said he and the others would spend the night in Mekele but that they would leave at dawn. They felt uncomfortable in the town and they were anxious to get back to their families with the proceeds from the trip. Since Mekele had grown in size and sophistication, there wasn't the same demand for salt as there had once been. These days, explained Kefla, the people of Mekele want refined salt, and they can afford to have it imported.

'It's not good for us,' he said. 'One day, everyone will want it. That will put us all out of business and we'll probably starve to death.' He paused and then, looking me squarely in the eye, he grinned. 'Maybe that's when God will have mercy on us and turn all the salt back into gold.'

That evening Samson and I invited Kefla and the others to a meal at a small restaurant. We had endured hardship and were ready to taste luxury. I ordered just about everything on the menu for my guests and made quite sure that they didn't catch sight of the bill. It came to far more than they had earned from the entire journey. That night Samson and I slept on soft mattresses and showered in hot water. I had thought of asking Kefla and the rest of the team to join us in the hotel, but Samson had insisted they'd be embarrassed. Instead I'd offered them some money, but they'd refused to take it, even when it was handed over by Samson. They were too proud. So, in the end, I'd presented each of them with clothing and pieces of equipment from my kitbags.

In the morning, after a good night's sleep, we went down to the reception desk. I wanted to send someone to find Bahru and the Jeep. The doorman said something had been left for me during the night. It was a package wrapped in sacking, about the size of a brick. I opened it. Inside was a neatly cut piece of grey salt.

After a long search we found Bahru in the back of the Emperor's Jeep parked in a lane off the main roundabout. He was fast asleep, and the front of his shirt was encrusted with dried vomit. I banged on the door and he sat up like a zombie woken from death. Four days of debauchery had taken its toll. I wondered how he had funded it all. Despite his hangover, however, he seemed pleased to see us and said he'd been doing some research. He had heard that the Italians had dug a series of test trenches for gold about fifty miles north of Mekele. I was so surprised at Bahru's initiative that I gave him a handful of tattered *birr* notes almost without thinking. That seemed to cure his hangover instantly, and within minutes our bags were loaded aboard the Jeep and we were jolting along a rutted country road. The dust churned up by our wheels was like talcum powder and it got into everything, but the surrounding landscape made up for it.

The President was right to be proud of his homeland. The high-lands of Ethiopia are beautiful, and I found myself staring in amaze-ment at a vast sweep of land covered in lush vegetation. Never before in Africa had I seen such astonishing fertility.

Tigray's people seemed as fertile as their land. Wherever we looked there were children herding sheep and cows with long horns, old men whipping their donkeys forward, women working in the fields and more children foraging for kindling. The Tigrayan people look quite different from the other Ethiopian tribes. They are fine-boned and svelte, and they stride about as if they are walking on air.

The road sliced through passes walled by great granite bluffs, so perfectly formed that they looked as if they had been carved by man. Then the granite cliffs gave way to sandstone and to open fields where crops of *teff* rustled in the breeze.

An hour out of Mekele it started to pour with rain. The water turned the dust into a thick soup, and the Jeep began to skid about. Bahru said his informant had given him directions to the gold trenches. Even though he was quite sure where he was going, I forced him to stop and get directions from a young boy who was out in the rain hurling stones with a sling shot. His teeth were chat-tering with cold, and his arms and legs were covered in goose-bumps. I asked if he knew about the trenches. He said he did and would show us the way. They were at a place called Werkamba.

'That's good news,' said Samson. 'It means "The Place of Gold".'

Before we reached Werkamba, the mud became too deep for the Emperor's Jeep to continue, so Samson and I decided to leave Bahru in the Jeep and walk with the boy through the downpour. The mud was the colour of oxtail soup and as thick as porridge, and in places it came up to our knees. I had brought along a cam-ouflage green army poncho and so kept reasonably dry, but Samson had no waterproof clothing and was soaked within minutes.

Werkamba was a village of about ten houses built of stone, each with a finely woven thatched roof. The boy said that a big mining company had been looking for gold in the area. (I found out later that it was Midroc, the company that also operated the Lega Dembi mine.) Villagers dread the discovery of gold on their land because then the government nationalizes it and they are forced to leave. Samson said that farmers do all they can to pretend that their land has no gold, though some of them mine illegally, digging narrow tunnels to reach the seam. I even heard of a farmer who built a hut over the entrance to his mine-shaft. He managed to keep the shaft secret for more than a year, but word eventually got out. The government seized the land and he was thrown off it.

In the village we were given freshly roasted coffee by the boy's mother and she told us what had happened. Engineers had come the month before and taken soil samples. A foreigner had also come. She was worried, she said. They were all worried. I asked if they did any mining themselves. The woman held her son's head to her chest and looked at the ground, but she didn't reply.

The new test trenches were set alongside the old ones made by the Italians, a couple of miles east of the village. They were no more than a yard deep, suggesting that the gold was close to the surface. Samson pointed to the veins of marble-like quartz that ran through the rock. Where you find those, he said, you find gold. It was unclear whether the Italians had actually mined the area. When I looked the place up later at the Geological Survey in Addis Ababa, I could find no record, but I knew that significant mining was taking place across the border in Eritrea.

I had brought the Gold Bug metal detector along with me. At last there was no danger of being arrested by officials or being mobbed by excited hordes of illegal miners. We assembled the unit and swept the test trenches once the rain had started to ease off. The machine squealed piercingly wherever the head was pointed. Samson raised his eyebrows. Then he knelt down in one of the trenches, probed with his fingers and selected a lump of soil.

'Look at this,' he said, crumbling it with his fingertips, 'it's got gold in it.'

He suggested we spend a couple of days at the trenches looking for nuggets. Gold is one of the hardest metals to find with a conventional detector, largely because the machine picks up nodules of iron, known as 'hot rocks', but specialized detectors such as the Gold Bug can compensate for iron in the soil. The metal detector has come a long way since it was invented by Gerhard Fisher in the early 1930s. Fisher was a German *émigré* and a close friend of Albert Einstein. When he showed his first model of a detector – the 'Metallascope' – to Einstein, the great scientist reputedly forecast that it would be a commercial failure.

Though I was tempted by Samson's suggestion that we look for nuggets I knew I couldn't. Before setting out in search of Solomon's mines, I had privately sworn an oath that I would not try to make a profit from the gold business. Instead we took a few soil samples to satisfy our curiosity and then we hurried back through the rain to the Jeep.

That evening in the town of Adigrat, perched on the border with Eritrea, I planned the next stage of the journey. I was keen to get to Tullu Wallel, to locate Frank Hayter's mine-shafts. We took out the map and had a good look at the route. There was quite a distance to cover down the western flank of Ethiopia. But before we could find out the truth behind Hayter's claims, there was one more place to visit. A friend had told me about a monastery called Debra Damo. In its vaults there were said to be secret texts that told of King Solomon. I was happy to give the place a miss and head straight for Tullu Wallel, but Samson said that visiting a monastery was an act of piety, and that it would bring us luck. I found Debra Damo on the map, right on the Eritrean border. It wasn't far from Adigrat.

We set off soon after dawn. The rain clouds which had brought such discomfort the day before had vanished and now the landscape was bathed in sunlight. Bahru put his foot on the accelerator and the Emperor's Jeep hurtled along, swerving round potholes and bouncing over ruts. We were on the main road to Axum, but there was very little traffic. Instead the road was full of cows and sheep grazing the verges. After an hour of driving Bahru misjudged a turn and hit a sheep head on. The poor animal was trapped under the Jeep. Despite this, Bahru refused to stop immediately for fear of encountering a furious farmer. Only once we were some distance from the herd did he pull over and get out to cut the mangled carcass from the chassis.

Another hour passed, with similar near misses. Bahru seemed exhilarated by his recent kill and refused to slow down, smiling evilly when I shouted at him. Then we came to a village where the road was full of people and animals heading for the morning market. Bahru seemed to accelerate deliberately, and people and animals leapt for safety. One sheep was too slow and there was a sickening thud as our wheels caught it. The animal's owner managed to jump in front of the Jeep – a brave act in a country like Ethiopia where most vehicles have unreliable brakes – and we were all catapulted forward as Bahru slammed into first gear. Thankfully, the farmer wasn't injured, but before we knew it, the entire village was pressed around the car. They wanted blood.

I told Bahru that he was on his own. He would have to get out and face the mob. His perpetual grin wavered and his lower lip began to tremble. The crowd peered in through the windows. Some of them were arming themselves with stones. Others were trying to rock the Jeep from side to side. I yelled again for Bahru to get out. Gathering his courage he climbed out of the window and up on to the bonnet. Then he bowed his head and pleaded with the farmer. I could not hear what he was saying, but his body language was eloquent. He was begging for mercy.

The villagers worked to free the sheep from the wheel arch. Then they daubed the Jeep's filthy white bodywork with the animal's blood. The farmer was shouting at the top of his voice. Samson said he was demanding compensation. He wanted cash, lots of it. Still standing on the bonnet, Bahru tried to talk his way out of the situation. He was the kind of man who could talk his way out of anything. Samson translated. First Bahru blamed the sheep for its stupidity. Then he blamed the Jeep's brakes. After that he blamed the poor condition of the road.

The villagers said they were sick of dangerous drivers. The dead sheep was no more stupid than any other sheep, and the road was bad because of the government. They were, they said, going to make an example of Bahru. They'd make sure he never injured another helpless animal again.

I prodded Samson in the back. He stopped translating and, with great reluctance, climbed on to the bonnet as well. I watched them through the windscreen: two grown men, throwing themselves at the mercy of the crowd. Every so often they would turn and point to me. Instead of lessening the villagers' rage, this seemed to anger them even more. I began to wonder if my companions were offering my head in exchange for the dead sheep.

Then Bahru fished out his wallet from his back pocket. Like a conjurer performing a trick, he demonstrated that the wallet contained no money. The only thing inside it was a driving licence. He offered it to the farmer, promising to leave it as collateral until he next returned to the village. The villagers talked among themselves, debating whether to take the licence. At length they agreed. The farmer put it in his top pocket and shouted a string of insults. Samson and Bahru clambered back into the Jeep. They looked very relieved. Bahru threw the Jeep in gear, waved to the crowd, and sped off. Then he burst out laughing.

'What's so funny?'

'Those people are as stupid as their sheep!' he exclaimed. 'I've got lots of fake licences for times like this.'

A few miles from Debra Damo a withered old man hailed us for a lift. He was so frail that I feared he might die in the back seat. His curly hair was as white as bleached whale bones, and all his teeth were missing. He said he was eighty-five years old, and he had been to the monastery a thousand times.

'What about its treasures, the books about Solomon?'

The man ran a thumbnail down the ridge of his nose.

'Yes, there are books,' he said. 'They are written in Ge'ez, the old language. They are very precious and they are guarded by the monks.'

'Will they show them to me?'

'Of course, but first you must get to the monastery.'

I had heard that no women were permitted to set foot in Debra Damo, and that the ascent kept a lot of men out too.

Shortly before we reached the mountain Bahru stopped to wash the sheep's blood from the bonnet. He said that if it hadn't been for me, he would have killed a lot more animals. It took his mind off the tedium of the drive. Like a Danakil warrior forbidden to hunt for testicles, he felt that his rights had been curbed by political correctness.

Debra Damo is perched on top of an *amba*, a flat-topped mountain, that rises 8,400 feet above the surrounding land. The track that leads to it is hideously rough, and when the Emperor's Jeep refused to negotiate a giant pile of boulders, we were forced to abandon it. The last stretch entailed crawling on our hands and knees up an enormous rockfall.

We eventually reached the foot of the mountain in the early afternoon but I could see no way up it. There was no path, and the cliffs towering above us offered no footholds. I told Samson to ask our fragile passenger which was the best route. The man put his hands over his ears and laughed a great toothless laugh, which echoed around the rocks like the ripple of distant thunder.

When he could laugh no more, he sat down in the shade and fell asleep. I feared he was another madman and was about to give Samson more orders when a strange thing happened. Someone whistled from halfway up the cliff. We looked up, blinking into the light. A hand was waving and pointing downwards. We shouted up questions, but before they were answered the man up the cliff threw down a plaited leather rope. It was as thick as my wrist, and it stank of rotting meat.

Telling Samson that he was more athletic than me, I made him go first. He wound the rope around his waist, but before he could start to climb, he was lifted from the ground. I could only marvel at the strength of the men who were hauling him up. Samson rose higher and higher with jolting movements, his hands frantically clawing at the rockface as his head was battered against its walls. At first he whimpered with fear, but then, as the height increased, the whimpering turned to groans and then to a chilling scream. I called up to him, telling him to be brave. Then suddenly Samson vanished.

Shading my eyes, I tried to work out where he'd gone. There was no sign of life. I shouted to the old man asleep in the shade but he didn't wake up. So I called up to the rock face. A moment later the plaited rope reappeared. I'd brought far too much baggage as usual. How was I going to get it and myself up? As if in answer to my question, a second rope appeared, thinner than the first but also made of sinewy leather. I tied it round my bags' straps and then they too began to rise.

When the bags were no more than a speck in the sky, the voice called down again. Then the hand pointed at me and at the thick rope. I wound it around my waist, securing it in a reef knot. But before I could adjust it comfortably, I found myself being pulled upwards. As I rose higher and higher, the rope cut into my sides, squeezing me like a boa constrictor crushing its prey. I breathed out, gasping, and found I couldn't breathe in again. Then I began scrabbling desperately for fingerholds in the cliff. But every time I found a fragile purchase in a crevice, the rope tore me away, jolting me upwards. It was as if a group of enormous fiendish jinn were at work.

The walls of the cliff were polished and grooved where the rope had rubbed across them over the centuries. A few more minutes and I was nearing the top. I could hear voices now, a young child and a cluster of men. Then there was the sound of Samson urging me on. The last twenty feet were so terrifying that my hands still sweat at the memory. I felt as if I was being cut in half, and the sight of the ground far beneath me made me feel sick with vertigo. A minute more and it was all over. I was pulled into a doorway and lay there on my belly, shaking and whimpering.

A skinny figure was looming over me. He was wearing dark green trousers and a royal blue overcoat, darned in places with white thread. On his feet were sandals made from rubber tyres, and on his head was a white cotton cap. His nose was long, his ears were pointed, and his mouth was hidden by a tuft of white beard. He looked like Asterix the Gaul, and like Asterix he obviously had a magic potion.

Samson introduced me to Asnake. His modest appearance belied his extraordinary strength. When I commented on his muscles, he roared with laughter.

'God gives me strength,' he said.

'He gives us all strength,' added Samson piously.

'Doesn't anyone ever fall down the precipice?' I asked.

'Oh, yes,' he replied airily, 'people die all the time.'

A child priest appeared. He was huddled in a white shawl and his feet were bare. He said his name was Eyba and that he would escort us to the monastery. A narrow path led round the edge of the cliff and up to the plateau above. Still shaking, Samson and I began to worry about getting back down the cliff face, but Eyba simply smiled and told us to look at the view. We could see for many miles in every direction. The afternoon light played on the hills, bringing them alive. Beneath us there were dry riverbeds, copses of trees and farmsteads, and in the distance we could see a mountain range veiled in mist. I could even make out Bahru asleep on the roof of the Jeep. Eyba pointed to a crest of hills in the foreground. He said they were in Eritrea.

Up on the plateau, a herd of fifty oxen were grazing in long grass. I was about to ask Eyba how they'd got there but Eyba had more important things on his mind. Had I been to America? he asked. I replied that I had.

'I am going to America,' he said earnestly.

'But aren't you a monk? Surely you'll spend your life here.'

The boy sniffed, then wiped his nose on his arm.

'In America there are Christians, aren't there?'

Samson answered for me.

'Many, many Christians, and many, many churches!' he exclaimed.

Eyba led the way through a maze of wattle and daub walls. As he walked, he foraged under his *shamma* and brought out a familiar sheet of paper. It was a Diversity Visa form for the United States. I rolled my eyes.

'I think they will need me in America,' he said.

Debra Damo was supposedly founded by Abba Aregawi, one of the famous Nine Saints of Syria who fled persecution and arrived in Ethiopia in about AD 451. A legend says that Abba Aregawi stood at the base of the mountain, wondering how he could ever climb it. But God called to a serpent which lived on the top of the mountain and told the creature to lower its tail and pull the priest up.

For fifteen hundred years a company of monks have inhabited the remote monastery. They are brought as children by their parents, who believe that good fortune will be conferred on the family if a son devotes his life to God. Until recently, Ebya said, there were also three hermits who spent their lives in silent prayer. No one ever saw them, but when they died, their bodies were taken to the far side of the mountain and thrown into a cave.

'I will show you the bodies,' he said.

I was impatient to look at the secret manuscripts which spoke of Solomon, but I knew it would be discourteous to refuse. So we made our way to the edge of the plateau and down a narrow track that clung to the rock face. Eyba cheerfully clambered over a tree growing out of the cliff. Samson and I followed, not daring to look down. Then the young priest gestured to a narrow cave entrance and, before I could stop him, he slipped inside, calling out to us to follow.

At the back of the cave lay several skeletons. One still had black and rotting flesh attached to it. The stench was appalling. Eyba picked up a femur and waved it around. He said big birds flew into the cave and fed on the rotting bodies.

After another terrifying clamber back along the path, we reached a cistern. Over the centuries the monks have carved a number of them out of the plateau, some as deep as sixty feet, to collect water on the rare occasions when it rains. Eyba said the water was very fresh. He scooped up a cupful for me to drink. Just in time I noticed that the water was alive with maggots and I hastily passed it to Samson.

It was early evening by the time we were taken to the church. The building was square in shape and made of small rectangular stones. It stood behind a wall and was surrounded by trees and patches of dried grass. It is said to be the oldest church in Africa.

As we took off our shoes outside a monk waited in the doorway. I pushed Samson forward to begin the lengthy salutations. The monk welcomed us in a whisper. He said he had been waiting for our arrival for many months, and he thanked God for delivering us safely to Debra Damo.

The antechamber of the church was decorated with wooden panels carved with images of elephants and giraffe, camels, gazelle, lions and snakes. There were paintings, too, vividly coloured. One showed Abba Aregawi being pulled up the mountain by the serpent. Another depicted Saint George dispatching the dragon. In a third the Queen of Sheba was arriving at the court of Solomon.

'Solomon,' I said.

The monk's face lit up.

'Ah, Solomon.'

'A wise king,' I replied.

'Yes, wise, very, very wise.'

'And rich.'

The monk smiled.

'*Very* rich,' he said.

I instructed Samson to ask about the secret manuscripts. The monk gazed at the floor.

'There were many books,' he said, 'but recently there was a fire in the library. Only a few now remain.'

'Where are they?'

He pointed towards a door leading to the back of the church.

'In the Holy of Holies.'

'I'm looking for King Solomon's gold mines,' I said. 'And someone told me that you might be able to help me in my quest.'

The monk turned to a wooden lectern standing in the middle of the anteroom and pulled off a mottled green cloth. Beneath it lay a very large book bound in scarlet leather.

'Is that the *Kebra Negast*?'

The monk opened the book at random, revealing neat hand-written columns of rounded black letters. The script was Ge'ez, the ancient language of Ethiopia. He did not answer my question, but he did speak.

'God appeared to Solomon in a dream,' he said, 'and asked him what special power he wished for. The young king replied that he yearned for wisdom so that he might be able to distinguish between good and evil. God blessed him with wisdom. Then Solomon built his great temple in Jerusalem, layering the walls with the purest gold, Ethiopian gold.'

He paused to turn the page with both hands.

'Word of Solomon's wisdom and fortune spread across the oceans and the seas,' he went on, 'and it came to the ears of Makeda. She wanted to look into the wise king's eyes and to hear of his learning. So she travelled with a great caravan through the desert, from our land to Judah.'

'Where in Ethiopia did Solomon get his gold?'

The monk did not reply but he continued to talk.

'And Makeda came to Jerusalem and rested in Solomon's palace, which was also fashioned from gold. She gave him precious beakers and fine objects and much gold, pure gold. And she asked him hard questions, and he answered them. Makeda was stirred by the king's wisdom and power. And Solomon was moved by the queen's beauty. So he held a banquet and sprinkled the food with salt. Makeda ate much and that night she slept in a bed beside Solomon's own.

'Between their beds was a jar of water. Solomon said he would not touch Makeda if she agreed not to use what belonged to him. But in the night the queen was overcome with thirst. She reached for the jug of water and drank from it. Solomon jumped from his bed and took the queen, for she had stolen what was his. Makeda returned to Ethiopia, where their son Menelik was born.'

'But what of the gold, Solomon's gold?'

Again, the monk turned the pages of the book.

'I will tell you of the gold.'

'Where did it come from? Which part of the country?'

'From the west,' said the priest, 'from the land of Shangul.'

'*Beni Shangul?*' I repeated, remembering that Dr Pankhurst had spoken of the place and had remarked on the quality of its gold.

The monk nodded.

'Yes, that is right. I myself come from Beni Shangul. The people who live there know about the mines of Makeda.'

'You mean the mines of Solomon?'

'No, they were not the wise king's mines. They were the queen's, for this was her kingdom.'

I asked him to tell me more, but the audience was at an end.

'It is time to pray,' he said.

Without another word, he disappeared into the main body of the church. I called out, asking for more details of the gold, but there was no reply.

Eyba led us out through the enclosure and back to our shoes. It was dark now, and the air was flickering with fireflies. We stayed at Debra Damo for another day, but we did not see the monk again. Ebya said that the monks preferred to spend their time alone rather than speaking to visitors. If they had wanted to talk, he said, they would never have joined the church.

Before we plucked up courage to descend the cliff and make our way back to the Emperor's Jeep, I had to know the answer to a question. The herd of oxen grazing on the mountain still baffled me. As no women or female creatures of any kind were allowed to enter the monastery, it wasn't possible to breed cattle there. I knew, too, that there was no track or secret path up the mountain. The only way to get to the top was by rope. I asked Ebya how the oxen were brought up.

'That is very difficult,' he said. 'When we want to bring an ox up we lower down a pair of big ropes. Then we tie them around the ox and all the monks come out to pull it up the mountain.'

Ebya broke off to take a deep breath and his eyes widened.

'The ox makes a terrible noise.'

11

Prester John

'And the windows of the halls and the chambers be of crystal. And the tables whereon men eat, some be of emeralds, some of amethyst, and some of gold, full of precious stones; and the pillars that bear up the tables be of the same precious stones.'

Sir John Mandeville, on the palace of Prester John

IN A CAFÉ on a back street in the ancient town of Axum I met a man who told me he was a god. I have spent time with deities in human form in India – the subcontinent has hundreds of them – but this was the first time I'd met a godman in Africa. His name was Michael and he was a former Rastafarian from Liverpool. His skin was the colour of dark apricots, pocked with mosquito bites, and his features a blend of African and Caucasian. He smoked hand-rolled black tobacco cigarettes, one after another, and he spoke in a slow rhythmic voice. Every few minutes he would get down off his seat and go and spit in the gutter outside.

'There's a bad taste in my mouth,' he said.

'From the tobacco?'

'No, from the troubles of the world.'

Michael was different from the deities I had come across in India. He took the business of being a god very seriously indeed. Although there are exceptions, Indian godmen are generally an easy-going bunch. I've heard them likened to snake-oil salesmen for they perform miracles, heal the afflicted and generally entertain. In a small village with no television, no cinema and no doctor, their arrival is the social event of the year. I watched as Michael took a long drag on his cigarette and expelled a plume of smoke through his nose. Some people are incidental smokers, but Michael was an expert. I asked him if he'd always been a deity.

'It was in me,' he said, 'but it was not wakened because I was sleeping. My eyes were blind and my ears were deaf to the truth. I followed the Way of Rasta. I found love with my brothers. I dreamed of a reunion with The People. But still I was blind.'

'How did you learn to see, then?'

He scratched at a scab on his arm.

'Ras Tafari came to me in a dream. He told me that I was his successor, that I was to leave Liverpool and journey to the Promised Land.'

'To Africa?'

'To Ethiopia.'

'That must have made the Rastafarians angry,' I said, 'because they regard Ras Tafari as their Messiah.'

'Yeah, man, there was bitterness: the sourness of ignorance.'

'Do you have a following?'

Michael lit another cigarette and was soon engulfed in a cloud of impenetrable smoke.

'A prophet needs followers,' he said, 'but a god walks alone.'

'What about miracles, can you do any?'

'I'm not a circus performer. I am the reincarnation of Ras Tafari.'

Samson kept quiet, but I could tell he wasn't relishing the foreigner's company. He took a very dim view of bogus deities, and kicked me under the table when Michael went out to spit in the gutter.

'This man is the Devil in disguise,' he said, voicing his disapproval, 'let's go quickly before he lures us into the desert.'

'Maybe he *is* a god,' I said, unable to resist teasing Samson. 'Shall I test him?'

When Michael returned, I said that my friend Samson was having trouble believing his divinity.

'Can I ask you a question?'

'Okay, man, ask me.'

'I'm here in Ethiopia searching for something. Can you tell me what it is?'

Michael's face seemed to retreat into the haze of smoke, and the silence that followed made Samson shift uneasily in his chair.

'I will tell you,' Michael said at some length. 'You are looking for . . .'

He paused.

'Yes . . . what are we looking for?'

Samson and I stared into his eyes, waiting.

'You are looking for . . .'

'Yes?'

We leant forward on the edge of our chairs.

'For a cave.'

I burst out laughing. I have seen all kinds of mind-reading per-formances in India, but even so I was impressed by Michael's routine.

As far as Samson was concerned, Michael's answer was proof indeed that he was the Devil in disguise, and he jumped up and ran outside.

'Will we find the cave?' I asked.

'Oh yes,' Michael said, almost as an afterthought, 'you will find a cave.'

Samson brooded all afternoon. He was angry that I had talked to the godman, and said I should be more selective in the people I mixed with. Though I liked to think we'd become firm friends, I knew deep down that he was only accompanying me because I had offered him sound employment. As far as Samson was concerned I was just another foreigner in pursuit of a lunatic quest.

Virtually everything in Axum seemed to be named after the Queen of Sheba. Legend has it that she made her capital there, though that seems improbable. Makeda died long before the rise of the Axumite kingdom. Nonetheless, the faltering tourist trade clung desperately to the myth. The hotels, the trinket stalls and the res-taurants all claimed links with the Queen, if only in name. There was even a local brand of chewing-gum named after her. Most of the archaeological sites were also attributed to her. The tourist guides had rechristened a stagnant pool on the edge of Axum as 'Sheba's Baths'. A jumble of rubble nearby was reputedly 'Sheba's Palace', and the stelae field opposite was supposedly her grave.

Samson's thoughts weren't on the tourist sites. He was thinking about a devil called Michael. I had once studied basic mind-reading with an Indian magician called Hakim Feroze, and I knew that there were all sorts of ways in which information could be extracted from an unwitting victim – who would then be astonished to be told what he thought had been secret. Even so, I found myself preoccupied by a premonition that I'd find a cave.

Most travellers spend days in Axum and they all have the same ambition: to be the first foreigner to set eyes on the Ark of the Covenant. The Ark is said to be kept in the Holy of Holies, in the compound of the Church of St Mary of Zion. I knew it was only indirectly related to my quest, but before we left Axum, curiosity drove me to pay the small entrance fee and enter the compound in which the Ark is kept. At the entrance to the church we passed lines of beggars waiting for tourist handouts and for God to answer their prayers. The hostilities with Eritrea had driven most of the tourists away. I must have been the first foreigner to visit the church that month. The beggars fell on me like locusts, holding out arms covered in suppurating sores or disfigured by leprosy.

The Church of St Mary of Zion, built by Haile Selassie in the 1960s, is an extraordinary example of hippy kitsch. Opposite it stands a curious square-shaped shrine in which the Ark itself apparently lies. The domed roof has lost many of its green mosaics, and the railings around the building are chipped. In the doorway hangs a crimson velvet curtain. The penalty for any layman attempting to enter is death, and I decided not to chance my luck.

Instead I asked Samson if I could see the royal treasures that are kept in the compound behind bars. They were guarded by a black-bearded priest who I knew must be very important because he was wearing Ray Ban Aviators with reflective lenses, and a black felt hat. Only a theologian who was very sure of himself would dress like that. He barked at Samson.

'What's he saying?'

'He wants more money.'

Ethiopian priests may be very pious, but they have an insatiable appetite for handouts. I was about to protest at such extortion but the priest tapped a yellow steel cabinet behind the bars and then grinned at me.

Unable to resist, I handed over a few notes and the priest began the long process of unfastening the locks. Then he pulled the cover open to reveal a very large gold cross and five or six imperial crowns, the oldest of which was apparently made in AD 400. Seconds later, he replaced the cover and snapped the locks shut.

'Your time is up,' he said.

★

The next morning both Samson and Bahru asked if they could have a lie-in. They'd eaten a questionable bowl of *asa wot*, a spicy fish stew, and they had been up most of the night as a result. I had been more fortunate. The day before I had discovered some tins of food at the back of a poky tourist shop. They had clearly been there for some time, because they each bore the letters CCCP and were stamped with a red star. Most of them had no labels, but I thought they'd be a welcome change from the interminable diet of *injera* and *asa wot*. That evening, unbeknown to Samson and Bahru, I'd dined on Russian corned beef.

Despite their pleas, and delighted that the corned beef had had no ill-effects, I insisted we hit the road early. I knew that the trek to Tullu Wallel would be arduous and I didn't want them to think they could down tools at the first sign of trouble. So we loaded the bags aboard and drove out of Axum before dawn. Already the road was packed with people and animals, all heading towards the town. Some of them must have been walking most of the night. Our headlights didn't work so to my annoyance road-kill was inevitable. By six o'clock Bahru had racked up an impressive total, even by his standards – two rabbits, a dog and a pair of sheep.

As we snaked up into the Simien mountains, the gradient increased sharply, as did the frequency of punctures. We no longer had a jack, so every time there was a flat tyre we had to wait for the grunt of an overloaded truck. Sometimes no vehicles passed for hours. I told Bahru that a Formula One racing team can carry out an engine overhaul and change all four wheels in a matter of seconds. He looked at me as if I was mad.

The tedium of waiting by the side of the road was relieved by scenery so spectacular as to defy our senses. The mountains reared up in a series of jagged peaks, and their slopes were carpeted with trees and ferns, grasses and mosses. There were waterfalls, too, plunging through the woods and dropping like sheets of diamonds to the valleys below.

During the long rains in the highlands of Ethiopia it is impossible to keep things dry. The most valued possession of the children who herd sheep and goats is a plastic bag. During good weather it is folded into a peaked cap. During the rains it becomes a transparent overcoat.

It is in these mountains that Prester John was once said to live.

Tales of this mythical Christian monarch, who ruled a blissful kingdom surrounded by pagan lands, kept generations of Europeans spellbound and, as the centuries passed, the myth evolved. Prester John, it was said, was descended from Solomon and the Queen of Sheba. He governed forty-two lesser kings and ruled a land where centaurs, Amazons and a race of 'shrinking giants' roamed. Through his kingdom there ran a river which bore precious stones, and theft and poverty were quite unknown. His palace was roofed with gems and its walls were adorned with translucent crystal. No traveller, it was said, was ever refused entry, and each day in the palace thirty thousand guests sat down to dine at a magical table carved from emeralds whose powers prevented drunkenness.

Prester John himself wore clothes fashioned from salamander skin, but despite his wealth he was as humble as any man alive. His only enemy was the new faith, Islam, against which he waged war with his army of superhuman cannibals.

In one corner of his kingdom issued forth the Fountain of Life. It restored the vigour of youth to any man who drank from it. Prester John had drunk from it many times, and though he was five hundred and sixty-two years old, he showed no signs of ageing.

For a thousand years the tale of Prester John dazzled all who heard it. Like Timbuctoo, the notion of such a place was intoxicating to Europeans, and many thousands of adventurers set out in search of the kingdom. Some went of their own accord. Others had little choice.

The Portuguese sent their *degradados*, convicted felons, to search for Prester John in the early 1500s. It was their last chance of gaining redemption. Those who succeeded in finding him and who returned to Portugal would be pardoned. None of them ever came back. But it was said that two Portuguese travellers who successfully disguised themselves did manage to pass through the Muslim lands surrounding Prester John's kingdom. Eventually they presented themselves to the king, who was so enchanted by them that he refused them permission ever to leave.

High in the mountains we stopped at a village to get the punctures repaired. There was an Ajip petrol station with an old Italian-made hand pump, but they'd run out of petrol years ago. The mechanic took one look at the Emperor's Jeep and his eyes lit up. He knew we'd be good for business. Before he did any work he treated us all to coffee and brought out chairs. I was struck by the level of customer service, considering there wasn't any competition for miles around. The mechanic said the road down the mountain was very hazardous indeed. We would need good tyres and brakes. Since Bahru had sold three brake pads the Jeep had been using a single brake. Still, we had managed to cover hundreds of miles without serious mishap, and it seemed an extravagance to spend money on any more. A second cup of coffee was served, and the mechanic became more persistent. If we didn't have the vehicle overhauled, he said, we would never get past the next village but one.

'Is the road that bad?'

'Of course the road is bad,' said the mechanic, 'but the problem is the villagers. They are evil. They put boulders in the way and you have to stop very fast. You see, they like driving cars off the road. Then they strip the chassis clean.'

Bahru looked tense.

'I have heard of that place,' he said. 'The drivers in Addis Ababa talk of it. They call it "The Place of Death".'

'Come on, it can't be any worse than elsewhere in the country,' I pointed out.

Bahru shook his head.

'This time the danger is real,' he said.

So we stopped the night there, while the Emperor's Jeep was refurbished. The engine was tuned and tested, third-hand brake pads were fitted, the tyres were replaced, and the leaking radiator was plugged. Working all night by the light of a paraffin lamp, the mechanic even fixed the faulty starter motor.

We slept on the floor of the village's only bar. A legion of over-dressed girls swanned up and offered their services. For such a modest village there were a lot of them. Basic economic principles of supply and demand hadn't yet culled their numbers.

At six the next morning the mechanic woke us. The Jeep was better than new, he said. Bahru asked how much money he owed. The mechanic said something in Amharic. Samson grimaced. It was quite clear that Bahru didn't have enough money to pay the bill. But he didn't seem concerned. He invited the mechanic to sit down with him and play cards.

'But I don't have any cards,' said the mechanic.

'I do,' said Bahru, and with that he produced a pack of cards from his pocket.

'If you win,' said Bahru, 'I will pay you double what you are asking for, and if I win, I won't pay anything.'

The mechanic looked down at his oily fists and considered the proposition.

'All right,' he said at last.

Bahru dealt them each nine cards. I'm not sure what game they were playing or how many hands it entailed, but it appeared to be some form of poker. We clustered round and looked at both men's hands. Word of the game gradually spread. A wave of anticipation rippled through the village. Despite the early hour, people filtered in. Within a few minutes the garage was packed. All eyes were on Bahru and the mechanic. Some of the villagers placed side bets on who would win. It was the first time in Ethiopia that I'd seen a craze for gambling.

The first hand went to the mechanic. He burst out laughing as the crowd pressed tighter. It was his turn to deal. He shuffled, and shuffled again. Then he dealt them both seven cards. Bahru glanced at the top card on the remaining pile. It was face down. He took it. Then he took another. And then another. The mechanic's cool expression faltered, and Bahru laid a winning hand on the table. The cards were dealt again, and again Bahru won. Then the mechanic won a hand. Samson called for the audience to quieten down.

'Last hand,' he said.

Seven cards were dealt to each man. The mechanic snapped his into a fan and pressed them to his nose. He seemed confident. Bahru picked up his cards and glanced at them. Then he took a card from the pile, looked across at me, and winked. The mechanic looked up at the ceiling and began to whistle. I could tell he was close to winning. In my mind I went through the consequences if we lost. They were grim. Then, just before the mechanic took a card, Bahru stood to his feet and slammed his hand on the table. The crowd went wild. He had won.

Fifteen minutes later we were rolling through the countryside again. The mechanic had been very sporting, despite a significant loss of earnings. Bahru steered the Jeep through the next village, taking care not to run down any animals. A new, virtuous side of his character had emerged which I had not seen before. We drove on in silence, negotiating the hairpin bends. Quite suddenly Bahru slammed on the brakes as we rounded an oblique turn. Without them we would have gone over the cliff. In the middle of the road there was a boulder, partly camouflaged with branches and foliage. Samson and I climbed down and pushed it over the edge. Exhilarated at the thought of cheating death and the murderous villagers, I asked Bahru how he was so sure he'd win at cards. He changed into third gear and peered into the rear-view mirror.

'Marked cards,' he said.

The greatest red herring for anyone searching for King Solomon's mines must be Henry Rider Haggard's novel of the same name. The book is a *tour de force* of Victorian literature, a swashbuckling tale which has appealed to generations of young men. Its characters are larger than life, fearless, and charged with an insatiable lust for adventure. But Rider Haggard's story is so embedded in fiction that it is of little use as a guide to finding ancient gold mines.

The book's real achievement is more subtle. It may not have led men to riches, but it has inspired them to leave their ordinary lives behind and go in search of adventure. Between the wars thousands of young European men flocked to Africa. Their purpose was always the same – to hunt big game and to track down treasure. Many had little in the way of education or training, but some did have solid academic credentials. One such man was a young Polish Count called Byron de Prorok. He was intrepid beyond measure, an adventurer and an amateur archaeologist. If there was ever a real-life Indiana Jones, it was he.

De Prorok had spent years during the 1920s in North Africa, excavating in the high Atlas mountains, on the banks of the Red Sea, and at the site of Carthage, in what is now Tunisia. But his real obsession was Ethiopia. While in Carthage he claimed to have bought an old parchment map that showed an ancient slave route up the Nile to Khartoum, then eastward to Ethiopia. De Prorok believed the slaves had worked in gold mines near Beni Shangul and then transported the yellow metal westwards, back to Egypt.

I didn't have much faith in de Prorok's treasure map. It sounded about as genuine as the one I'd bought from Ali Baba. De Prorok, however, was determined to discover the ancient mines. In 1934, leading an expedition that was both well-funded and well-equipped, he set out from Khartoum in the Sudan, and crossed into Ethiopia at Kurmuk by what he called 'the back door'. He had difficulty in getting permission from Emperor Haile Selassie to travel through the west of the country and, when eventually permission was granted, de Prorok was forbidden to carry weapons.

Frank Hayter had travelled in secret and alone, but de Prorok brought along archaeologists and photographers, scientists and taxidermists, porters and a retinue of hangers-on. The Count knew how to travel in style, and the tale of his journey to Beni Shangul might well have come from the pages of *King Solomon's Mines*. He claimed to have discovered ancient gold workings, and shafts carved into the mountains where emeralds had been mined long before. He spoke, too, of legions of children enslaved by a fiendish warlord known locally as the Mad Sultan Ghogoli. The despot forced them to work in the mines where they were guarded by brutal warders, who wielded hippopotamus-hide whips. The Sultan was rumoured to be a hundred years old, and to have a thousand wives. Anyone who crossed him was strung up on a tree by the thumbs until he fell away from them. Ghogoli was more than a little reminiscent of Rider Haggard's own antagonist, Gogool.

Beni Shangul was not far from Hayter's mine-shafts, so I decided to head to Tullu Wallel via the Beni Shangul region. I had managed to get a copy of de Prorok's account of his expedition, *Dead Men Do Tell Tales*, before leaving for Ethiopia. It bore many similarities to Hayter's own description of the area in *Gold of Ethiopia*, which I took as a positive sign. Hayter noted that de Prorok had discovered positive proof that the Pharaohs had obtained gold from north-west Ethiopia. In fact the Count had actually taken gold samples from the west and had tested them against ancient Egyptian gold. He found the samples to be virtually identical.

The Jeep's renovation in the highlands had been a godsend. But no sooner had some problems been solved than new ones surfaced. First the fuel pump failed, then we had a blown gasket and yet more punctures. The last straw was when one of the front tyres burst on a blind bend. Bahru wrestled desperately with the steering-wheel as the vehicle lurched out of control, eventually managing to bring us to a juddering halt on the edge of a ravine.

Once we had celebrated having survived, Samson climbed on to the roof rack to untie the last good wheel. He threw it down to the ground for Bahru to catch. But the driver's vision was clouded by an overdose of *qat*. He clutched at the air, and the wheel went over the cliff and into the ravine below. Samson volunteered to climb down and retrieve it. He was gone for four hours.

By dusk we reached Gondar, the seat of Ethiopian power from 1632 until the middle of the nineteenth century. Despite its glorious past, my first impressions of the town were not favourable. It started to pour with rain the moment we arrived, and it didn't stop until we left. Much of the intervening time was spent hunting for lodgings and a place to eat. All the hotels were inexplicably full. Someone said something about a Pan African football match, but I found it hard to believe that the continent's great football teams would converge on Gondar.

The manager of the only hotel in town with spare rooms took my money and led me to a peephole in the wall.

'Look through there,' he said.

'What is it?'

'Just look!'

He grinned. I put my eye to the hole and looked. Then I blushed and drew back quickly. A white woman and a black man were locked in an intimate embrace.

'She's Israeli,' said the manager bitterly, 'and she's staying in there with her Ethiopian guide.'

'Maybe they're in love,' I said.

The manager shook his head abruptly.

'It is *not* love.'

In the morning we ate breakfast in a large café with orange walls and a bright blue ceiling. The waitress ferried espressos to our table, and asked if we'd heard about the Israeli woman.

'That's gossip,' snapped Samson righteously.

'Maybe they're in love,' I said, repeating myself.

'No, no,' replied the girl, 'it is *not* love.'

After a meal of crusty bread rolls dipped in thin gravy, we inspected the castles for which Gondar is famous. Sometimes on a journey you arrive at a town which is famed for its architecture, a place about which countless books have been written. But after casting an eye over it all, you wonder if you're missing something. The royal enclosure, which contains the castles and palaces of Gondar, had been stripped bare. The buildings were empty shells, and all trace of their former residents had vanished.

Samson trudged behind me, enduring both the rain and my astringent comments on one of his nation's greatest treasures. He suggested I look beyond the ruined walls and think of their history. He was right. The ground on which we walked was once regarded by the European powers as an Avalon, an enchanted seat of sovereignty. The Portuguese, the French, the British and others sent their explorers to present their credentials to its emperors. Many of them never completed the journey and those that did endured extraordinary hardships.

The most famous early explorer to arrive in Gondar was James Bruce, the Laird of Kinnaird, and a man of considerable private wealth. He set off from Scotland in search of the source of the Nile and eventually reached Gondar on St Valentine's Day, 1770. Bruce was a great hulk of a man, standing six foot three, stout as a barrel, with a mane of bright red hair. He was a crack shot and a fine horseman, and he was also a severe hypochondriac. Contemporary accounts said he was easily offended and had a violent temper. When he grew angry his nose would start bleeding quite spontaneously.

Hardly a single white man had ventured to Ethiopia since the Portuguese had left three centuries before. Bruce found himself in the middle of a barbaric civil war, but he managed to get to the headstream of the Blue Nile, although he mistook it for the main source of the river. The journey back to Britain was one of almost unbelievable hardship. Before returning home Bruce stopped at various European spas to cure his malaria, and to receive treatment for the guinea worm which riddled his right leg. He made the mistake of announcing his discoveries to the court of France. This was seen by the English as a direct snub. London wits, including Dr Johnson (who loathed the Scots, and who was regarded as an authority on Ethiopia although he'd never been there), tore Bruce's story to shreds and turned him into a laughing stock. A broken man, the Laird retired to his Scottish estate and years later wrote a long, ponderous account of his adventure.

My interest in Gondar lay not in the ruins, but in some of the city's inhabitants for it is here that the last of the Ethiopian Jews, known as the Beta Israel, once lived. A great deal of misinformation surrounds the Ethiopian Jews. Remarkably few academic studies have been conducted on the subject, and much of the work published is of questionable scholarship. Judaic scholars are not even certain when the Beta Israel arrived in Ethiopia. Some have put the date as early as the tenth century BC while others contend that they arrived as late as medieval times. Although it is a tempting idea, only the most dubious scholars believe that the Ethiopian Jews arrived during the reign of Solomon. The Beta Israel themselves believe that they are the descendants of Menelik I, the son of Solomon and Sheba. Others have postulated that they are the tribe of Dan, one of the ten lost tribes of Israel, or that they failed to cross with Moses when he parted the Red Sea, and so fled southwards out of Egypt.

For centuries the Ethiopian Jews survived encircled by Christianity. Commonly known as *falashas*, they were totally isolated from the world of mainstream Judaism. They were unable to read or speak Hebrew or to learn the Talmudic scriptures. Their religious life was based on the Torah, the first five books of the Bible, and they kept to a kosher diet and observed the Sabbath.

Sometimes they were persecuted, and at other times they were left alone. Almost always they lived in their own villages, sequestered away from the Christian community. Many of them must have converted, for fear of losing their lands in times of persecution; in doing so, they affected Ethiopia's own unique blend of Christianity. In ancient times there may well have been hundreds of thousands of Beta Israel in Ethiopia. Yet gradually their numbers were decimated through persecution, conversions, famine and disease.

The Beta Israel made the news headlines in the mid-1980s and early 1990s when almost every one of them was airlifted to Israel. Operation Moses in 1984, and Operation Solomon in 1991, were two of the largest mass airlifts in history. No one is quite sure exactly how many Ethiopian Jews were moved in the evacuation, largely because the operations were so hurried. But it is thought that about forty-five thousand left in the exodus.

The strangest thing I have read about the Beta Israel was written by C. H. Walker, a former British Consul to western Ethiopia. He remarked that they were unsurpassed as craftsmen and that the local Christians didn't trust them. Walker said the most feared section of the Beta Israel were the *Buda*, the religious hierarchy. They were believed to have the power to turn themselves into hyenas, and to transmit the Evil Eye. At night, in animal form they would ravage graves and feed on the dead. In human form they would typically wear a gold earring, quite unique in design. Walker said that hyenas were frequently shot and found to have the same curious rings pinned through their ears. Was there, I wondered, any connection with the hyenas of Harar?

A couple of miles from Gondar we came to a hand-written sign in white chalk which advertised that we had arrived at the 'Falasha Village'. It was the kind of place that must have attracted many tourists before the evacuations, but now there were none. Bahru braked sharply and pointed to the sign. The village appeared to be deserted and all the houses were empty. Even the blacksmith's foundry and the workshops, which would once have produced the ironwork, pottery and baskets for which the Ethiopian Jews were renowned, had been abandoned.

A boy of about seven wearing pink wellington boots and an outsize T-shirt was standing by the road playing in a deep puddle. I went up and asked him if there were any Jews left. He kicked his foot towards a thatched hut, partly hidden in a grove of banana trees.

'She is in there,' he said.

As Samson and I walked over to the hut, a woman spotted us and began to lay out a series of crude fired-clay figurines. Then she smacked her palm against mine, and welcomed us to her house.

'We have come to meet the Beta Israel,' I said.

The woman looked at the figurines and then at me.

'They have gone to Israel,' she said, 'and they have left me behind.'

'Are you the *only* Jew here?'

She nodded, her eyes drooping sorrowfully.

'They left me alone.'

'But there was plenty of warning. Why didn't you get evacuated?'

'I was sick, so they wouldn't take me. They said they would come back. So I am waiting here, and selling these figures which I make.'

The figures were all very similar. A third of them represented a man, another third a woman, and the rest a man in bed with a woman.

'These are Solomon,' she said, 'and these are Makeda, and those ones there are Makeda visiting Solomon.'

After we had admired her work and Samson had bought a figure for his girlfriend, the woman, who was called Rachel, took us to see the synagogue. It was a plain circular building and above it rose a large Star of David. Rachel said she never went into the synagogue now that she was alone. She stayed by the roadside most of the time, waiting for tourists or, better still, for the Israeli officials to come and get her. Then she led us to her *tukul*.

We took off our shoes and went in. The walls were papered with old newspapers printed in Chinese characters. The floor was made from dried mud, and the only piece of furniture was a long, rickety bed. So the three of us sat in a line on it.

'The Israeli Embassy people came to meet me,' said Rachel, 'but they told me I was too late to come to their country. I would have to wait here until the next evacuation.'

'When will that be?'

Rachel coughed into her hand.

'I don't know, but they said they would come and get me when it happened. They promised.'

Samson asked her about Solomon.

'King Solomon and Makeda had a son,' she said softly, 'and he is our ancestor. He was Menelik.'

'Can you read the Talmud?'

'No, we don't have it. We have never had it. But we have a book of prayers in Ge'ez.'

I told Rachel that I had been to Jerusalem, to the place where Solomon's Temple had once stood. I said that I'd met some Ethiopian Jews, and that they were still adjusting to the great change in their lives. Many of the Ethiopian men were in the army, and others were living in very poor conditions despite handouts from the state. Every Israeli, it seemed, knew of their plight.

Rachel got off the bed and looked me straight in the eye.

'These Beta Israel you met in Jerusalem,' she said, 'did they speak of me?'

Halfway between Gondar and Bahir Dar, which nestles on the banks of Lake Tana, Bahru charged through a vast sea of grey vultures. Within seconds there was carnage on the road. Most people avoid vultures, but not Bahru. As the wheels sliced through the vultures' ranks, crushing wings and breaking beaks, I prayed that the slaughter wouldn't have ominous consequences later on. Samson said vultures were the messengers of the Devil. Killing them was a virtuous act, though diabolic retribution would probably follow.

As the road ran along the eastern bank of Lake Tana, we caught our first glimpse of the water. The late afternoon sun reflected on it, transforming the surface into a dazzling sheet of gold. Lake Tana is the kind of place where you could easily spend a lifetime navigating the inlets and visiting the monasteries on its banks and on the islands which lie scattered across its waters. Samson begged me to let him make a pilgrimage to some of the churches. He wanted to ask for God's protection now that we'd spilt vulturine blood. I would have loved to stop as well, to journey to the island of Dega Estefanos where the Church of Saint Stephanos contains the mummified remains of five former Emperors of Ethiopia in glass-sided coffins.

Samson wasn't thinking about sightseeing so much as survival. He predicted a catastrophe if we didn't stop and pray. The vultures were already beginning to take their revenge, he said. To take his mind off the matter, I pulled out the map and went over the route. We didn't have time to stop. We had to go further west, to Beni Shangul, and then head south to Tullu Wallel. There would be plenty of opportunities to pray later, I said.

We spent the night in Bahir Dar. The town was one of unexpected beauty, quite unlike anywhere else I had been in Ethiopia. Palm trees lined the wide avenues, which were brushed by cleaners sweeping with long palm fronds. There were little boutiques selling knick-knacks and banks offering foreign exchange, basket-sellers hawking their wares, and policemen in immaculate uniforms. Samson took a deep breath.

'I think this is the most beautiful place in the world,' he said, 'I will bring my girlfriend here when we are married.'

Samson was still a long way from his honeymoon. The subject of marriage was one which preoccupied him. He spoke of wedded bliss continually. A man who was married, he said, was a man who had been touched by angels. Samson was the kind of person who would make a good husband. He was considerate and generally good-natured, and he didn't smoke, drink, gamble, chew *qat* or swear. But his girlfriend came from a different social class. Her family had a big house in a good suburb of Addis Ababa. They even owned a car. Samson was a taxi-driver who had lived in a shack until it had been burned to the ground. He had never met the girl's parents during the three years they had known each other. Worse still, he and his girlfriend were so fearful of being found out that they had to avoid being seen together in public. This need for secrecy put a great strain on Samson.

Bahru dropped me at the Ghion Hotel in Bahir Dar, and my bags were unloaded and ferried to the room by a porter with a clubfoot. Samson said he wouldn't need a bed for the night. He was going to seek out the nearest church.

'There is much to pray for,' he said.

'Are you still thinking about the vultures?'

'Yes, the vultures,' he replied, 'but I am thinking of angels as well. If I pray very hard, all night, maybe they will fly down and touch me with their wings.'

12

The Mad Sultan

'The trail led up a wild valley in which we were astonished
to find hundreds of slaves at work riddling gold in the
riverbed under brutish foremen armed with whips of
hippopotamus hide.'

Count Byron de Prorok, *In Quest of Lost Worlds*

THE YELLOW AND white line which ran westward to Beni Shangul
looked harmless enough. Michelin's map-makers sitting in their
cosy offices in Paris could have had no idea of the true condition
of the road. I made a note in my journal to write to them as soon
as I returned home. Then I reminded myself that it was the rainy
season, a time when inoffensive tracks become surging rivers of
mud. Bahru clenched his teeth and accelerated at full speed. The
wheels span furiously, propelling the wretched Emperor's Jeep
through the slime. Neither he nor Samson said very much. I could
feel them ganging up on me, bound by their common nationality
and by their reluctance to continue the journey. Both men were
eager to return to the capital, and they knew instinctively that the
road was about to get even worse. A glance at the route into Beni
Shangul confirmed it. The yellow and white streak would soon be
replaced by a narrow pencil line, indicating an unmarked track.
I ripped the legend off the map and stuffed it down behind the back
seat.

Despite the dreadful driving conditions, Samson was feeling
better. Since leaving Bahir Dar two days before, I had let him stop
at any church we passed for a quick bout of prayer. Sometimes even
the harshest employer has to veer towards lenience.

De Prorok's book, *Dead Men Do Tell Tales*, had been written
decades before, but it spoke of a wild, untamed people living in a

hostile land. The countryside hadn't changed since de Prorok's time, but I hoped the indigenous tribes had grown more friendly. However, everyone I'd asked *en route* had said that only a madman would dare to make the journey to Beni Shangul, and eventually I'd stopped asking for people's opinions because they didn't do much for general morale.

The only comfort was that the Mad Sultan Ghogoli must surely be dead by now. De Prorok went into every chilling detail of the despotic ruler's regime. Ghogoli governed Beni Shangul as a semi-independent kingdom, paying only lipservice to Haile Selassie, and he retained complete control over the gold mines in his territory. His rule was absolute. The lightest form of punishment was castration, in which he clearly delighted. If any of his slaves were found swallowing gold, they were buried up to their necks in ant hills with their noses and ears cut off, or they were hung from posts until they were dead. When Ghogoli was feeling benevolent he permitted a wrong-doer to be executed by his nearest male relative, with the rest of the family looking on. The walls of his palace were said to be festooned with the dried 'body parts' of his enemies. De Prorok was too polite to say it, but I knew he was talking about genitalia.

The Sultan's favourite punishment was the so-called 'human candle'. This was reserved for those who questioned his authority. I'd heard that Haile Selassie had frowned on the practice but had been powerless to stop it. One reason for its persistence was that it was popular with the locals. No one could see enough human candles, just as bull-fighting aficionados can't get enough of their sport.

The punishment began with Ghogoli's guards lighting a slow fire beneath a cauldron filled with tallow. The prisoner was then stripped naked and his hands were tied behind his back. Next the guards dipped thin cotton bandages in the tallow and wound them around the unfortunate victim. De Prorok likened the process to Egyptian mummification. When the prisoner had been completely swathed in lengths of cloth, from the chin down to the backs of his knees, a thicker strip of tallow-soaked cotton was woven through the layers across his back, and left to hang down like a wick.

On the Mad Sultan's command, the wick was ignited. With the crowd cheering enthusiastically, the bandages smouldered, smoked, broke into flames and then blazed. As he burned, the victim ran about, screaming. If he tried to run away, the guards would lash him with their swords. De Prorok was intrigued by the punishment: 'Gradually, the smell of burning flesh increases, but there is a limit to human endurance. The victim goes mad. In the intensity of the suffering, he does not know what he is doing. The pungent odour of roasting meat is unmistakable. At last his suffering is ended, from insanity he goes into unconsciousness and then into his death throes.'

I decided to keep all mention of the Mad Sultan to myself, for fear of inciting a mutiny. With every hour that slipped by, Samson and Bahru questioned the wisdom of our expedition. I, too, queried my line of work. Why, I asked myself, couldn't I have a more normal career like most of my friends? But before I could give it any more thought, Samson pointed to the road. Ahead of us lay a stretch of water. Bahru eased the vehicle to a stop, like a rider pulling up his horse before an especially high fence.

It was impossible to tell how deep the water was, but it looked very muddy, and every so often a bubble of methane would rise to the surface and burst. Samson got out, took off his trousers and waded in. When the water was up to his waist he leaned out and dipped a long bamboo stave into the middle of the ooze. It disappeared without trace. All around the edges of the bog there were discarded rocks and splintered pieces of wood, indicating that other vehicles had got stuck here. Bahru wrung his hands together and bit his lip. Then a look of determination stole over his face.

'He's not seriously going to try and drive through it, is he?' I asked Samson.

'For Bahru this is a matter of honour,' replied Samson wearily.

The driver got back into the Jeep and reversed about fifty feet. A second later he was charging at full speed towards the water. It was nothing short of suicide. Samson and I yelled for him to stop as we waved our arms. But it was too late. The vehicle was grounded in the middle of the bog, with Bahru slouched behind the wheel, a broken man.

For three hours, we struggled to free the Emperor's Jeep. Bahru stripped off all his clothes – even his underpants – and swam down to wedge stones under the wheels. Samson and I cut bamboo and razor grass, and put them in place. But it was no good. Every attempt at escape failed and settled the vehicle still deeper in the bog. By the end the Jeep had sunk to its bonnet, our hands were lacerated and we were all covered from head to foot in thick, noisome mud.

Eventually I gave up and sat down by the edge of the quagmire in despair. A few minutes later we heard three children in the distance. They were chewing sticks and giggling. They sat down beside me and stared at the Jeep. Then some more children turned up, followed by a pair of women, and after them half a dozen men. Before we knew it an entire village had surrounded the bog. They were laughing and pointing, but none of them offered to help.

'These are bad people,' said Samson under his breath.

'Ask them to give us a hand.'

He rattled off a sentence in Amharic. The crowd jeered and gesticulated and shook their heads.

'They want money,' he replied.

'How much?'

'Two hundred *birr*.'

'That's nearly twenty pounds!'

Samson looked at the bog and then at the crowd.

'They are bad people,' he said again.

We tried to negotiate the price down but they were well aware that we had no other choice. When, eventually, we settled on a price only a little lower than the original demand, it became apparent that they were professionals. They worked together, each taking a job. The men found stones and the women cut down more bamboo poles, while their children opened a sluice to drain away the water. Twenty minutes later the road was clear.

I handed over the money.

'They will feast tonight,' said Samson.

We drove on through the twilight and then the darkness. The moon rose high above us, a vanilla disc of light. If the track was bad during the day, it was ten times worse at night. We still had no headlights, and the sides of the track were lined with impenetrable thickets of bamboo. In some places the potholes were as deep as plague pits. We begged Bahru to stop, declaring that we could camp in the Jeep for the night. But he refused. His pride had been dented.

A few minutes before midnight we reached a hamlet that was little more than a cluster of thatched huts. Samson went to find us somewhere to sleep. The villagers had been woken by the sound of our engine and soon they were crowding around the car. Samson got out and spoke to them.

'They are miners,' he said, 'working a gold seam two miles to the north. They have invited us to stay the night here.'

We were welcomed by a lantern swinging in the cool nocturnal air. I could smell tobacco burning and see the whites of eyes illuminated in the pastel yellow light. When they saw my face, the miners ducked their heads and shook my hand vigorously. A pot of meaty stew with macaroni was prepared, and a short-wave radio was fished out of a box and switched on with the volume turned up. It sounded like Radio Moscow.

The leader of the miners, Lucas, sat beside me in his hut. The lantern was hung above his head, drawing moths to it. We flailed our arms to knock the insects away from the food, but Lucas and the others didn't seem to care that a number of them had flapped into their stew. One of the men stirred the dish with a goat's thigh-bone, and then everyone started to eat from the communal dish. Lucas urged me to take the best pieces of meat and then reached into the stew and selected a bone for me to chew, holding it to my lips.

I slept more deeply that night than I think I have ever slept before. The miners could easily have slit our throats, pilfered our equipment and run off into the hills. But they had a greater source of prosperity, gold.

Dawn was accompanied by the sound of chickens scratching and children playing, and was followed by another communal dish of macaroni, high on moths and low on meat. Lucas said he would take us to where they were mining gold.

We left the Jeep at the camp and set out into the undergrowth. Rain during the night had lowered the temperature but had brought out horseflies and mosquitoes. Lucas explained that the area close to the hamlet had already been mined out. So now the men were working a stretch across the river. The operation was quite different from the mine near Shakiso. For a start it was much smaller, involving no more than about twenty men and their families. Unlike Bedakaysa, the miners worked as a group, each man and each woman looking out for the next. An unknown visitor turning up at the Bedakaysa mine in the middle of the night would have been courting death.

Soon the bamboo thickets gave way to wild mango and thorn trees. I followed close behind Lucas, anxious not to fall down an old mine-shaft. There were dozens of them pitting the ground, each about three feet in diameter with passages that linked them to others.

Though he wore only a frayed tweed herringbone jacket with turned-up cuffs, Lucas was an impressive figure and stood well over six feet tall. As I struggled to keep up with him I asked if they were finding gold.

'There's plenty for all of us,' he said, 'but we find it hard to get a fair price. Addis Ababa is a long way away, so usually we sell it to dealers who take it across the border and up to Khartoum.'

'What's the quality like?'

Lucas grinned, then wiped the sweat from his neck with his hand.

'It's the best gold in Ethiopia,' he said, 'ninety-nine per cent best quality. Ever since men have lived here they have mined the gold.'

'How long is that?'

Lucas thought for a moment.

'Since time began,' he said.

Half an hour later we came to a series of freshly dug tunnels. There must have been more than fifty of them, stretching over about an acre of ground. Lucas slipped off his jacket. Three or four of the tunnels were being worked, with young boys standing at ground level and catching the wicker baskets of earth as they were sent up. Another group of boys, younger than the first, ferried the soil down to the river where the women panned it. The operation was small in scale but efficient.

Lucas said the tunnels ran along a rich seam and that they always had a hole at each end so as to ensure an escape route if the roof caved in.

'Are there cave-ins?'

'Often,' he said, 'especially in the rains when the ground is so wet. There's nothing we can do except make sure we prop up the sides of the tunnels with wood. Last week one of the men was almost killed. We dug for many hours. But he was a strong man, thank God, and he survived.'

Samson stripped off his shirt, kicked off his shoes and jumped down the tunnel, disappearing like a ferret down a rabbit-hole. He clearly hadn't forgotten his mining days. Lucas asked if I wanted to go down. I took a small torch from my camera bag and followed him into the shaft. It went straight down like a well shaft. For someone unused to the work, clambering down was an unnerving experience. Lucas made it look so easy. He glided down the thirty-foot hole without giving it another thought. Behind him, I was wheezing and struggling. Eventually the shaft levelled out and led to a passage, little more than three feet in height, that continued for fifty feet, before diving down again, this time in a steep slope. It reminded me of the cramped passage which leads to the heart of the Great Pyramid of Cheops at Giza. We crawled on our stomachs over soil that had been tamped down by innumerable bodies. The light from my torch was dim and in the end I switched it off. It was easier to shut my eyes and rely on the sense of touch.

After a great deal of crawling I heard voices. Samson had reached the mine face and was calling out.

'This is the seam,' said Lucas, pressing my hand to a jagged wall of soil. 'There is much gold here. You can smell it, can't you?'

I turned on my torch and then breathed in. All I could smell was red African earth and sweat. Lucas showed how the miners chipped away at the seam with a sharp iron pike. Most of them didn't bother with lanterns or torches. Years of tunnelling had given them a sense of their surroundings. Like moles, they had no need to see.

Back on the surface, after a gruelling ascent, I followed the procession of children who shuttled the baskets and pans from the mine face to the river. The boys were apprentices. One day they would continue the work of their fathers, as their fathers had done before them. But first they had to scurry back and forth like rats through the tunnels. In our society we regard the idea of child labour as deplorable, but most of the world knows no other way. Children's miniature frames and nimble movements make them the obvious choice for tunnelling.

Down at the river twenty-five women were sweeping the round wooden pans in the flow. They became uneasy when they spotted me but then relaxed when they saw Lucas by my side. A couple of girls were bathing on the rocks and rinsing their dresses. They shrieked for us to turn away until they'd slipped back into their clothes. Others were singing. Samson said it was a song of lost love. Each woman wore a miniature gourd, no bigger than the bowl of a pipe, strung around her neck. In it was kept the gold dust for which they worked so hard. Squatting on their haunches, the women swirled water around the great pans until all the soil was gone, leaving no more than a speck or two of gold. Vast quantities of dirt have to be sifted to produce even the smallest trace of gold dust. For every grain of it a gallon of sweat is lost.

During the rains the river is high, providing the water needed to pan the gold, but in spring and autumn the water level drops. Then the villagers work in the fields instead.

I asked if the government ever tried to restrict their mining.

'The officials are fearful of this place,' said Lucas. 'They think that we will cut their throats and kill them. And they know about the Devil in the mountain.'

'Which mountain?'

Lucas pointed a finger to a double peak in the distance. It resembled the so-called Sheba's Breasts in Rider Haggard's novel.

'The Devil is up there on Gorba,' he said. 'The peak on the right is male, and the one on the left is female. The Devil is on the female hill.'

'Have you seen him?'

'No, I haven't,' he said, 'and I don't wish to. The people who have been there have all died. Sometimes they climb up and disappear. Even *faranjis* have gone up there and disappeared.'

Just as Ethiopian caves are frequently associated with gold and treasure, mountains are often linked to the Devil. I had read a description of another Devil mountain in the Simien range, written by Paul Hartlmaier, a German travelling in Ethiopia during the 1950s. He said the Devil supposedly dwelt near the village of Addi Arkai, on a mountain called Amba Hawasa. The locals believed that anyone stupid enough to venture up the mountain would be cast into the chasm below. Whatever the case, such tales are an effective method of keeping inquisitive visitors away.

I wondered if Frank Hayter or Count de Prorok had ever explored the mountain of Gorba. After all, de Prorok had searched the area before the Mad Sultan's army chased him away. He had found a river called Werk Warka, literally the 'River of Gold', at which hundreds of Ghogoli's child slaves were toiling. De Prorok said the slaves were in a pitiful condition and that anyone who ran away and was caught was flayed alive by the guards' hippopotamus-hide whips. Near the river the Count found chambers full of graves. When his team excavated them they discovered ancient human bones, embalmed skeletons, a number of amphorae, and necklaces similar to those found in ancient Egyptian tombs.

The Ethiopian porters were so terrified of opening the graves that de Prorok and the other Europeans had to leave the camp during the night and exhume the bodies alone. The Count thought the bones might have belonged to Egyptian gold miners working the area even before the time of Solomon, and he claimed to have come across what looked like an obelisk, made from porphyry. As if that wasn't enough, de Prorok also said he'd found an ancient emerald mine at Beni Shangul.

The Mad Sultan's forces hounded the expedition out of the area before the obelisk and their other discoveries could be removed. I asked Lucas and his fellow villagers if they knew of Werk Warka, and if they had heard of ancient graves and an obelisk. They all laughed at the question.

'Take my advice,' Lucas said as we walked back to the hamlet, 'don't waste your time with these things. Go back to your country and forget about the gold and the emeralds.' He stopped and turned to face the twin peaks of Gorba.

'Why?'

'Because the Devil is watching you.'

Christmas swayed across the yard, brushing a chicken away with her broom, each stride starting at the hips, buttocks moving legs. Her feet were bare, calloused like the hull of a ship which has been at sea for many months. She fluttered her eyelashes at Samson and sighed deeply. He said the woman wasn't his type, and in any case he was faithful to his girlfriend. But the bar owner's wife had fallen head over heels in love.

Samson and I had shared a room at the back of the bar, in a village called Mengay, two days on from the mining hamlet. The road had deteriorated even further and I dreaded the journey ahead.

The room at the bar had cracked mud walls, a high tin roof and a pair of rope beds. During the day, light would stream in through a glassless window. There were bats roosting in the darkened corners where the tin roof met the walls. At night they would flutter out of the window to hunt for insects above the trees. There was also a gap of ten inches below the door, under which chickens would scramble in their perpetual search for grain.

That night I was so tired that I fell into a deep sleep. In the early hours a live creature armed with many claws plunged the thirteen feet from the tin roof on to my chest. I sat up screaming and gasping for air. It was the bar's cat stalking bats.

Next morning I asked Christmas about the bats.

'The Death Birds!' she cried. 'Did they bite you?'

As I probed for puncture marks on my neck, she served Samson an immense bowl of spaghetti topped with chicken livers. It was on the house, she said, massaging her fingertips flirtatiously into his shoulders.

The village was near Asosa, virtually on the border with Sudan, and it was flooded with refugees, some of them maimed and missing limbs. Although the Ethiopian population were sensitive to the plight of their Sudanese cousins, there was tension between them. The refugees were eligible for handouts from aid organizations, whereas the local Ethiopians were given nothing.

In the West we have little concept of poverty. But on Ethiopia's border with Sudan, its full meaning is all too apparent. These people are stranded in limbo, from one generation to the next. They have barely enough food to survive, and never enough to escape. They cannot afford to buy rags to clothe themselves, to send their children to school or to buy medicine if they fall sick.

'Now you can understand why gold is so alluring to these people,' said Samson. 'They have nothing else to hope for.'

In the afternoon a blind woman was led up to the bar's veranda where we were sitting. The child leading her took her hand and placed it on my shoulder. Her arms were emaciated, her face haggard, her mouth empty of its teeth. The dress she was wearing was ripped down the sides and the back. She spoke in a voice so loud that we assumed she was deaf.

'She's saying that she's heard there is a *faranji* here,' said Samson. 'She has something to sell for the right price.'

'What?'

The woman shouted something.

'Some coins.'

'Can she show us?'

The woman untied a pouch tucked into her dress and handed it to me. Somehow I knew what was in the pouch even before I opened it. There were twenty of them – large silver coins, all bearing the same date, 1780. I had bought a bag of identical coins years before while living in Kenya as a student. They are known as Maria Theresa dollars or *thalers* (the word from which 'dollar' is derived) because they were first minted during the reign of the Austrian Empress, between 1740 and 1780. For decades the coins were the currency of Ethiopia, where the image of the Empress was believed to be that of the Virgin Mary. What was strange, however, was the fact that though the coins were minted in many different years, Ethiopians only trusted the ones stamped with the date 1780 and considered all the rest to be fakes. So all later versions were marked with the same date. The Austrian mint has recently started to produce the coins again. They are still dated 1780.

Bahru needed to get the Jeep's chassis welded, so we were forced to spend a second night in Mengay. When we told Christmas, she quivered with delight.

Evenings in remote Ethiopian villages tend to be quiet. No one has much money to spend on carousing, although Bahru always managed to find a card game in which to use his special deck. I never stopped him, for if I condemned what was his only source of revenue, he'd have turned to me for funds.

Samson and I went for a walk. He was desperate to get away from Christmas, who was busily preparing him yet another vast meal. We passed a row of run-down shops – a baker's, a tailor's and a kiosk selling soap and wire wool, mosquito coils and matches – and then a bar, marked in the usual way by an upturned cup on a stick. A little further on, towards the end of the village street, we saw a crowd gathering. Samson asked what was going on.

'A miracle man,' said a passer-by.

The villagers lined up in an arc, waiting for the miracle man to begin, the atmosphere electric with anticipation. 'He's from Sudan,' said one man. 'He can do miracles,' said another.

I've been interested in illusion for a long time but I'd never heard of any miracle workers plying their trade south of the Sahara, so I persuaded Samson to stay and watch.

The magician lit a pair of paraffin lamps dangling from the lowest branches of a tree and then laid out a striped blanket, removed his shoes and welcomed the crowd. As he stepped into the pool of light cast by the lamps I got a better view of his face. Very dark and softened with age, it was friendly and trustworthy. Samson said the man, whose name was Petros, didn't speak very good Oromo. His native tongue was Arabic.

Petros said he would perform four miracles. First he would throw ordinary water on to the ground to make a fire. He poured a cup of clear liquid on to a patch of soil near one corner of the blanket. A stream of smoke spiralled up, and then the ground burst into flames. The crowd cheered and clapped and Samson nudged me in the ribs.

'A miracle!' he exclaimed.

Next Petros declared that he would stop his own pulse. A woman from the front row put her fingers on the miracle man's wrist and announced that his pulse had faded and then disappeared altogether. Again the audience went wild, slapping their hands on their thighs and laughing out loud.

For the third miracle Petros said he would eat glass. He broke a clear light-bulb with his shoe, placed a shard of glass on his tongue and then crunched it up and swallowed it. Samson slapped me on the back.

'Isn't this incredible?!' he shouted, as all around us the villagers clamoured for more.

Petros said that he would do one last miracle. The *pièce de résist-ance* would be to turn a rod into a snake. Samson's eyes lit up. He knew the miracle well. It was first performed by Aaron at the court of the Pharaohs. The miracle man turned his back for a moment and drew a rod from a cloth bag. It was about three feet long and the colour of black olives. He asked the crowd what they saw.

'It's a stick,' they said in unison.

The magician tossed the stick on to the blanket. At first nothing happened. But then, slowly, it began to move and eventually it slithered away. I can hardly begin to describe the effect this had on the crowd. Men, women and children leapt up and ran about in awe, unable to believe what they had seen.

I made the mistake of bragging that I knew how the tricks were done. Samson thought I was demeaning the miracle man.

'Explain the miracles to me,' he said.

'All right. For the first trick he made a fire without any matches.'

'Fire with water,' said Samson, nodding.

'Well, I think you'll find he sprinkled some potassium permanganate on the ground and poured glycerine on to it.'

'What about the second miracle, stopping the pulse?'

'You put a walnut or something small and hard in your armpit and squeeze. It stops the blood's circulation in your arm.'

Samson scratched his head.

'Okay, but he ate glass.'

'If you eat a banana first and then grind up the glass with your back teeth, it gets embedded in the banana and passes through the intestines harmlessly.'

We had come to the last trick. I knew this would be sensitive because Aaron's miracle had been recorded in the Bible, and Samson took the Bible very seriously indeed.

'Turning a rod into a snake,' I said, 'is sometimes regarded as the oldest piece of conjuring in existence.'

'Aaron did it himself,' said Samson, 'it's recounted in Exodus,' and he gave me chapter and verse.

'It's easier than it looks,' I said. 'The trick is that there is no rod, just a snake. If you stretch the snake out and press down hard on its pituitary gland, the poor thing thinks that an enormous predator is standing on top of it. So it goes into shock. But when you let it go, it comes to and wriggles away.'

'You think you know all the answers, don't you?' said Samson bitterly.

Feroze, the conjurer who taught me magical illusion, advised me always to carry a few simple tricks on my travels. He said they would alleviate boredom and might help get me out of a sticky situation. In the West we tend to underestimate the effect of magic tricks. We all know they're just that − tricks. But transplant the same illusions into a small village off the beaten track and you can drive people wild.

In the early years of the last century an indefatigable Englishman called John Boyes set out for East Africa. An old friend of Frank Hayter, he had been inspired by Rider Haggard's *Allan*

Quartermain. In the book, which is a sequel to *King Solomon's Mines*, the hero goes in search of a lost white race north of Mount Kenya. Boyes intended to follow Quartermain's own route down into the Rift Valley. Very few white men had ever been accepted into the indigenous Kikuyu tribe before, and a number had recently been massacred.

When Boyes arrived at the first Kikuyu stronghold, he audaciously declared that he was a god, and he told the locals that he could not be killed. Such a claim might seem suicidal, but Boyes had a plan. Before the first spear could be hurled in his direction, he told the villagers that he would prove his power by drinking boiling water. He poured some water into a cup containing effervescent liver salts. The water bubbled furiously, and Boyes gulped it down, to the amazement of the tribesmen. Then he pulled out his phonograph, wound it up and played a record. That, he said, was an evil spirit trapped in a box.

In his book *King of the Wa Kikuyu*, Boyes claimed that tribal people from miles around came to pay homage to him as a result. Eventually he became their monarch, with five hundred thousand warriors under his command.

As we continued our journey, the rains grew heavier. In places the mud was so deep that it came up to the door handles, and traversing it with treadless tyres was a vile experience. Still, despite his enthusiasm for trapping wildlife under the wheels, and his constant *qat*-chewing, Bahru proved himself a skilled driver. While Samson would fall into a gloom of despondency, Bahru never complained. He was a man who lived from one minute to the next. Nothing fazed him. Sometimes we'd turn a bend to see a seemingly impassable stretch of track before us: a battlefield landscape of holes, mud and quicksand. Then, stuffing some *qat* leaves in his cheek, his eyes lighting up in delight, he'd stamp on the accelerator and charge through the quagmire and out the other side.

On the way to Nejo, our next stop, dense forest gave way to a patchwork of fields. The ground was clearly full of minerals, for each rocky outcrop gleamed with iron and quartz. The soil was fertile too. Samson said that if you planted a walking-stick here it would grow into a tree a hundred feet tall. Then he reminded me that, as all Ethiopians know, this was where the Garden of Eden had been.

Eventually the road levelled out and its surface improved. There were less potholes and less mud. Best of all, the rain had stopped. When I exclaimed at our good fortune, Samson said it was because God was watching over us. No sooner had he spoken than Bahru jammed on the brakes and the Emperor's Jeep skidded to a halt.

'Is it a flat tyre?'

Bahru shook his head.

'We can't go on,' he said.

'What's wrong? The road's fantastic.'

Turning off the engine and pulling out the key, Bahru said his luck had run out. Samson and I looked at him.

'Just like that?'

He nodded meekly.

'Just like that,' he said. 'If we continue we will die.'

A few miles before, when the road was indescribably bad, we would have taken his sudden alarm seriously. But things were looking up. Despite us offering to push-start the Jeep so we could drive the short distance to Nejo, Bahru was adamant. He wouldn't drive another yard. So Samson had to drive while Bahru sat in the front passenger seat, hunched up, his knees pulled up against his chest.

An hour later we were slipping down Nejo's muddy main street, past buildings with corrugated iron roofs and cement walls. We pulled up at a bar. Kerosene and sawdust had been sprinkled on the floor to keep away the flies. I ordered Bahru a large glass of *araki*. He slugged it down and asked for another. Still a cloud of depression hung over him. Samson told him to pray: beseeching God was the only path to redemption. Bahru said he needed a third drink. Then he asked to be left alone.

I had heard from several sources that Nejo was the site of ancient gold mines. Frank Hayter's friend Captain Bartleet had written of ancient mines in the Wollega area, and the Swiss engineer and prospector Alfred Ilg (the same man who had proposed a railway from Djibouti to Addis Ababa and made a shoe to prove his skill to Menelik) was certain that he'd found the remains of ancient gold mines a few miles from the town.

After being granted a concession to mine gold near Nejo, Ilg returned to Europe to raise capital. Then, in 1901, he formed a company in Antwerp, naming it the 'Mines d'Or du Wallaga'. Ilg's concession, which was granted for fifty years, extended in a radius of eighteen miles around Nejo. The adventurer Herbert Weld Blundell visited the area in 1906. Commenting on the 'lively and curious aspect' of the place, he reported that the mine produced about eighty thousand American dollars' worth of gold a year and that the Emperor received half of this as his share.

Samson and I went from one shop to another asking if anyone knew where the ancient gold mines were. Our questions were met with suspicion and no one would give us a straight answer. As I became increasingly frustrated, Samson begged me to stay calm. Foreigners searching for gold mines made people nervous, he said. At last we gave up and went to a small hotel which served European food. The place was empty because the owner refused to employ prostitutes. As far as most Ethiopians are concerned, a hotel or bar without whores is a bad joke.

The owner was unusually light-skinned, and he tiptoed around the table as I harangued Samson on one of my pet themes – the gap between utter failure and absolute success is often as narrow as a hair's breadth, and in our quest for King Solomon's mines we had to leave no stone unturned. Samson couldn't stand my sermons, but he put up with them all the same.

When I had finished, the owner presented us with our macaroni and introduced himself. He said his name was Berehane and he'd heard we were looking for gold. He pointed to a faded sepia photograph hanging in a frame on the back wall. It was of a white man.

'That was my grandfather,' he said, 'Signor Antillio Zappa.'

I couldn't believe our luck. Zappa had been a gold miner and a friend of Frank Hayter in the 1920s, and he was mentioned in many of the books I'd read on pre-war Ethiopia. Berehane sat with us as we ate and said that most people made fun of his mixed ancestry. Half-castes are disliked, but those with Italian blood are especially despised.

When we'd finished eating Berehane jumped up and returned a minute later holding a battered leather case. We opened it up and began to leaf through a jumble of papers that had belonged to Zappa. There were black and white photographs of men panning and others building sluices. There were diaries, too, written in a spidery hand, some in English, others in Italian. Samson unfolded a set of maps and typed geological reports. But Berehane wanted us to see something else. He handed me a sheaf of letters. They bore wax seals and an embossed lion standing beside a flag, printed on brittle, yellowed paper.

'They are from the Emperor to my grandfather,' he said. 'You see, they were friends.'

Early next morning Berehane took us to where his grandfather Antillio Zappa had mined three-quarters of a century before. We soon left Nejo behind us. Ahead lay rolling hills surrounded by a patchwork of fields in which farmers whipped oxen pulling home-made ploughs. The sky was inky black, threatening rain, and a pair of crows flew overhead, calling 'Werk, werk!'

'Do you here that?' said Samson. 'They are saying *werk*, which means gold. It's a good omen.'

After some time we came to an exposed hillside. Berehane pointed to a vast crater the size of a football field.

'This the old mine,' he said.

'How old is it?'

'Gold was mined here thousands of years ago,' he said. 'That's why my grandfather came here. At one time there were hundreds of men digging and panning. But there isn't much gold left now. Sometimes the farmers find small nuggets, but they sell them quietly. Everyone fears that the government will take their land away if they hear of gold being found.'

It was very likely that Zappa had dug where ancient gold mines had once existed. But all trace of any ancient mines had long since disappeared. Even the crater excavated by Zappa was far less deep than it would once have been, for the soil was soft and erosion during the rains swift. Despite the lack of evidence, I liked to think that the Pharaohs and, later, Solomon, might once have obtained gold from the hills near Nejo, from Signor Zappa's mines.

13

Used Mules

'God has given us mules but no roads to ride on.'

Ethiopian proverb

BACK AT THE bar, Bahru was lying in a heap in the corner. He was too drunk to stand. The gaggle of resident prostitutes said he had drunk a whole bottle of *araki* and had no money to pay. They asked why he was so dejected.

'His luck has run out,' said Samson coldly.

The women looked sympathetic and tutted to themselves while we helped Bahru to his feet, paid his bill and got him a room. Then we went off to buy some supplies.

If we were going to make an attempt to find Hayter's mine, we'd need some specialized gear. My big worry was being able to illuminate a large cavern, as torches only give an isolated beam of light. I wanted to buy a pressure lantern which would run on kerosene. We also needed blankets, waterproofs for Samson, nylon ropes, a portable stove, some polythene sheeting, marker posts, mallets, and a sack of old clothes that might be bartered for food along the way. Fortunately, most of these items were readily available across Ethiopia. Shops seemed to remain reasonably well stocked because no one had any money to buy anything. In fact goods would stay on the shelves for years before a customer with cash turned up.

After a prolonged search we managed to buy almost everything except a waterproof coat for Samson. We'd found one high-quality waxed canvas jacket and Samson's face had lit up when he saw it hanging in a polythene wrapper at the back of the shop. He'd hinted that it was his size and that it was just the thing to keep him dry, but it was much too expensive. Instead, he had to make do with a black bin-liner with holes cut for his arms and head.

Most of the garments on sale at Ethiopian used clothing stalls have come from Europe or America, but they are hopelessly unsuited to the harsh African conditions. Such flimsy clothing may be fine in the West where we rotate dozens of outfits, but in a place like Ethiopia clothing soon gets worn out. It kept striking me that someone ought to supply the market stalls with durable army surplus gear. Military clothing lasts forever and is extremely cheap. I was surprised to find my idea wasn't original. In the 1920s, the geologist and gold prospector L. M. Nesbitt said that a destitute European in Ethiopia had wanted to import army surplus clothing from Marseilles, though the plan had come to nothing.

I asked the man who was selling the waxed jacket if he had any pressure lanterns. He stuck a finger in his ear and jiggled it about. He had had one once, he said. It had been on the shelf for twenty years so he'd not reordered when eventually it was sold. For the rest of the day we searched through virtually every kiosk, shop and stall in Nejo looking for a pressure lantern. Towards the end of the evening we came to a shoe shop on the outskirts of town. I wasn't going to bother going inside, but Samson hoped to talk me into buying him a new pair of boots. Amidst the clutter of worn-out shoes sat a frail-looking man in a peakless pink baseball cap. I said we were looking for pressure lanterns. The salesman rummaged under the counter and brought out a box covered in soot. We opened it up and there sat a pressure lantern in almost mint condition.

'Two hundred *birr*,' he said.

It was a huge sum, almost twenty pounds, but I knew it was essential to have the right equipment. So I fished out the notes and slid them across the counter. Money spent on good-quality gear is always money well spent.

We returned to the bar to find Bahru sitting on the end of his bed, his knees pressed up to his chin. He had run out of *qat* and he was suffering from withdrawal symptoms. I showed him all the gear we'd bought.

'We're going to need every bit of it to get to Tullu Wallel,' I said. Bahru stared at his feet.

'I'm not going to Tullu Wallel,' he muttered.

'You don't have to come up the mountain, you can park nearby.'

'I'm not going anywhere.'

I couldn't understand what had come over the man. He'd not

shown signs of depression before. I offered to pay for his meals and to buy him a bale of the wicked green leaves. I even offered him more money. But he wouldn't budge.

So, the next morning, with great reluctance, Samson and I unloaded our belongings from the Emperor's Jeep and stood by the side of the road. We waited there for eight hours, until late morning turned into evening, but not a single vehicle passed by.

That night in the bar I treated Bahru to some more *araki* and gave him a gift, a bar of Greek-made chocolate. He cheered up a little and challenged a drunk in the bar to a game of cards. I winked at Samson.

'That's our old Bahru,' I said.

Bahru slapped the marked deck on the table and told the drunk to cut it. They played a few hands, with Bahru inevitably winning. But then the drunk pulled a knife and accused him of cheating. He snatched the pile of cash on the table and said that if Bahru challenged him for it, he'd stab him. The whores intervened and broke them up, and Bahru crept to his room, his head low, his arms dragging down at his sides.

'My God,' said Samson, as Bahru left, 'maybe his luck really has run out.'

Next day we hauled the baggage back to the roadside. Three hours later a brick-red Landcruiser skidded to a halt beside us. It was the only vehicle we had seen moving since morning. The driver said he could drop us at Begi, seventy-five miles west of Nejo. After that we were on our own. I peered into the back of the Landcruiser. All I could see were dozens of arms and legs and faces squirming in discomfort. Samson hugged Bahru and then I too embraced him. It was a sad moment, but we had no choice. We had to continue without him. The next minute our bags were thrown up top and we squeezed into the tangle of limbs.

Anyone who has ever travelled in East Africa knows the joy of *matatus*, the ubiquitous communal vans that are the main form of local transport. They make even the worst overland bus journey seem luxurious. In a *matatu* the concept of personal space doesn't exist. Passengers are pressed together so tightly that they become a single entity, with multiple heads, legs, hands and feet. If you sneeze, the entire organism shudders. You find yourself counting the minutes, wondering how you can stand another second. But time slips by, punctuated by flat tyres and pee stops. It seems incredible to me now, but there were twenty-four people pressed inside that Landcruiser, not including the three men clinging to the roof.

The hours passed and I grew used to having someone's elbow in my back, and a candyfloss of hair pressed against my face. Samson had a long conversation about the Old Testament with the person squashed up beside him. I was sitting near him, but I didn't feel like chatting. The fact that we had left Bahru behind, so far from his home, bothered me. The first rule of an expedition is that every-one should stick together. If Stanley had been leading the party he'd have thrown Bahru in chains and had him horse-whipped. But then things have changed since Stanley's day.

Begi lies on a flat plain of grassland with hills to the south and east. It's the sort of place at which, in more normal circumstances, you'd never stop, but there had been no time to check the maps before climbing aboard the Landcruiser. The driver appeared to think the small town was near Tullu Wallel, so we took his word for it. The few locals who watched us extricate ourselves from the back of the vehicle looked alarmed, and I half expected them to rush over and tell us we'd made a terrible mistake.

Then our bags and equipment were tossed down on to the edge of the road and, before we could look up, the *matatu* had driven off towards the border with Sudan.

I always try to get the best maps before going to a new country because generally, with the exception of India whose National Survey produces fantastically detailed maps, the last place you can get good maps is in the country itself. Michelin produces the most detailed series of civilian maps for the African continent, scaled at 1:4,000,000. I also had all the American tactical pilotage charts for Ethiopia. The one that covered the western region was segment K-5D, on a scale of 1:500,000. Although there weren't many place names marked, it gave valuable relief information.

We looked at the maps and it immediately became clear that we were twenty-five miles north of Tullu Wallel. It would have been much better to approach from the south, as the road there runs nearer the mountain, but it was too late to turn back.

There was a single bar in Begi which served warm Pilsen lager and doubled as a brothel. The whores were sitting in the shade of the veranda, picking their teeth and plaiting each other's hair. They looked over at us and then looked away. A foreigner and an Ethiopian with a Bible stuffed under his arm weren't the kind of people who generally required their services. We dragged our belongings into the shade and asked the girls where we could hire mules. They screwed up their faces, and then one of them pointed silently across the street to a rickety wooden kiosk.

Inside, a man was asleep on a chair with a kitten curled up on his chest. All around him were stacked empty gin bottles. He woke up, disturbed by the opening door knocking over part of his stock. His cheeks and chin were covered in grey stubble, his eyes sagged down, and most of his nose was missing. He greeted us. We greeted him.

'Mules,' said Samson, 'we're looking for mules.'

'How many do you want?'

Samson asked me for a figure.

'Lots,' I said, 'we'll need lots of mules.'

The man seemed pleased. He brushed the kitten away, stood up and called out of the door. A young boy came running. The man barked orders and the boy ran off.

'It's hard to get good mules,' he said. 'Why do you need them?'

'To go to Tullu Wallel.'

His face froze.

'The mountain?'

'Yes.'

We stood there in uneasy silence. The man peered at me. I don't know why but I feared blinking, as if by doing so I'd be revealing secret information.

'The Devil lives on the mountain,' he said.

'Oh.'

'He'll kill you and eat your brains.'

'Ah.'

There was an awkward silence.

'Are you missionaries?' he asked at length.

I looked at Samson, who was still holding his Bible.

'Yes . . . yes, we're missionaries,' I said devoutly, grasping at straws. 'We have come to get the Devil off Tullu Wallel. We're going to kick him all the way back to Hell.'

The old man dipped his noseless head in appreciation.

'That is good,' he said. 'Then you will need fine mules.'

'The very best,' I responded, 'for we are doing God's work.'

The gin-bottle man told us to come back a little later. His contact in the mule business would need time to get there. We sought refuge from the late afternoon rain back at the bar. The girls sat about waiting for the evening's clients. There's something very strange about African drinking dens during the day. They're like discos when the house lights have been turned on. There's something not quite right about them.

Samson opened his Bible at random and began to read the Psalms. I had expected my announcement that we were missionaries would infuriate him. But he was delighted and took the disguise very seriously.

One of the girls was serving drinks. I asked for a cup of coffee. There's nothing like village coffee in Ethiopia. The only problem is you have to wait for it. A good cup can take up to two hours because it is made from scratch. After an hour of sitting around, I went into the yard behind the bar to see how things were progressing. The girl told me to be patient. The water supply had been cut, she said, which meant she had had to trek to a well a mile away. Then firewood needed to be collected. Only after that could the slow process of roasting the coffee begin.

When the beans had turned from pale green to dark brown, she held them up to my face for me to smell them. After that she tipped them into a mortar and ground them to powder. Only then could the cup of coffee be made. Almost two hours after placing the casual order, it finally arrived. It was the freshest, most delicious cup of coffee I can remember.

In the late evening the gin-bottle man sent his son to fetch us. His mule contact had turned up. We strolled across to the kiosk and were introduced to Tadesse. He was one of the most evil-looking men I have ever set eyes on. If I'd been told he had just chopped up his children and danced on their graves, I wouldn't have been the least surprised. He had wicked, shifty eyes, high cheekbones, and a long waxy tongue which emerged from his mouth between sentences, like that of a tree frog catching flies. The gin-bottle man spoke highly of the muleteer, saying he was the only man who knew the mountain.

I asked Samson what he thought.

'We don't have to climb Tullu Wallel to find the Devil,' he said. 'He's standing right here.'

The muleteer's eyes flickered from side to side. He was waiting for our answer.

'Where are the mules?'

He said he would take us to them once they had been rounded up. I asked how long that would take.

'One or two days.'

'That seems like a very long time.'

Tadesse looked at me hard.

'Ethiopian mules are very wild,' he said.

We arranged to inspect the animals at first light. If they still hadn't been caught, I would view them through my binoculars. Business turned to the mountain itself. When I inquired if Tadesse was afraid of Tullu Wallel, he didn't say anything; he just laughed manically.

'He is a good man,' said the gin-bottle man. 'You will grow to like him.'

'Are his mules strong?'

The gin-bottle man rubbed the hole where his nose ought to have been.

'They're as strong as the mountain,' he said.

We thanked him for the introduction and turned on our heels to go. But I couldn't leave yet. There was something I had to know. Unable to contain myself, I made Samson find out how he'd lost his nose. The gin-bottle man glanced down at the table, and I felt embarrassed at having asked.

'A long time ago,' he said, 'I had an argument with my wife. She bit it off and ran away.'

On the way to the mules I bragged about my equestrian experience. I told Tadesse and Samson that my Pushtun ancestors prided themselves on their skill at *buz-kashi*, the Afghan national sport played on horseback with a headless goat. Polo is said to have developed from the game. The horses get so charged up that they bite each other if they get the chance. I went on about how I myself had been raised with horses. The animals were in my blood, I said.

Of course it was all a lie. As children we did have a pair of vicious donkeys called Boney and Claude, but they rolled under the fence one day and were never seen again. Anyone mad enough to try saddling them up would have been torn to pieces.

Everything I know about horses was passed on by an old family friend. An indomitable Swiss, he had decided that he'd trek with horses from Ulan Batur, in Outer Mongolia, to Vienna. He bought a pair of ponies from a horse-dealer in a suburb of the Mongolian capital. They were wild animals with sores all over their backs. The locals told him to pee on the sores. He soon found this was no easy feat. But when he did manage it they reared up and ran away, leaving him stranded in the frozen wastes of Mongolia. When, after many adventures, he arrived back home, I asked for his advice.

'Always pick your animals very carefully,' he said.

Those words rang in my mind as we walked the three miles to where the mules were grazing. There were eight of them, and Tadesse still hadn't managed to catch them. However, their backs were covered in saddle sores, which meant that they must have been ridden at some point.

I asked the price.

Tadesse pointed out the high quality of the saddles and the harnesses.

'There's not a finer mule for a hundred miles,' he said. 'I'm only charging ten *birr* a day for each.'

That was about eight pounds a day for all eight. It sounded like a bargain, so we took the lot.

Samson didn't understand why we needed so many animals but I justified the decision by saying that I expected injuries. It was going to be a long, hard trip. There were sure to be fatalities. In fact my reasons were different. There's nothing like a pack of mules to give one a sense of entourage.

The night before we left Begi with the mules, I re-read Frank Hayter's description of finding the mine-shafts at Tullu Wallel. A *dejazmacth*, a nobleman, had told him of a legend. It said that the ancient kings of Ethiopia had obtained their gold from two places in the west of the country. The first was Beni Shangul, and the second was at the base of Tullu Wallel. Both sets of mines were, he warned, 'guarded by the spirits of the old rulers of this country'. The tip-off sent Hayter's head spinning. He left at dawn the next day and, after days of trekking, he finally reached the twin peaks of Tullu Wallel, which he called Sheba's Breasts.

The party continued their approach, pushing through a dense bamboo forest, and eventually reached the eastern flank of the mountain. There Hayter claimed to have discovered fourteen stone portals covered in vegetation. 'They were the entrances to under-ground caves,' he wrote, 'and not natural entrances either, for the stone uprights and heavy lintels that squared the openings had been fashioned by the hands of man.'

Hayter's two books on Ethiopia contain many black and white photographs. There are pictures of gold prospectors and mule cara-vans, of lepers and encampments and tribal ceremonies, and there are innumerable shots of Hayter himself, dressed in pith helmet and safari suit. The only image missing from his books is the one of the actual mine entrances. However, Hayter's friend Captain E. J. Bartleet, who retold the tale in his own book *In the Land of Sheba*, includes an extraordinary photograph. At first glance it looks very ordinary, but on closer inspection you begin to appreciate its sig-nificance. At the top right of the picture there is a natural cave opening. But a few yards away, at the bottom of the photograph, there is the upper part of what looks like a man-made stone entrance. It is partly hidden by vegetation but it is unmistakable, and it appears to lead to a mine-shaft.

That night, before setting off for Tullu Wallel, I sat on my bed in the brothel, shining the beam of my torch on the picture from Bartleet's book. A man was screaming in the next room. At first I thought it was the cry of passion. Then I remembered that Samson had taken the room next to mine and that he was devoted to his long-suffering girlfriend. So I got off my bed and knocked gently on the door, irritated that Samson should be making so much noise. The screams turned to a long, low groan. I pushed the door open. Samson was lying on the floor, sweating profusely and clutching his abdomen. I asked what all the fuss was about. From what I could understand, he claimed to be in a great deal of pain. I hoped it wasn't a burst appendix. I remembered reading a book about climbing Everest. It had said that top climbers always have their appendix out before starting the ascent. I kicked myself for not thinking of it before. We were a man down and our assault on Tullu Wallel hadn't even begun.

Unsure of what to do, I went and asked the Tigrayan whores. They spoke no English, so I clutched my stomach, stuck out my tongue and pointed to Samson's room. The girls looked puzzled, and one of them nodded and stuck out *her* tongue. Then they walked off into another room, and a great deal of muffled shouting followed. I went back to Samson. A moment later there was a thump on the door. A tall, athletic-looking man wearing nothing but underpants was standing in the door frame. He said in English that he was a doctor. I pointed to my travelling companion. The doctor jabbed a finger into Samson's belly.

'Probably the appendix,' I said knowledgeably.

'No,' he said, 'it is intestinal worms.'

I asked how much we owed for the diagnosis.

'Fifty *birr*.'

The doctor said he would send one of the prostitutes to get medicine. Then he returned to his room. He clearly had unfinished business to attend to.

After the disturbance I went back to Bartleet's book and ran over the facts again. The story seemed to fit. My American tactical pilotage chart indicated that Tullu Wallel did indeed have two peaks, reaching a height of 10,738 feet. The distances Hayter had given from Gambela and Gore were about right too. And, more importantly, like Beni Shangul just to the north, the area was well known as an ancient source of gold. But the question that haunted me was why Hayter hadn't published the photograph of the cave entrance in his own book. Bartleet had scooped him, publishing the account of the find in 1934, a year before Hayter's book appeared. In his account, Bartleet explained that he was supposed to go on the adventure but fell ill and had to stay behind in Addis Ababa. So Hayter went alone, and Bartleet never got to see the fourteen portals or the mine-shafts for himself. I assumed that Hayter must therefore have taken the picture but chose not to publish it himself. Perhaps he feared it would help others identity the place.

I had insisted we leave Begi at dawn. An early start on the first day keeps untested men and mules on their toes. Moreover, I didn't want Tadesse to think I was a walkover, even though I'd agreed to pay his opening rate for the pack animals.

Tadesse had roped in his two sons, whom he said would work for free. The boys grinned wickedly. They had their father's genes. The younger one carried a sharp bamboo stave which he used to poke the poor mules' behinds. When he wasn't poking, he was sharpening the stick. The other boy didn't have any interest in being a muleteer, despite his father's hopes. He had heard of a place called America, he said, where he could get money for free.

After taking a couple of sachets of yellow powder prescribed by the doctor, Samson said his symptoms had gone away. I felt rather guilty about not delaying our departure, but he exclaimed that he was fighting fit again. I think he was embarrassed that he had worms.

Tadesse herded the mules to the front of the bar. They huddled together, eyes staring and hooves stamping. Despite this feigned fear, I could tell they were longing to escape. They were wild animals and resented labouring for humans. I had seen the same deranged look in our donkeys' eyes the day before they ran away.

The kitbags were soon strapped into position with leather thongs, and then the younger boy shaved a sliver off his bamboo shaft and plunged it into one of the mule's backsides as if to let them know who was boss. I looked over to see if the gin-bottle man was up but, like everyone else in the small town, he must have been fast asleep.

There is something about walking with mules that stirs me. I've travelled with camels and yaks, and even llamas, but mules are quite different. I've been bitten by a llama and spat at by more than one angry camel. Donkeys are less hostile but you always get the feeling that you're doing them an injustice. Mules on the other hand are built for rough work and thrive on hardship.

Samson was pleased to be heading for the mountain. He kept dropping hints about his new role as a preacher. I took him aside and said that we weren't really missionaries. In case he hadn't realized, I said, I wasn't even a Christian.

The track from Begi veered to the east and skirted a hill called Gimi. We were very close to the border with Sudan, which lay on the other side of the hill. I was worried that we might be arrested as spies, for border areas in Africa tend to be patrolled by secret police. If we were arrested, I told Samson to hold his Bible high in the air and declare that we were working for God. If interrogated, I planned to pretend I was a recent convert to Christianity. Everyone knows that converts are the most fanatical followers of a faith.

We continued walking well into the afternoon. The saddles were in poor shape, but at least they kept the flies off the mules' sores. The animals took every opportunity to stop and eat, and I knew they were all on the lookout for an escape route. As we trudged along, the humidity rose until finally, in the afternoon, it began to rain. We sought refuge under a bank of trees and waited for it to pass.

Tadesse asked me if I was really a missionary.

'Of course I am,' I replied firmly.

'Then why do you talk about treasure so much?'

'The Bible,' I said, 'that is the treasure that we are talking about.'

The muleteer narrowed his eyes and gave the order to move on.

'The Devil will be waiting for us,' he said.

We slept the night at Gidami. My feet were sore and Samson's arm ached from carrying the Bible all day. We'd walked for almost twenty miles. However, the mules seemed to be in high spirits. Samson took Tadesse and his sons to get some food and asked me if I would join them but I declined. An old English explorer whom I had once met near Hunza, in the Karakoram range, had passed on a valuable tip. He said that you have to turn yourself into a mythical figure early on in a journey: that is the only way of establishing your authority. The explorer's method was simple. He told me not to eat, at least not in public.

'I never chow with the natives,' he explained, 'not because I think I'm above them or because I don't like the food. They see me going on day after day without anything in my stomach, and they think I'm superhuman. Try it out some time, old boy.'

I'd been waiting to put this into practice for years. I unpacked my kitbags. In them I still had eight of the tins I'd bought in Axum. Samson couldn't understand why my luggage was so heavy and I'd let him assume it was full of books. That night I gorged myself on a can of corned beef. It's an explorer's staple. Count Byron de Prorok and many other travellers in Africa all swore by their inexhaustible supply of 'bully beef'.

During the night a spider wove an enormous sticky web over my face. As a die-hard arachnophobe I was very disturbed by the event. None of the others could understand why I was so alarmed. Unable to convince them of my horror of spiders, I decided to bolster my spirits with another surreptitious tin of corned beef.

After a couple of hours of walking, Samson and the muleteers were ready for breakfast. They sat down to eat some crusts of bread and a few bruised pieces of fruit. Tadesse couldn't believe I wasn't hungry.

'The Lord fills my stomach with His goodness,' I said, looking over at him meekly.

That day we altered course, heading east, and Tadesse pointed a broken fingernail at the distant horizon.

'That's Tullu Wallel,' he said.

I stopped and took a deep breath, and then glanced over at Samson. He was sucking his lower lip. Tadesse's eyesight was either remarkably good or remarkably bad. When I looked I couldn't see anything except for tall razor grass and the tops of trees. Only after another hour of trudging through rain did I see Tullu Wallel. It was fitting that I caught my first glimpse of the Devil's abode in such horrible weather. Samson and I let the mules go on. We both needed a moment to stare at the mountain. The summit was lost in cloud, brooding and mysterious, but it quite obviously had twin peaks – Sheba's Breasts, as Hayter had called them. Before we set off again Samson said a prayer. He looked up at the heavens and prayed that God would look after us and deliver us safely from the mountain.

I asked Tadesse how long it would take to get to Tullu Wallel.

'Maybe one day, maybe four days,' he replied.

It was an appropriate answer to a stupid question. Time didn't matter. We were nearing the mountain and that was all that counted. Above us, in the trees, baboons swung from branch to branch, taunting us. Tadesse picked up some stones and flung them at the animals.

'They are the Devil's disciples,' he said. 'Beware of baboons.'

I didn't tell him of Frank Hayter's curse, but I was thinking of it as we passed the baboons. Hayter believed completely in the spell that was put on him by an Abyssinian monk, when he'd captured a hundred sacred baboons and shipped them back to London Zoo.

That was back in 1924. He later wrote: 'Let me put my feelings in a nutshell. Ten years ago I was a very fit man indeed, fit enough to enter the ring and defend my title as boxing champion of Herefordshire. Today I am no more capable of flying without wings than of boxing. And I am only thirty-three.'

During my research I had tried to find some trace of Frank Hayter's family. He said that he married his cousin who bore him a son. I did manage to obtain copies of his birth and marriage certificates, but I do not know when he died. His last published book, *The Garden of Eden*, appeared in 1940. After that the trail goes cold. I wrote to hundreds of people all over the world called Hayter, but none appeared to be related to the explorer. Even so, I am sure that somewhere, in some forgotten attic, his notebooks and journals must survive.

Tadesse said the mules needed time to graze. We untied their packs and let them chew on the long grass. The muleteer's sons decided to pass the time by throwing more stones at the baboons. I said it was probably unwise to aggravate them, as they could be cursed.

'Of course they're cursed!' exclaimed Tadesse. 'That's why we throw stones at them.'

I asked Samson to go over to a clutch of low mud huts nearby and see if anyone knew about Tullu Wallel.

'What should I ask?'

'Ask them if they fear the mountain.'

He was gone for an hour and when, eventually, he came back to where we were sitting, he looked rather unnerved.

'I think you had better meet these people,' he said.

'Why?'

'Come and see.'

The seven huts were arranged in a horseshoe, with a fire smoking in the middle. The central yard was shaded by a thorn tree. Under the tree sat a man, a woman and about six children. The man greeted Samson and then stood up when he saw me.

'You must sit down,' said Samson.

I sat down. The children giggled, their mother smiled and their father nodded.

The parents were about thirty but looked sixty. Three decades of village life in western Ethiopia turns the skin to leather and callouses the hands and feet until they are almost unrecognizable. The man said his name was Jambo and that his wife was called Sara. We shook hands and Jambo offered me some berries. They were plum-coloured and pippy. I ate a few and praised them. The children giggled again. Sara smiled. Jambo nodded. Then I said how happy I was to have come to their home. We sat in silence. I was waiting for Samson to say something, but he didn't.

'Tullu Wallel,' I said after some time.

I was expecting more giggles, more smiles, more nods. But Jambo and his family looked alarmed.

'A bad mountain,' said Jambo sternly.

'The Devil . . .'

'He lives there!' he shouted, pointing away to the distance.

'Have you ever been there?'

Sara looked nervous.

'Of course not!'

'They kill animals in honour of the mountain,' said Samson gently.

I asked if this was true.

Jambo nodded. 'Yes, sometimes we kill animals.'

'Does it keep the Devil happy?'

'Yes, when we kill animals, the Devil is happy.'

'What if he is not happy?'

Jambo fell silent for a while and then spoke.

'It is not good when the Devil is angry.'

I asked Jambo when he was planning the next sacrifice. He passed me some more berries.

'No money to buy chickens.'

'If you had money would you make a sacrifice?'

Jambo leapt up from his seat. Yes, they'd make a sacrifice immediately, he said. He had remembered that the mountain required an offering urgently.

'What happens if no sacrifice is made?'

Jambo shook his head.

'Trouble.'

I fished out a wad of low-denomination notes. Explaining that we were missionaries, I said we had come to kick the Devil back to the farthest reaches of Hell. But before we routed him, we would give him one last meal.

Jambo grabbed the cash, passed half of it to his wife, and barked at her as gruffly as he could. She returned a few minutes later with a rather mangy pair of chickens. Within moments Jambo had broken their necks, hacked off their heads and plucked them. The children crowded round. I sent Samson to bring Tadesse and his sons. We would spend a night camping out at Jambo's place.

It wasn't long before a watery stew had been prepared. Tadesse, his sons, Samson and Jambo's family all dug in.

'Don't you have to hold the meat up to the mountain and say a prayer?'

Jambo gnawed at a bone.

'We have already done that,' he said.

'Eat, eat!' said Sara.

'I've made a vow not to eat anything until the Devil has run away from Tullu Wallel.'

With that I got up and walked off into the darkness. I had an appointment with a tin of corned beef.

When the watery stew had been eaten, I asked Jambo to take a look at the photograph of the mine entrance in Bartleet's book. He held the red binding up to his nose, and his family clustered around.

'It's the entrance to a shaft,' I said. 'Can you see the stone doorway?'

'The shaft,' said Jambo, 'that is the place where the Devil lives. You must not go there.'

'But I told you, we're missionaries. It's our job to get rid of the Devil so that you can live in peace.'

The farmer threw a chicken bone to one of his dogs.

'The Devil will bite off your heads,' he said.

'We know there is danger,' I replied. 'But God will protect us.'

Jambo stood up and walked over to one of the huts. A few minutes later he returned and sat down beside me. There was something cupped in his hands. It was made from leather and was the size and shape of a film canister.

'Tie this amulet around your neck,' he said. 'Inside there is a spell written on paper. It is written in Ge'ez, and it will give you extra protection.'

Jambo wiped his face with his hand. Then he stared into the fire, as if he was looking into the future.

'Remember one thing,' he added, 'the Devil is very clever. Missionaries have been to Tullu Wallel before. Like you they said they were very strong but . . .'

'But what?'

'But they never came down from the mountain.'

14

Tullu Wallel

'A good traveller has no fixed plan and is not intent on arriving.'

Lao Tzu

FRANK HAYTER SAID the mine-shafts were located at the base of the eastern flank of Tullu Wallel. By this I assumed he meant the east breast of the mountain. All the next day we walked through fields in which ripe ears of wheat reflected the sun. The land was almost empty of people. Samson thought that most locals preferred to farm other land.

'Many of them won't even eat this wheat,' he said. 'They think it's poisonous, so they sell it to people down in Gambela.'

We took regular breaks to let the mules rest. I was sure that the climb up the mountain wouldn't have improved much since Hayter's day. The animals would need their strength. Tadesse didn't approve of my reluctance to work the mules hard. He said that if we were too kind, they would become even lazier and wilder than they already were. As it was, he said, they weren't carrying enough on their backs.

'If people see that I'm walking with half-laden mules,' he said, 'they'll laugh at me.'

'Why?'

'They'll say that my mules are weak.'

Until late that afternoon none of us bothered to ride. While the ground was far from flat, it wasn't a great strain to walk. Only on the last stretch towards a village did I decide my legs needed a rest. All eyes were on me as I struggled to mount the most docile of the animals. I'd chosen her because her eyes lacked the glint of savagery present in those of the males. When I asked what her name was, Tadesse shook his head.

'These are animals,' he said, 'they are not people; they don't have names.'

So I called her Clarissa.

Tadesse, his sons and Samson had listened intently to my tales of ancestral horsemanship. With my usual flair for hyperbole I'd gone a bit far. In the end I had just about claimed to have been born on the back of a horse. They longed to see the great equestrian in action. But riding a mule in the wilds of western Ethiopia called for special training, training I didn't have. I couldn't get my balance at first and blamed it on the saddle, the uneven stirrups, the terrain, and then on Clarissa. More than once I ended up on my back on the ground, wounded and humiliated, to the delight of the mule-teers. But with time I learned the basics of balance, and that Clarissa would protect me if I just clung on.

At the next village we passed around the photograph of the mine entrance. The oldest man, who was blind, virtually deaf and hunch-backed, pricked up his ears when he heard the words Tullu Wallel.

'He's saying that he knows the mountain,' said Samson.

'Has he ever been up there?'

Samson translated the question. The man nodded.

'Yes, he has.'

'When was that?'

'A long time ago.'

'When?'

'It was when the Italians were here.'

'Did he see the mine-shafts?'

'He says he did see a cave,' said Samson, 'a big cave.'

'What was inside?'

I was waiting for him to say 'the Devil'. But he didn't.

'There were bats, many bats.'

'Anything else?'

'Yes,' said the man, 'there was . . .'

'What? What else was there?'

'There was gold.'

I smacked my hands together and gave Samson a double thumbs-up. Tadesse looked over at us suspiciously.

'I thought you were missionaries,' he said.

'Yes we are, but the Devil is attracted to gold. So if we find *gold*, we'll find *him*.'

'Ask the man if he'll climb the mountain with us and show us the cave.'

Samson translated.

'He says he's too old, too frail.'

'But we can strap him to a mule. We've got plenty of them.'

The hunchback croaked an answer.

'He says he wouldn't go back up there for all the money in Ethiopia.'

'Why not?'

'Because of the curse.'

I am all for curses and superstition, but there's a point at which they start getting in the way. That point had arrived. I explained we were missionaries, that we were doing God's work. He remained unmoved. I rustled a large denomination note, but still he wouldn't budge. He shouted something to Samson.

'He says that anyone who goes up Tullu Wallel is hit with misfortune afterwards. When he came down from the mountain his father died from malaria. Then his brother dropped dead. No one knew why.'

'But that could have happened naturally. There's a lot of illness here.'

Samson had more information to pass on.

'Yes, but the wives of the two men he climbed the mountain with both died in childbirth.'

I unfolded the map and asked for accurate directions. If the informant wouldn't accompany us, at least he could advise us how to find the mine. The man's blindness and inexperience with maps were a severe handicap. He didn't want to talk about the route, only about the curse. That was the one thing I didn't want to hear about because I knew it was beginning to worry Tadesse and his sons. Without Tadesse we'd have no mules. And without mules we'd have no entourage.

I gave the order for us to move out. It was unpopular with Samson, who was complaining of blisters. The boys didn't want to go further either, but they wouldn't admit that they were afraid.

We took to the path again. Clarissa dug her hooves into the dirt and soldiered on. I rapidly developed a respect for her as she compensated for my pathetic riding skills. The track led up to higher ground. We were all aware that the rains would start in the mid-afternoon, so we were eager to keep going for as long as possible. I kept an eye out for a village where we could spend the night, but there wasn't any sign of human life.

Samson asked me if I thought Bahru would have left for Addis Ababa. It hadn't been long since we had parted from him, but it now seemed an age away. We reminisced about him as we moved ahead, recounting the many near-misses and his addiction to *qat* and marked playing cards. Then my mind turned to the subject of Ophir. Western Ethiopia was as remote as it was possible to be. Solomon's men might have acquired gold from nearer the coast, but I knew there were trading routes from central Africa to the east coast and that they had been used for centuries. And, of course, western Ethiopia is close to Nubia, from which the Egyptians mined gold long before the time of Solomon.

When it came, the afternoon downpour fell harder than on any other day. The mules didn't seem to mind very much. The water cooled them, and they could drink from the pools that collected on the path. But torrential rain is a great hindrance to humans. Unlike on the Indian subcontinent or in the Amazon, in Africa the rain seems to cool the air temperature dramatically and soon you find yourself quivering with cold. I put on my army camouflage poncho, spreading it out at the bottom to accommodate Clarissa's hindquarters. Samson donned his black bin-liner. He resented me having the best equipment. As for Tadesse and his sons, they didn't have any waterproofs, so they just got soaked.

The worst thing about the rain was that it turned the soil into a quagmire. In some places we were walking up a torrent of dark brown mud and I began to worry that the mules might miss their footing. As it was they tripped and stumbled, and then, quite suddenly, one of them toppled over. With the memory of the lame camel in Afar fresh in my mind, I jumped down to help Tadesse attend to the poor animal. It was in a forlorn state. Tadesse grappled with the harness and managed to inspect its legs. Fortunately, none were broken, but the mule was shaken and the accident unsettled the other animals.

In the late afternoon we took refuge in a grove of wild gum trees a hundred yards from the track. I was concerned that we were nowhere near a village, but Samson pointed up to the high branches of the trees.

'Look at those,' he said, 'that means that there are people near here.'

About twenty large wicker baskets were tied to the topmost boughs. Samson said they were for honey. The local people hang them in the trees and leave them there for months. Eventually honey bees swarm in some of them. Then the bravest men in the village climb up and harvest the honey. Tadesse boasted that his family had been honey-hunters for generations, but that they had progressed up the social ladder to herding mules.

Samson was right about there being people nearby. As the light began to fade, we came to a settlement. It was much larger than the other villages we had seen since leaving Begi. There was a line of small shops, a market area, a blacksmith and even an official. Within minutes word of our arrival had spread, and the official stepped from the comfort of his shack to confront us. He wanted to know why we had come and he demanded to see our identity papers. When the rain had stopped, he dragged his desk and chair into the central square and interviewed us formally, as the inquisitive villagers clustered round. I said we were missionaries and that we had come in peace. The man said he was going to search our luggage. That was the last thing I wanted. Whenever my kitbags were examined valuable items seemed to disappear. Worse than that, I didn't want him to find the metal detector.

The official dropped a heavy hint that on his pitiful wages it was hard to afford a quantity of *araki* befitting a man of his standing. I wondered what that quantity might be. We led him to the bar and plied him with the local brew. He managed to down fifteen glasses. Then he passed out.

That evening we were put up by one of the villagers in his hut. As before, Samson and the muleteers invited me to eat, but I refrained. The Devil still hadn't been routed, I said, so I could not eat. They didn't say anything, but I could tell they were moved by my lack of appetite. When he had eaten a monstrous amount of *injera* and *kai wot*, spiced goat stew, Samson questioned the villagers about Tullu Wallel. The first man to talk said that a *faranji*, a white man, used to live up on the mountain. He couldn't say precisely when, but it was in the days when the Emperor was still in power. Maybe it was Hayter, I thought to myself.

'Did he see the white man himself?'

The informant said it was long before he was born.

Everyone else we spoke to had a tale to tell about the curse. Some of them had ventured up the mountain in their younger days in search of gold. They had all borne terrible misfortune as a result. One man had been stung by a thousand bees, another had been poisoned and had nearly died, and a third told of how his wife had gone mad after gathering sticks there.

After hearing all this, I knew we were going to have trouble getting more people to join our team. For the climb itself we required one man for each mule. I didn't know how long we would be on the mountain, but I was certain that we would need to take food and extra supplies. Samson broached the subject, asking for volunteers. He said we'd pay generously. The villagers shook their heads, and one woman grabbed her two sons by the ears and marched them back to their hut. We said we were missionaries, and I likened us to St George on his quest to slay the dragon.

'The only difference is that our dragon is much bigger,' I said, 'he's the Devil.'

The villagers were unimpressed. A curse was a curse, and no amount of inducement would make them risk the wrath of the Devil.

That night the Russian corned beef sat heavily in my stomach. I was apprehensive about what we might find on Tullu Wallel. For a long time the mountain had been an obsession, and now at last we were going to ascend it. I found myself thinking about Frank Hayter more and more, and I went over his descriptions of Tullu Wallel yet again.

At dawn we rose and loaded the mules. It was pouring with rain. I slipped on my poncho, and Samson wriggled into his bin-liner. We were just about to head off, when four men approached us. They said that they had decided to come with us.

'Aren't they frightened?'

The men, all in their early twenties, looked petrified, but one of them spoke for the others.

'It is time for the fear to end,' he said.

They each took the reins of a mule and led the way towards the mountain. The rest of us followed behind. As it was still dark I walked beside Clarissa. After an hour of trudging uphill, the first glint of light brought life to the undergrowth. The mist was low, hanging over Tullu Wallel like a death cloud, but I found myself stirred with new energy. At last, our motley band of mules and men had been transformed into a fully fledged expedition.

We headed straight for the mountain, which seemed to beckon us towards it. The rain didn't let up for a minute, which made the going very slow. I stayed at the back of the procession. I might have been the inspiration behind the expedition, but I was a novice at muleteering. We crossed fields and forded rivers, but we didn't seem to get any nearer to Tullu Wallel. I began to wonder if the mountain was a mirage, alluring yet unreachable.

Tadesse stopped three times during the morning to adjust the leather straps that bound the packs and saddles to the mules. In the rain the thongs stretched and had to keep being tightened. Clarissa's reins were tied to my hand and she battled on beside me. Samson was less appreciative of the experience. His blisters had got worse and I could tell that he was missing his girlfriend and Addis Ababa greatly.

For most of human history, man has walked with animals. Nothing is more natural, but the last century has erased our communal knowledge of that past. Now we think of wheels and tyres rather than legs and hooves; we think of miles per gallon and engines overheating, not of hay and animal fatigue. An internal combustion engine may be one of man's greatest achievements, but it is a noisy, polluting beast of a thing. Spend a few days trekking with pack mules through the forests of western Ethiopia, and you realize there's no comparison.

The woodland began quite suddenly. We forded a stream and ascended a steep bank, with Tadesse's sons jabbing their sticks angrily at the mules. Before us stood the forest, like a great curtain on the edge of a stage. I knew straight away that I would emerge the other side a different man.

We entered the forest and the morning sun disappeared. I have been in thick jungle before, but even the Upper Amazon couldn't compare with this. I stared up at the tops of the trees. They formed an unbroken canopy above us, each tree rising from a snarl of roots and mud, their long vine-covered trunks rearing up into a sea of green.

The smell changed too. There was the scent of wild garlic, and the musty aroma of moss and leaf mould. There was lemon mint as well, which grew wild. I chewed it and found it helped stave off thirst. We moved in a single file, stumbling over roots and low branches, and slipping and sliding in the mud. The track wound round trees and up and down gullies, zigzagging back and forth. The four local men said they had never come into the forest before. Only the most courageous honey-gatherers ventured there. In some of the taller trees we saw more honey baskets trussed high in the branches. There was little time to think of the diabolic danger ahead. Our first worry was the mules.

Tadesse kept telling me to ride, but I dismounted early on after almost being garrotted by a low branch. Somehow Samson managed to stay on his mule most of the time. He had hidden talents as a horseman. Thankfully, the tree canopy high above us gave us some protection from the torrential rain, but the mud was appalling. Mules are always the butt of man's humour, but the hours we spent battling through the muddy floor of the forest proved to me their extraordinary worth, and I found myself appreciating the writings of Dervla Murphy more than ever. An old hand with mules, she has trekked over mountain ranges and through forests with them, but to read her you would never guess just how difficult such a feat is.

The mud had been up to our thighs for a couple of hours but we soldiered on. I noticed that the mules had an uncanny ability to find the best route, and Tadesse's sons encouraged me to let Clarissa find her own way. But by late morning, even Clarissa was finding the mud tough going.

I suggested that we unpack the animals and carry some of the equipment ourselves. Tadesse balked at the idea. He seemed to thrive on the mules' discomfort.

'People will not be able to say that my animals are weak now!' he shouted.

Leading pack mules through thigh-deep mud is a slow business. I wanted to try another route, but the local men said there was no other track leading to Tullu Wallel. Their certainty surprised me, especially as none of them had actually been to the mountain before. I was also worried about the ermoli tick. De Prorok had written that it worms its way under a mule's skin and lays its eggs there. If not extracted, it can cause a terrible infection.

In the middle of the day we stopped at a stream. Samson opened one of the packs of food and passed it around. I drank some water but didn't eat anything. Tadesse and his sons were beginning to regard me with wonder. They asked Samson in whispers how I could keep going day after day without eating. Samson said that God filled my belly and gave me strength, so I had no need for food.

A few miles on we hit a patch of bog. Tadesse was at the head of the line, leading a large male mule. Suddenly the animal began to sink into the mud and it started to bay, fighting to keep its muzzle from going under. The local men knew what to do. They yanked the animal sideways by the bridle and the girth straps, and the mule crashed on to its side on firmer ground, its legs kicking furiously. One of Tadesse's sons stabbed it with his stick to make it get up. I swiped the boy on the back of the neck and told him to give the animal a minute to regain its strength.

Then, quite suddenly, the forest came to an end. Though we now got wetter than ever, having left the protection of the tree canopy, morale began to rise. In the late afternoon we reached a hamlet. At first it looked uninhabited, but we soon discovered that a group of honey-gatherers lived there along with their herd of goats.

The head of the hamlet came out to greet us. Straight-backed and wrapped in an emerald blanket, he invited us to spend the night. Our exhausted mules were unpacked and fed, and the rest of us, cold, wet and hungry, slumped down on the ground outside the huts.

At my prompting Samson asked the headman about the mountain.

'We don't go up there,' he said, 'not even to get honey.'

'Why not?'

'The danger.'

'You mean the Devil?'

The headman didn't reply.

'We're missionaries,' I said boastfully, 'and we've come to kick him back to Hell.'

Still the headman remained silent. I sensed that he was regretting ever having invited us to stay in his home, but hospitality is of paramount importance in Ethiopia. Still ignoring Samson's questions, he told his wife to prepare food for the guests and then he led us into the hut which he shared with his goats. We huddled round the fire and tried to dry our clothes. The problem with army issue kitbags is that they are made of canvas and everything in them gets soaked through when it rains. I emptied out one of the sacks and looked for clean underwear. The local men and Tadesse's sons watched in disbelief as I sorted through my belongings. They hadn't brought along any extra gear, not even a toothbrush. I found myself apologizing, but then I remembered the pressure lantern, which still hadn't been used. I gave it to Tadesse along with the kerosene and told him to get it working. His eyes lit up with glee.

While the food was being prepared, I stuffed an unlabelled tin down my trousers and said I had to go to the loo. Then I trotted out into the rain and found a quiet spot to open it with my pen-knife. The tin was full of sweetened prunes.

Back in the hut the lamp's instructions had been trodden under foot. God knows who ever came up with the design for pressure lanterns, but you need a Nobel prize in physics to work them out. Tadesse took the entire thing to pieces and laid the component parts out on my damp sleeping-bag. We all clustered round and marvelled at just how many pieces there were. When the puzzle was finally put back together the muleteer was left with a handful of odds and ends. Declaring them to be surplus to requirements, he tossed them into a corner. Next he filled the fuel tank to the top with kerosene and pressured the unit by pumping the handle. He pumped and pumped until his shoulder ached. Then he primed the lamp with alcohol and, his eyes glinting, struck a match and put it to the wick.

What happened next took us all by surprise. The lantern shot flames high into the thatch and then exploded. The headman emitted a shriek as he realized that his hut was on fire. It was an awkward moment. We were burning down our host's house, a situation which any guest seeks to avoid.

Fortunately the rain had drenched the roof so the fire was slow to take hold, and Tadesse's sons managed to put out the flames quite quickly. The second problem was Tadesse's burns. He held his hands to his face, whimpering. I prized his fingers away. To my relief his injuries weren't serious. Of more concern was the fact that we now had to sit in almost total darkness.

After dinner Samson lit a candle, took out his Bible and read us a passage from the Book of Chronicles. We were all huddled around the smouldering fire, with the goats pressed together in a single woolly mass. In the background I could hear an infant crying, and outside the rain continued to fall. Samson chose the passage in which Solomon welcomes the Queen of Sheba as his guest. I snuggled up in my soaking sleeping-bag and thought how fortunate I was to have found Samson. He had a knack of reinventing himself. He'd been a prospector, a gold miner, a taxi-driver, a guide and a fixer *extraordinaire*. And now he'd become a missionary, albeit in disguise. I thanked God for sending me Samson and then, lulled by his reading, I fell asleep.

An English childhood introduces you to heavy rain, but even that doesn't prepare you for the monsoon of East Africa. We set out at five in the morning having thanked the headman. I left some supplies in payment for the damage done to his hut. The mules were laden and the men readied, but an early start in pouring rain had dampened our spirits. Samson was particularly miserable. He had had only a thin nylon blanket to sleep under, and it was soon drenched. He hadn't slept at all and his stomach hurt. I suspected that the intestinal worms had returned to haunt him. To make matters worse, his bin-liner raincoat had melted when the thatch caught fire, so now he had no protection against the rain.

It was still very dark when we left the hamlet. I tried to raise morale by suggesting that the end was nearly in sight. Tadesse and his sons said they'd have to be getting back to Begi soon – they had important affairs to attend to at home. Even the local men were reluctant to continue. Soon Samson was clutching his stomach and complaining about the rain. Tadesse began to bark angrily at his sons, and the local men lagged behind at the back of the procession, their heads down. It was time for a little magic.

I halted the caravan and unpacked one of my kitbags. From the bottom I took out a medium-sized glass jar, with a sprinkler built into the top. The men didn't say anything, but they were clearly wondering what was going on. I asked them to line up and stick their tongues out. It was an unpopular command, largely because of the heavy rain. I ordered them to trust me. Samson went first. I sprinkled a few grains of the white powder on his tongue and told him to swallow.

As soon as his tongue retracted, his face lit up. He smiled and then he burst out laughing, and begged for more. The others grew jealous and wanted some too. I sprinkled a little of the miracle powder on Tadesse's tongue, then on those of his sons, before giving a dose to the other four men. They loved it.

'It tastes all meaty,' said Tadesse.

'It's delicious!' exclaimed Samson. 'What is it?'

I didn't tell them, except to say that it was magic from Peru. That was partly true. I had been sold the powder by a man in the small town of Nazca in the Peruvian desert. It was monosodium glutamate.

Morale rose sharply after that. I enticed the men on by promising them more of the magic powder. They couldn't get enough of it. Samson said it tasted like the *kai wot* that his mother made back in Kebra Mengist.

An hour later we reached the eastern slope of Tullu Wallel. At the next magic powder break I made an announcement. I told the men to be brave, declaring that we would vanquish the Devil and drive him from his cave. But they were changed men already. They no longer had any fear. Their blood had been fortified by the mysterious effects of monosodium glutamate.

We started climbing. Hayter had said that the cave lay at the foot of the eastern slope. So when we were a little way up I gave the order to fan out in pairs and search for the mine-shafts. Earlier that morning the men wouldn't have dreamed of looking by themselves. But now they were buoyant. We left the mules with one of the local men and began the search.

For six hours we combed the mountain. With the muleteers' spirits bolstered I felt that at last we were within reach of Frank Hayter's mine-shafts. I had promised a sack of magic powder to the first man who set eyes upon the cave. But with time the team's enthusiasm levelled off and then died away completely. No amount of monosodium glutamate could compensate for the wretched conditions. The rain was torrential and didn't let up for a minute. It hampered the search, as did the bushes armed with barbed thorns, and the area's infestation of ticks. The men would have stormed away, but there was nowhere to storm off to. Instead, they took every opportunity to make the extent of their discomfort known.

At 5.14 p.m. Tadesse screamed louder than I have ever heard a grown man scream. Samson and I ran towards his voice, stumbling over rocks and roots.

'The cave! The cave!' he shouted.

'Where?'

'Over there! The entrance to a cave!'

I congratulated the muleteer and rewarded him with an extra dose of monosodium glutamate. He licked his lips and said it had been a communal effort. We examined the cave entrance, while Tadesse's sons fetched the mules. It was far larger than anything I had imagined. I whooped loudly and slapped Samson's hand in a high five. We had found it. We had found the entrance to Solomon's mines.

I thought fast. We would need ropes, flashlights and the Gold Bug. Once the mules had been brought over, I unpacked the kitbags and pulled out a red nylon rope. Attaching it to myself and Samson, I said that we would go in alone while the others paid out the rope. The order went down very well with the men who clearly didn't envy us our task. Tadesse asked what the metal detector was for. I told him it was a special machine for detecting the Devil. Then Samson said that the flashlights had run out of batteries, and the pressure lantern was too dangerous to risk using again. I racked my brains and asked myself what Henry Morton Stanley would have done.

'Cut down bamboo staves,' I shouted. 'Rip up the blankets and make fiery torches.'

The men set to work. Samson was less than happy at having his blanket shredded, but it was in a good cause. We wound the cloth round the sticks, dipped them in kerosene, and set them alight. Then I gave Samson a last sprinkling of magic powder and together we entered the cave.

The smoke from the torches set the place alive with bats. There were thousands of them, just like the ones we had encountered in Dire Dawa. Our torches gave off more fumes than they did light, and it was impossible to see more than a few feet ahead. I led the way, with Samson's hand on my shoulder. At last, I thought, we were entering the ancient mine-shafts. But then, after twenty feet, we hit a rock wall and the cave came to an abrupt end. With the bats still swooping and diving around us, we searched for a passage-way or a brick wall or a door. But there was no way forward.

15

Return to the Accursed Mountain

'There is no greater pain than to recall a happy time in wretchedness.'

Dante, *Inferno*

SEVEN MONTHS LATER I was back in Ethiopia. Tullu Wallel had haunted me ever since I'd left its accursed twin peaks. Although I'd tried to get on with new projects, resuming normal life was impossible. I had to complete the search. I knew that somewhere on the mountain's slopes lay the answer to the riddle of King Solomon's mines. As before, there was only one way to find out. I was going to have to return to Tullu Wallel.

Usually, there is nothing more pleasing than returning to a place where you have endured hardship. But as the plane taxied towards Addis Ababa's airport terminal, I felt a lump in my throat. My toes curled up in my shoes, and my heart raced. I was mad to have come back and I knew it. The only certainty was that there would be much more hardship ahead before I flew home to Europe.

A familiar figure was waiting at the arrivals gate. He was dressed in some of my old clothes, his hair was cropped short, and he looked despondent. It was Samson. When our eyes met neither of us smiled. The journey ahead was about unfinished business. This was not a time for pleasantries. Samson took my bags and led the way to his taxi. He didn't say whether he'd been surprised to get my message. In fact he didn't say anything at all.

As the taxi neared my hotel, I muttered my first words.

'I had to come back,' I said.

'The mountain?' whispered Samson.

'The mine-shafts, I can't stop thinking about them. I know that I can find them.'

Samson ran the wheel through his hands before applying the brakes gently. The taxi glided to a halt.

'Tullu Wallel will kill you,' he said. 'Take my advice. Go back to Europe and stop thinking about Solomon's gold.'

The words echoed advice given to Hayter when he ventured back to Ethiopia to search once more for the mountain's mine-shafts. That was sixty-five years before my own journeys. On his death-bed, Hayter's old companion 'Black' Martin whispered to him: 'Leave Tullu Wallel and Abyssinian gold alone, or you will live to regret it, as I have done.' Black Martin, who was afflicted by an Ethiopian curse, died a few days later.

Perhaps I should have taken the advice, but I didn't. Instead I made a beeline for the accursed mountain, dragging Samson with me. I was struck with a strong case of *déjà vu*, for we tracked down Bahru and roped him and the Emperor's Jeep in as well. Bahru's luck had eventually returned and he had made his way back to Addis Ababa. We found him lying in a daze in the back of the Jeep, his eyes bloodshot, his mouth packed with *qat*.

The days that followed were far harsher than any other journey I have ever undertaken. We struggled through mud, sleet and torrential rain. The mules and muleteers battled on despite the dreadful conditions. Our clothes, blankets and supplies were drenched early on and never dried out. The skin on my feet began to rot away, and my shins felt as if they had been flayed with whips. Samson was in no better condition. His intestinal worms had returned with a vengeance.

My obsession with Frank Hayter's mine-shafts was destroying not only me but those with me. Most journeys have a clear beginning, but on some the ending is less well-defined. The question is, at what point do you bite your lip and head for home?

On the last morning, after a truly wretched night, we sat crouched in the lee of a hardwood tree dreaming of being far from Tullu Wallel. Our spirits were broken. I took stock of the situation. The rain was coming down in sheets. Most of the food was gone and the batteries were dead. The kerosene was finished, and the last of the drinking water had been consumed. Samson was clutching his belly and moaning. I had fallen into an ants' nest and my back was badly bitten. Being eaten alive by soldier ants is indescribably painful. The mules had started to buck whenever anyone went near them. The muleteers' faces were drawn, the palms of their hands raw and bleeding. I wondered if things could get any worse, and at that moment the rain turned to hail. I knew then that my search for Hayter's mine-shafts was at an end.

Taking a deep breath, I staggered to my feet and ordered the retreat. As we turned on our heels and began the long, miserable trek back towards the main road, I smiled wryly to myself. Frank Hayter's secret was still safe, as was the exact whereabouts of King Solomon's mines.

Glossary

Abyssinia: former name for Ethiopia

amba: a flat-topped mountain

Amharic: the language of the Amhara tribe, widely spoken in Ethiopia
    and often regarded as the national language

amole: a uniform block of salt, once used as currency in Ethiopia

araki: an alcoholic drink, usually distilled from maize

asa wot: a spicy fish stew, made with freshwater fish

berbere: a highly spiced sauce common throughout Ethiopia in which
    meat dishes are served

Beta Israel: the tribe of Ethiopian Jews

birr: the national currency of Ethiopia: at the current rate of exchange,
    12 *birr* equal £1

Buda: the religious hierarchy of the Ethiopian Jewish community
    believed to have the ability to transmit the Evil Eye

dejazmacth: a local nobleman

dink: the ancient Egyptian word for a dwarf, which is also found in
    various tribal languages in Ethiopia

doro wot: a spicy chicken stew, often served with hard-boiled eggs

enset: the 'false banana' plant, cultivated in Ethiopia and prized for its
    edible stem

falasha: one of the community of Ethiopian Jews, most of whom now
    live in Israel: the term is now regarded as politically incorrect

faranji: colloquial term for a foreigner

Ge'ez: the ancient language of Ethiopia, still understood by the country's
    priesthood

ghamelawallas: sweepers in Calcutta and other Indian cities who buy the
    dust from the floors of jewellery workshops

injera: Ethiopian bread made from *teff* flour, upon which a communal meat stew is served

kai wot: a spicy lamb stew served in a *berbere* sauce

Karo: a tribe from south-west Ethiopia whose warriors paint their bodies in elaborate patterns

Kebra Negast (*The Glory of Kings*): sacred text of Ethiopia, which contains a detailed account of Solomon's meeting with Makeda

Makeda: the Ethiopian name for the Queen of Sheba

makwamya: ritualistic prayer sticks used by the Ethiopian clergy

matatu: a communal taxi or minivan, popular in East Africa

mensaf: a Bedu dish of meat cooked in milk and served with flavoured rice

Mursi: a tribe from south-west Ethiopia, famed for the curious clay lip-plates that they wear

Oromo: one of the main tribes in Ethiopia, or their language

qat: the mildly narcotic leaf chewed in the Horn of Africa and in southern Arabia, sometimes called *chatt* in Ethiopia

shamma: a cotton shawl, worn throughout Ethiopia, often with a delicately embroidered border

shiftas: bandits

sistra: an Ethiopian musical instrument, possibly of ancient Egyptian origin

tabot: a replica of the Ark of the Covenant

teff: a grain popular in Ethiopia, from which *injera* is made

thaler: a Maria Theresa dollar, once used in various African countries as currency, and still minted by the Austrian government

tukul: a wattle-and-daub or simple stone hut

werk: the Amharic word for gold

zill-zill tibs: shredded beef strips fried and served with sauce

Bibliography

All books were published in London unless otherwise stated.

Solomon and Sheba

Budge, E. A. Wallis, *The Queen of Sheba and Her Only Son Menylik* (Medici Society, 1922)

Littman, Enno (ed.), *The Legend of the Queen of Sheba in the Tradition of Axum* (Bibliotheca Abessinica, 1904)

Philby, H. St. John, *The Queen of Sheba* (reprint, Quartet, 1981)

Phillips, Wendell, *Sheba's Buried City* (Gollancz, 1955)

Raymond, Captain E., *King Solomon's Temple* (Artisan, Thousand Oaks, Ca., 1992)

Toy, Barbara, *In Search of Sheba* (John Murray, 1961)

Biblical History

Feather, Robert, *The Copper Scroll Decoded* (HarperCollins, 1999)

Grierson, Roderick, and Munro-Hay, Stuart, *The Ark of the Covenant* (Phoenix Press, 2000)

Hancock, Graham, *The Sign and the Seal* (Heinemann, 1992)

Keller, Werner, *The Bible as History* (Hodder & Stoughton, 1956)

The Septuagint Bible (Falcon's Wing Press, White Hills, 1954)

Vermes, Geza, *The Dead Sea Scrolls in English* (Penguin, Harmondsworth, 1962)

Ophir and Punt

Bent, J. Theodore, *The Ruined Cities of Mashonaland* (Longmans, Green, 1895)

Burton, Captain Richard F., *The Gold-mines of Midian and the Ruined Midianite Cities*, 2 vols. (Kegan Paul, 1878)

——*Land of Midian (Revisited)*, 2 vols. (Kegan Paul, 1879)

Bibliography

Craufurd, Commander C. E. V., *Treasure of Ophir* (Skeffington, 1929)

Hall, R. N., *Great Zimbabwe* (Methuen, 1905)

——and Neal, W. G., *The Ancient Ruins of Rhodesia* (Methuen, 1902)

Keane, A. H., *The Gold of Ophir* (Edward Stanford, 1901)

Kitchen, K. A., *Punt and How to Get There* (Orientalia XL, 1971)

Peters, Carl, *The Eldorado of the Ancients* (Pearson, 1902)

——*Solomon's Golden Ophir: A Research into the Most Ancient Gold Production in History* (Leadenhall Press, 1899)

Rothenberg, Beno, *Were these Solomon's Mines?* (Thames and Hudson, 1972)

Stuart, J. M., *The Ancient Gold Fields of Africa* (Effingham Wilson, 1891)

Wicker, F. D. P., 'The Road to Punt', *Geographical Journal*, Vol. CLXIV, July 1998

Gold

Angier, Bradford, *Looking for Gold* (Stackpole Books, Mechanicsburg, Pa., 1980)

Bernstein, Peter L., *The Power of Gold* (John Wiley, New York, 2000)

Butler, Gail, *Recreational Gold Prospecting* (Gem Guides, 1998)

Cornell, Fred C., *The Glamour of Gold Prospecting* (Fisher, Unwin, 1920)

Goble, G. F., *Hints to Intended Gold Diggers and Buyers* (n.p., 1853)

Marx, Jennifer, *The Magic of Gold* (Doubleday, New York, 1978)

Randle, Kevin D., *Lost Gold and Buried Treasure* (Evans, New York, 1995)

Ethiopia

Baker, Samuel White, *The Nile Tributaries of Abyssinia and the Sword Hunters of the Hamran Arabs* (Macmillan, 1867)

Bartleet, Captain E. J., *In the Land of Sheba* (Cornish Brothers, Birmingham, 1934)

Briggs, Philip, *Guide to Ethiopia* (Bradt Books, Chalfont St Peter, 1998)

Blundell, H. Weld, 'Exploration in the Abai Basin, Abyssinia', *Geographical Journal*, Vol. XXVII, June 1906

Bruce, James, *Travels to Discover the Source of the Nile*, 5 vols. (J. Ruthven, Edinburgh, 1790)

Budge, E. A. Wallis, *A History of Ethiopia* (Methuen, 1928)

——*Bandlet of Righteousness* (Luzac, 1929)

Burton, Captain Richard F., *First Footsteps in East Africa* (reprint, Dent, 1910)

Demessie, Metasebia, *Bibliography of the Geology of Ethiopia* (Ethiopian Institute of Geological Surveys, Addis Ababa, 1996)

de Prorok, Byron, *In Quest of Lost Worlds* (Frederick Muller, 1935)

——*Dead Men Do Tell Tales* (Harrap, 1943)

Farago, Ladislas, *Abyssinia on the Eve* (Putnam, 1935)

Bibliography

Gordon, Frances Linzee, *Ethiopia, Eritrea and Djibouti* (Lonely Planet, 2000)

Griaule, Marcel, *Abyssinian Journey* (John Miles, 1935)

Harris, Major W. Cornwallis, *Highland of Aethiopia*, 2 vols. (Longman, 1844)

Hartlmaier, Paul, *Golden Lion* (Geoffrey Bles, 1956)

Hayter, Frank E., *In Quest of Sheba's Mines* (Stanley Paul Ltd., 1935)

——*The Gold of Ethiopia* (Stanley Paul, 1936)

——*African Adventurer* (Stanley Paul, 1939)

——*The Garden of Eden* (Stanley Paul, 1940)

Henze, Paul B., *Ethiopian Journeys* (Ernest Benn, 1977)

——*Layers of Time: A History of Ethiopia* (C. Hurst, 2000)

Jelenc, Danilo A., *Mineral Occurrences of Ethiopia* (Ministry of Mines, Addis Ababa, 1966)

Jones, A. H. M., and Monroe, Elizabeth, *A History of Abyssinia* (Clarendon Press, Oxford, 1935)

Nesbitt, L. M., *Desert and Forest* (Jonathan Cape, 1937)

Nicholson, T. R., *A Toy for the Lion* (William Kimber, 1965)

Pankhurst, Richard, *An Economic History of Ethiopia* (Haile Selassie University Press, Addis Ababa, 1968)

——*The Ethiopians* (Blackwell, Oxford, 1998)

Pankhurst, Sylvia, *Ethiopia: A Cultural History* (Lalibela House, Woodford Green, 1959)

Phillipson, David W., *Ancient Ethiopia* (British Museum Press, 1999)

Rey, C. F., *Unconquered Abyssinia As It Is Today* (Seeley Service, 1923)

Salt, Henry, *A Voyage to Abyssinia* (Rivington, 1814)

Spectrum Guide to Ethiopia (Camerapix, Nairobi, 1995)

Thesiger, Wilfred, *The Danakil Diary* (HarperCollins, 1996)

Trimmingham, J. S., *Islam in Ethiopia* (Oxford University Press, Oxford, 1952)

Ullendorff, Edward, *The Ethiopians* (Oxford University Press, Oxford, 1961)

——*Ethiopia and the Bible* (British Academy, 1967)

Weninger, Stefan, *Ge'ez: Classical Ethiopia* (Lincom Europa, 1993)

Miscellaneous

Alvares, Francisco, *A True Relation of the Lands of Prester John* (Cambridge University Press, Cambridge, 1961)

Barradas, M., *Tractus Tres Historico-Geographici* (1634)

Boyes, John, *King of the Wa Kikuyu* (Methuen, 1912)

Cashmore, E. E., *The Rastafarians* (Minority Rights Group International, 1992)

Coan, Stephen (ed.), *Diary of an African Journey: The Return of Henry Rider Haggard* (Hurst, 2001)

Bibliography

Davidson, Basil, *Old Africa Rediscovered* (Gollancz, 1959)

de May, R., *Narrative of the Sufferings and Adventures of Henderick Portenger* (Richard Phillips, 1819)

Haggard, Henry Rider, *King Solomon's Mines* (Cassell, 1885)

Hall, Richard, *Lovers on the Nile: The Life of Samuel White Baker* (Collins, 1980)

Herodotus, *The Histories* (Everyman's Library, 1910)

Kessler, David, *The Falashas* (Allen & Unwin, 1982)

Mandeville, Sir John, *Travels and Voyages of Sir John Mandeville* (c. 1356–7)

Shah, Sayed Idries, *Destination Mecca* (Rider, 1957)